BRIGHTON PLANNING DEPARTMENT
ENVIRONMENTAL GROUP APRIL 1979

BRIGHTON TOWN
AND
BRIGHTON PEOPLE

By the same Author

Fashionable Brighton, 1820-1860
The History and Architecture of Brighton
About Brighton
James Wyatt

Brighton Town

AND

Brighton People

by

ANTONY DALE

PHILLIMORE

1976

Published by
PHILLIMORE & CO., LTD.,
London and Chichester
Head Office: Shopwyke Hall,
Chichester, Sussex.

ISBN 0 85033 219 2

Text set in 11/12pt Baskerville

Printed in Great Britain by
Unwin Brothers Ltd.,
Old Woking, Surrey.

Contents

Illustrations

(between pages 120 and 121)

ACKNOWLEDGMENTS

Plates I, V, VIII, IX, XIII, XIV, XV, XVI, XIX, XXIII and XXIV are reproduced by kind permission of the Director of the Brighton Art Gallery.

Plates VII, X, XII, XXI and XXII are reproduced by kind permission of the East Sussex County Librarian, Brighton Area.

Plate XX is reproduced by kind permission of Howlett and Clarke, Brighton.

The originals of Plates II, III, IV, VI, XI, XVII and XVIII are in the possession of the Author.

INTRODUCTION

Most books about Brighton, including my own, have dealt with what might be called its highlights: the Royal Pavilion and its occupants; the great architectural estates like Kemp Town and their inhabitants. But these people were never real residents of Brighton. They only came for the season or at irregular intervals and then departed to their London mansions or their country houses. In their absence normal life at perhaps a slightly lower level and such local government as then existed in Brighton proceeded uneventfully.

It so happens that two main sources of information about this life and local government survive. This book is mainly based on these two sources. The first comprises the Minute Books of the Brighton Vestry from 1790 until the incorporation of the town in 1854, and in the case of burial grounds only, until 1856.

During this period the Clerk to the Vestry was the senior partner for the time being of Howlett and Clarke, the oldest firm of solicitors in Brighton. The Vestry books survived in the keeping of this firm until recently, when they were presented by them to the Sussex Archaeological Society. By the kindness of my fellow members of the Council of that Society I have been allowed to consult these Minutes.[1] There is, however, one mystery attached to them. When Dr. A. E. Wilson and the late Mr. W. A. Barron first spoke to me about the existence of these minute books they mentioned that these survived from the late 16th century until 1854. However, between that time and my investigation of the records, the earliest volume covering the years down to 1790 has disappeared. It was not among the volumes presented to the Sussex Archaeological Society, but Howlett and Clarke cannot

1. The Minutes are now in the East Sussex County Council's Record Office.

trace its existence either. I suppose that one day it will turn up.

The second source of information has been the Minute Books of the Brighton Commissioners for roughly the same period, namely from 1789 until the granting of a charter to the town in 1854, and, for the transfer of the remaining powers of the Commissioners to the new Corporation, until 1855. These records, by the kindness of the Brighton Town Council, I have likewise been allowed to consult. They also have their own mystery. The first local Act of Parliament setting up a body of Brighton Commissioners for the purpose of rudimentary local government was in 1773. But the minutes of their meetings only survive from 1789. There is no explanation of what has happened to the records between 1773 and 1789.

From 1789 until the second local Act of 1810 the minutes of the Commissioners' meetings covered also the activities of the workhouse. But this second Act set up a body of Directors and Guardians of the Poor who were until 1825, appointed by the Commissioners and thereafter elected by the Vestry. The Directors and Guardians of the Poor continued in existence until the introduction of the National Health Service in 1947. Their minutes would also be a very valuable record of social history. But these have not survived either in the General Hospital in Elm Grove, which is physically and geographically the heir to the workhouse and infirmary, nor in the Welfare Department of the Corporation, nor in the Reference Department of the Public Library, nor in the Town Clerk's office. Some day they will perhaps turn up in an unexpected Corporation limbo.

Both the Vestry minutes and the Commissioners' minutes record the development of local government from the most rudimentary beginnings to the nucleus of what we can recognise as such today. Throughout the whole period the public and to a certain extent the governing body themselves resisted the idea that the municipality, or what passed for such, should extend its activities more widely and above all opposed the expenditure of public money involved in the greater complexity of life. This may well have been the case in all other English communities of the period whose outlook was a very independent one.

But life and thought in Brighton had one very unusual characteristic. When the Prince of Wales first came here in 1783 he was a supporter of the Whig party. Brighthelmston, not being an ancient borough, was not then enfranchised. It therefore adopted his politics. When, as Prince Regent in 1811, he changed sides and continued the Tory government in power, Brighton did not change its views with him. For more than 70 years thereafter the town continued to be not only Whig in sympathy but even violently radical. Of this many passages in the Vestry Minute Books leave no doubt at all.

At the end of 1838, for instance, a copy of the famous People's Charter was pasted in the Vestry Minute book. This at the period would have been considered so 'left wing' as to be almost equivalent to Communism today. It was not until after 1885 that the town acquired the Conservative overtones that, since that time, have been normally associated with seaside places. This change is outside the scope and period of this book.

But, despite its radicalism, Brighton did not cease to be extremely royalist in outlook at the same time, even after the Court had made its last visit in 1845. It remained consistently grateful to the memory of George IV, even when he was out of favour elsewhere, as indeed it does today, and rightly so. The result is that one finds in the Vestry Minute Books a resolution passed in September 1841 in favour of vote by ballot and extension of the franchise only a few pages before a loyal address to the Queen on the birth of the Prince of Wales. This combination of radicalism and royalism is a most unusual one that can rarely be found elsewhere.

The relationships between the Vestry and the Commissioners were not at times too happy. Except perhaps between employers and employees, human beings have found no relations more difficult than those between

electors and elected. The former invariably consider that
the latter's only function is to carry out the former's
wishes. The latter reply that they are not delegates, but
representatives who are chosen to use their intelligence
and that this is well above that of their electors. Brighton
at this period was no exception to this rule. The situation
was not made easier by the extreme complacency with
which both sides expressed their sentiments. Both sets
of minutes are written in the picturesque and hard-hitting
language that makes their perusal extremely lively—a far
cry from the drably factual style of most modern minutes.

Part I
The Brighton Vestry

1.–1790-1810

In 1789/90 the municipal government of Brighton was divided between three separate organisations. The Town Commissioners were a body of 64 people set up by Act of Parliament in 1773 to provide for the paving, lighting and cleansing of the streets and to build groynes in front of the town in order to prevent coastal erosion which had engulfed the original Brighthelmston below the cliff.[1]

Secondly, the High Constable and two Headboroughs were elected annually on Easter Tuesday by a jury of inhabitants summoned by the Earl of Abergavenny as the Lord of the Hundred of Whalesbone. Their function was the appointment of constables or watchmen and the maintenance of law and order in the town.

Thirdly, there were the churchwardens and Overseers of the parish whose principal responsibility was the maintenance of the poor of the town, but who also exercised some other functions of local government.

The general law on the subject of the poor derived from the Vagrancy Acts of the last years of the reign of Queen Elizabeth. Each parish was obliged to be responsible for its own 'deserving poor', as they were called, and to maintain a poor-house or workhouse to contain them. In addition weekly sums of out-relief were also administered. As a consequence of the system, parishes were not willing to accept responsibility for those from other parts of the country, and the destitutes were consequently

1. See Part II, Section 1.

returned to their parish of origin to be a charge on that parish, often with considerable hardship en route. The 'able-bodied poor' on the other hand were 'set on work' wherever they were.

The Brighton Vestry books from 1790 onwards deal with the meetings of the churchwardens and Overseers of the parish. But until 1826, with the exception of one instance in April 1790, they do not ever record the election of such officers.Two parish wardens were, however, elected annually at a meeting held on Easter Monday immediately after divine service. This was summoned by the Vicar's warden on the previous day. The minutes of these meetings were kept on separate sheets of paper which have not survived. After the passing of the Vestry Act of 1818, which made provision for regular notice of meetings to elect churchwardens and Overseers of the Poor, no alteration was made in the practice followed at Brighton because the parish seems to have been under the impression that its own procedure derived from custom immemorial and dated back at least until 1580, when an ordinance of the Privy Council directed that two wardens should be elected from amongst the fishermen and one from the landsmen of the town.

But in 1833 a disputed election occurred, and at the usual show of hands one voter claimed a plural vote. The right was not admitted, but the parish subsequently, in 1835, consulted counsel, Sir John Dodson, concerning the procedure to be followed henceforth. He advised that no special custom entitled the parish to disregard the general procedure laid down in the Vestry Act of 1818.

The Overseers of the Poor were appointed by the magistrates out of a list of eligible persons submitted to them by the Vestry. In 1828 and 1829 a complaint was made that this list of eligible persons was submitted to the magistrates by the outgoing churchwardens and Overseers direct, without first being approved at a Vestry Meeting.

The election of the High Constable and the Head-boroughs, who were also honorary officers, is not recorded

in the Vestry books either. But in 1793 it was decided
that the High Constable should be paid £12 12s. a year
towards his expenses, including £4 4s. for the annual
dinner and his expenses in attending the Assizes and Petty
Sessions at Lewes. But in the following year this was
changed to £10 10s. for the expenses of his first day in
office, which included the dinner, and thereafter such
reasonable expenses as he incurred and were passed by the
parish. In April 1805 it was resolved that the officers of
the parish should be allowed their supper at the monthly
meetings.

In early years the Vestry occasionally met in the Town
Hall and after 1804 invariably did so. But between 1790
and 1804 it was generally their practice to hold each
meeting in a different public house. In this way they met
from time to time at the *Castle,* Castle Square; the *Little
Castle* and the *Three Tuns,* both in Little Castle Square,
which was to the south-west of Little East Street; the
White Horse, the *Greyhound,* the *Spread Eagle* (which
since 1816 has been called the *Sussex Arms,*) and the
Dolphin in Great East Street, as East Street was then
called; the *Star and Garter* in Little East Street; the *Old
Chimneys* (now the *Golden Fleece*) in Golden Lion Lane,
which is now the south-east end of Market Street; the
Black Lion and the *Cricketers* (which before 1790 was
called the *Last and Fish Cart*), both in Black Lion Street;
the *Gun* (later Harrison's Hotel) in Black Lion Street
Cliff, later East Cliff, which is now King's Road; the
Old Ship, the *New Ship,* the *Old Tun* and the *Seven Stars*
in Ship Street; the *Ship in Distress* (later the *Sea House*)
in Middle Street; the *King's Head,* the *George,* the *Half
Moon,* the *Carpenters' Arms,* all in West Street; the *White
Lion,* the *Unicorn,* and *Horse and Groom* (later the *Brick-
layers' Arms*), the *Blacksmiths' Arms,* the *Wheatsheaf*
and the *New* inn (which since 1830 has been called the
Clarence Hotel), all in North Street; the *Hen and Chickens*
(later the *Running Horse*) in Portland Street; the *Gardener's
Arms* in Church Street; the *Golden Cross* (later the *Marlborough*) in Prince's Street; the *King and Queen* in North

Row, now Marlborough Place; the *Catherine Wheel* (later the *Duke of Wellington*) in Pool Lane, now Pool Valley; *The Packet* (previously the *Sloop*) in Old Steine Street, now Steine Street; the *Schooner*, possibly in High Street; the *Crown and Anchor*, possibly in Margaret Street, though it is doubtful if that street had been completed by 1804; and the *Blue Anchor* whose whereabouts cannot now be traced. Most of these names are still very suggestive of a fishing town. Only 13 of these public houses still survive today on their original sites.

The Vestry acted as the licencing authority. In February 1801 an application was made to it for a new public house to be called the *Royal Crescent* inn. This was to be behind the new street of Royal Crescent which was then in course of erection. The application was refused on the grounds that sufficient public houses already existed in the town, though their number was not specified. But three years later it was stated that 42 licensed houses existed, and this was not thought sufficient for the town. Eleven more were therefore licensed.

The surviving Vestry Books begin with the appointment in January 1790 of William Attree as Clerk. But Bishop's *Brighton in the Olden Time* quotes an advertisement of the Commissioners signed 'William Attree' and dated 1 August 1773, so he had presumably held office since that date. His salary in 1790 was £10 10s. a year. By 1804 this had become £30 a year. William Attree and his brother John acted as solicitors for the Prince of Wales in the purchase of land for the Royal Pavilion. Their firm survives today as Howlett and Clarke of 8 Ship Street, and is the oldest firm of solicitors in Brighton. Partners in the firm throughout its different states (Attree and Son; Attree and Cooper; Attree, Cooper and McWhinnie; Attree, Clarke and Co., and so on) succeeded each other as Clerk to the Vestry until that office virtually ceased to exist with the incorporation of the town in 1854.

From 1808 onwards, if not before, a Collector of the poor-rate was appointed. The office was given to Jonathan Grenville, who was required to give security in the sum of

£1,000 and was authorised to retain a commission of three-pence in the pound.

The third principal officer of the parish was the Beadle or Cryer—an office not discontinued until 1877. In 1799 Nicholas Washer of 10 Jew Street was Beadle and Cryer, but in March 1800 he was succeeded by Thomas Waring, whose salary was £20 a year, plus his clothes. He lived at 3 Great East Street. His duties were to 'make the Poor Books, the Church Book, the Surveyor's Book and the Town Book'; on Sundays to attend the north and west galleries in the church (where the occupants of the work-house and the schoolchildren sat); to go round the town with the parish officers in order to make the militia list; and 'likewise to officiate as Headborough in the town but not elsewhere. 'In 1796 when a resolution was passed authorising the apprehension of all vagrants and beggars it was resolved that the Cryer should be paid one shilling for all vagrants apprehended by him. John Shelley succeeded Thomas Waring as Beadle in 1801.

In November 1792 surveyors were appointed to survey 'the new buildings and improvements of this town'. But this seems to have been only a temporary measure.

The Town Hall of the day was in Bartholomews, as is the present one, and had been built in 1727. An entry in the Vestry minutes of August 1791 gives an unfavourable idea of Bartholomews at the time as it recorded that 'hog-sties, stables and dung be removed' from there. The Town Hall contained a lock-up or 'black hole' for offenders against the law. From 1773 on the market was adjoining. A drawing by E. Hall in the possession of the Corporation shows the building as it was in 1823.

The workhouse had also been part of the Town Hall building since 1727. In October 1799 a committee was appointed to confer with the Vicar concerning the enlargement of the workhouse. A year later a plan was made to erect an extension in the yard, containing 24 more beds. As so enlarged, the building held about 150 people and remained in use until 1822. The Master of the workhouse was John Sickelmore. But the general supervision under

him was in the hands of a Governess who was paid £15 15s.
a year. In 1799 Mrs. Taylor, who had been Governess, died
and was succeeded by Mrs. Worgan.

Nothing reveals better the grimness of the treatment
given to the poor under the old parish system of relief
than the method by which medical attention was provided.
In 1803 the extremely unusual occurrence took place
that Dr. Bankhead offered to attend the poor free of
charge and did so for one year. But normally the operation
was put out to tender. The entry of 25 September 1797
frankly reveals the brutality or indifference of the contemporary approach: 'C. W. Newton, being the lowest
tender for medically farming the poor, be contracted
with for the same from 29 Sepr. inst. to Christmas 1798
at the sum of £37 10s.'. In other years the amount paid
after advertisements in the *Sussex Weekly Advertiser,*
was usually about £40 a year.

The Vestry books make clear that the unfailing annual
diet of the inmates of the workhouse was beef, split peas,
oatmeal, bread, butter, cheese, and beer. Annual contracts,
of which that in 1795 is very typical, provided for the
supply of shoulders, necks, and stockings of good ox beef,
a shoulder to each neck and stocking clear of bone and 12
pounds of beef suet to each lot at 2s. 3d. a stone; legs
and skin of ox beef at 1s. 4d. a stone; ox-heads at 2s. a
head; the best Waterford butter at 76s. a hundredweight;
good split peas at 16s. a bushel; good oatmeal at 12s. a
bushel; the best old Derby cheese at 51s. a hundredweight;
good amber malt at £2 10s. a quarter; good hops at 1s. 6d.
a pound; and good second wheaten flour at 9s. 4d. a
bushel. To the modern age it seems a different world
where, even for the poor, tea was not a staple and cheap
article of diet. It seems harder still to imagine life without
any form of hot beverage. The diet of the poor contained
nothing sweet of any kind and probably consisted of only
stew of beef, peas and oatmeal, plus bread, cheese, and
beer. The non-edible supplies contracted for were the best
brown soap at 80s. a hundredweight; good candles at
9s. 6d. a dozen; and good Newcastle coals at 36s. a chaldron.

The clothing was ordered by several dozen of each article or by contract for a year's supply. It consisted of brown serge coats, waistcoats and breeches, together with stockings, shoes, and hats for the men and boys; brown serge gowns and petticoats, together with stockings, shoes and trimmed hats for the women and girls. Shirts, shifts, stays, and flannel for petticoats, aprons and blankets must also have been acquired, though this is not mentioned, because these were amongst the articles distributed to the non-resident poor. According to Erredge's *History of Brighton* the only work given to the outdoor poor before the Poor Law Amendment Act of 1834 was the collection and crushing of oyster shells in a large iron mortar at a fixed price per bushel. The resulting material was then sold as manure and for the construction of garden paths. This form of hard labour was very common in workhouses both before and after 1834. Probably the most famous example was the crushing of bones in the Andover workhouse in Hampshire which was one of the worst features in the scandal affecting that institution in 1845.

The day-to-day entries in the Vestry books relate to the admissions to, and discharge from, the workhouse and to the distribution of various kinds of out-relief. This could be anything from 1s. a week upwards, but more often than not was about 4s. to 6s. a week. It could be as much as £2 2s. a week for a man and his family, or 1s. 6d. each for as many of his children as were able to work. If a woman chose to reside outside the workhouse it could be as little as 1s. a week to encourage or more or less force her to enter 'the House'. Similarly in April 1790 Robert Burgh who had hitherto been paid 1s. a week was 'taken into the Townhouse because of troublesome conduct'. Those who resided in the workhouse and worked could be allowed a proportion of what they earned 'as an encouragement'. The meeting of the Vestry on 13 January 1790 in fact recorded the discontinuation during pleasure of such an allowance to William Souter of 2d. a week out of the 1s. earned by him.

A grant of £1 10s. in lieu of clothes could be given, or rent paid. Whole outfits of clothes, or only individual garments were distributed. Occasionally more substantial articles like tools were given, or even a horse and cart. In one case a fisherman entered into a bill of sale with the parish for repairs to his boat. Most of these items were of a routine nature, and only the most unusual of them are of interest today.

Seductions and illegitimate births were a frequent subject for the Vestry books. The entries included acceptance of such offers as that of John Patterson in 1794 to pay the sum of 40s. for the lying-in of Elizabeth Coppard, who was then pregnant by him, and thereafter the sum of 2s. a week for as long as their child was chargeable on the parish; or of John Lelliott in 1799 to pay one guinea down for the child he had had by the widow Upton and 1s. 6d. a week for the future. But when the transgressing father belonged to a family of substance the parish did not hesitate to drive a better bargain. In 1790 a bond of £50 was accepted from George Lansdoll of Dorking to indemnify the parish against any issue of Mary Earl by John Lansdoll, who was presumably the son of George Lansdoll and under age at the time. If the identity of the father was not known at the time of the birth the mother was later taken before the magistrates at Lewes (Brighton did not have its Petty Sessions until 1812) to swear to the identity of the father. In a case where the mother died before the paternity of her child was established a friend to whom she was supposed to have revealed the identity of the father was taken before the magistrates for the same purpose.

In cases where men deserted their wives and children, leaving them as a charge upon the parish, the men were advertised for. One man was also indicted because he had, in addition, sold tools belonging to the parish which had been entrusted to him. In 1790 a deserted wife was allowed to live in a house in Bartholomews called 'Elisher's Hole', presumably adjoining the workhouse, and in addition was allowed 10s. a week for the support of her family.

Entries about the poor of other parishes who had to be transferred to their parish of origin are not as frequent as one might have imagined. Several entries on this subject were made on 26 November 1790 which are fairly typical of this kind of transaction. Mrs. West made application for relief on behalf of her son John and herself. They were taken before the magistrates at Lewes eight days later to prove the place of their legal settlement, and in the meantime were given 5s. relief. A shoemaker named Clark was also examined as to his place of settlement and removed thereto with his wife and family. Francis Measor was similarly taken before the justices to be committed to the House of Correction for having returned to Brighton from Keymer, which was the place of his legal settlement, after having been transferred there by a court order, and for being troublesome on his return to Brighton. Three other women appeared on the same occasion, two of them to be sworn to their parish, one of them being with child by Henry Newell, and a third, Sarah Davy, to be sworn as to the father of the child by whom she was pregnant.

An interesting entry in the Vestry books occurs in June 1805 when two of the Overseers named John Hargreaves and John Mills visited Birch and Robinson's cotton mills at Broughton Lodge, Backborough, Lancashire, to report on the state of health and morals of the Brighton children apprenticed there. There were 140 children at the mills, and 20 cows were kept for their sustenance. The Overseers were fully satisfied with the boarding house at the mills, which they found clean and comfortable. The children were fed on alternate days 'on milk diet and animal food'. The beef and butter met their approbation, but the bread they thought 'remarkably brown and tasted sourish, which we were informed was from the dough being raised by leaven'. They remonstrated with the proprietors on the subject, but were assured that it was good wholesome bread that would be passed by any doctor in the county. This assurance they appear to have accepted.

The Overseers found the children 'tolerably clad, the girls better than the boys', and their health good. Their employment was said to be 'far from being laborious'. But words have different meanings at different periods in history because these children worked about 14 hours a day except during a short period in the height of summer when, from want of water, they occasionally worked longer.

Of their moral condition the Overseers were unable to judge except that the proprietors assured then that 'not one act of bastardy has happened among the apprentices during their conducting the business, a period of twenty years'. They were less satisfied with the education of the children. This appeared to consist of instruction from a clergyman for two hours only on Sunday evenings. Therefore the improvement of the children 'cannot be much', and none of the Brighton children had been taught to write.

The Overseers' visit to the cotton mills was unannounced, and they arrived there in the absence of the proprietors. One has the impression that the Overseers were somewhat dissatisfied with what they found and made representations accordingly to Messrs. Birch and Robinson. But that the latter blandly replied that if the Brighton Overseers were not satisfied with the treatment of the children they could take them away, or the mill-owners would 'at a moment's notice transfer them over to any person they might appoint'. No further action followed. So one presumes that the Overseers accepted that anything was good enough for the poor in the usual tradition of the period.

Well-known names do not very often occur in the Vestry books. One that does is Queenie Thrale, daughter of Dr. Johnson's friends, Henry and Hester Thrale, who occupied a house in West Street, Brighton. On 16 February 1791 it was recorded that 'on the Application of Miss Thrale it is ordered that a poor Boy proposed by her be received into the poor House during the pleasure of the officers on being paid by the said Miss Thrale 4s.

weekly for his board'. A similar arrangment was made
in March 1805 by Nathaniel Kemp of Preston Manor and
later of Ovingdean Hall on behalf of a woman named
Lemons for whom he paid 3s. a week. Nathaniel Kemp
served on the committee which assisted the overseers. So
did Thomas Scutt of the Wick House, Hove, whose son,
the Rev. Thomas Scutt, was responsible for the development of Brunswick Square and Terrace. Samuel Shergold,
the proprietor of the *Castle* Hotel which adjoins the
Royal Pavilion, served in the same capacity. One of the
Overseers in the 1790s was William Wigney, whose bank of
Wigney and Co., at the corner of Great East Street and
Castle Square and whose brewery, Wigney and Sons in
Ship Street, were amongst the best-known commercial
enterprises of the period.

But probably the most celebrated name was actually
that of one of the inmates of the workhouse. This was
Phoebe Hassell or Hessell, the woman soldier who was
born in 1713 in the reign of Queen Anne and died in the
reign of George IV, having at the age of 15, fallen in love
with a soldier named Samuel Golding, whose regiment
was ordered overseas. She enlisted in another regiment
also bound for the West Indies and managed to preserve
the secret of her sex during the whole period of her
service. She was wounded in the arm by a bayonet at
the battle of Fontenoy in 1745. But it was not until her
lover was himself wounded and invalided home that she
revealed her sex to the wife of the colonel of the regiment and obtained her discharge. Phoebe and Samuel
Golding were then married and lived happily together
for 20 years. After his death she settled in Brighton and
married again. By 1792 Phoebe was 79 years old. Her
second husband, William Hassell, was still living. On
29 December in that year the Vestry book recorded a
gift of three guineas to them 'to get their Bed Netts which
they had pledged to pay Dr. Harrison for Medicines'.
By 1797 her husband must have died, for in that year
occurs a resolution that her rent should be paid and her
weekly allowances discontinued. At this time she partly

supported herself by selling gingerbread and apples from a basket at the corner of Old Steine and Marine Parade. On 9 March 1801 it was recorded that Harry Bridger, esquire, of Buckingham Place, Shoreham, 'be written to and informed that the Parish Officers of Brighthelmston will not be answerable for any Rent on Phoebe Hassell's account after Lady Day next'. Possibly Bridger was by then making her an allowance. In August 1806 she was allowed a pair of shoes and stockings 'and one change on leaving the poor-house'.

During the last years of her life, possibly from this date when she left the poor-house, Phoebe was granted a pension by the Prince of Wales. She lived to see him become King, and, as the oldest inhabitant in the town, rode in the Vicar of Brighton's carriage in the local procession on the occasion of George IV's coronation. She died on 12 December 1821, aged 108, and was buried in St. Nicholas's churchyard. Her tomb-stone was erected at the expense of the pawnbroker and later Town Commissioner, Hyam Lewis. It was recently restored and re-lettered by the Northumberland Fusiliers, successors to the 42nd Foot, who still consider Phoebe to have been a member of their regiment. A portrait of her hangs in their mess.

Public events occasionally make an appearance in the Vestry books. For instance, on 29 October 1798 it was resolved that books should be opened at the local banks to receive contributions 'for the relief of the Widows and Children of the brave Men who so Nobly fought and fell in the Service of their King and Country (or other relations depending on them for support) and of such as have been wounded in the British Fleet in the glorious Victory of Rear Admiral Lord Nelson over a superior French Fleet on the coast of Egypt on the 1st and 2nd of August 1798'.

A year later (21 November 1799) a deputation of fishermen attended the Vestry to request the officers of the parish to petition the Admiralty to take steps to get 10 of their number released from captivity 'who were early on the Morning of the 20th instant taken out of their Boats whilst Fishing off Seaford by two French Lugger Privateers and carried into some port in France'. A petition was sent to Sir Godfrey Webster, M.P., of Battle Abbey requesting him to lay it before the Lords of the Admiralty.

In May 1800 occurred an entry concerning the 'Hants Foncible Cavalry' which had been disbanded in Brighton. Some of the soldiers were ill at the time and had not been able to travel home with their wives and children. They had therefore become a charge upon the parish to maintain them or remove them to their parish of origin at a considerable distance away. In view of the great expense of either course the parish petitioned the Secretary of War to grant some relief on their account.

At the next meeting three days later, an address was drawn up and signed congratulating the King on his recent escape from an attempted assassination. This was exposed for signature by other inhabitants and then handed to the High Constable and to Thomas Pelham, Major General Lennox, and the Members of Parliament for the county, for presentation to the King.

2.—1810-1854

The Election of Town Commissioners

After the passing of the Act of 1810 the nature of the entries in the Vestry books entirely changed. The Vestry was no longer concerned with the daily administration of the workhouse. The responsibility for this passed to the Directors and Guardians of the Poor who were elected by the Town Commissioners. But the Vestry acquired the new responsibility of electing the Town Commissioners themselves who had previously been nominated by their own number.

The Commissioners still served for life or until resignation. At Vestry meetings election was by show of hands, but at a meeting on 21 September 1819 a ballot was demanded and took place. While voting was in process the doors of the room were closed and some qualified electors who presented themselves were denied the opportunity to vote. At the following meeting the election was disputed and declared void because it had been held by a ballot at which some voters had been denied the occasion to vote and some voters had voted for themselves. The Vestry proceeded to consult counsel named S. B. Burnaby. His opinion was that vote by ballot was not contemplated by the Act of 1810; that, if a ballot was held, admission could not be refused during the process to any qualified elector; but that electors could vote for themselves. He advised the Vestry to treat this particular election as void, and another was duly held. Henceforward election by a show of hands was resumed.

The Clerk

William Attree, who had been Clerk to the Vestry since 1790, died in 1810. He was succeeded by his son, Thomas Attree, who also assumed the office of Clerk to the

Brighton Commissioners. His salary in 1820 was £100 a year, though the Vestry Minutes do not record this. He had been born in 1778 at 8 Ship Street, where his father practised as a solicitor, and had been himself admitted as a solicitor in 1799. He practised there all his life and continued to live in Ship Street until, in about 1830, he built himself the house in Queen's Park which has since been called the Attree Villa. There he died on 7 February 1863, aged 85. He played a prominent part in the foundation of both the Brighton Dispensary and of the Sussex County Hospital. At one time he held so many local offices (Vestry Clerk; Clerk, Solicitor and Treasurer to the Brighton Commissioners; Clerk and Solicitor to the Directors and Guardians of the Poor) that his enemies called him 'the King of Brighton'. He also held until his death the remunerative office of Stamp Director for Sussex and Surrey.

Thomas Attree remained Clerk to the Vestry until 12 April 1830, when he was succeeded by his partner, Somers Clarke. The latter was born in 1802 and was the son of a clergyman. His youth was spent at Midhurst and Plumpton. After qualifying as an attorney he became managing clerk to Few and Co. in London, but moved to Brighton in 1827 as managing clerk to Thomas Attree's firm, then Attree and Cooper. On the retirement of Frederick Cooper in 1830 he was taken into partnership, and the firm became, Attree, Clarke and Co. At about the same time that he became Vestry Clerk he also assumed the office of Clerk to the Directors and Guardians of the Poor. He was also Clerk to the Local Land Tax Commissioners. He lived for about 20 years at 27 Oriental Place, and then, in 1848, moved to 57 Regency Square, where he remained until his death. He still held the position of Vestry Clerk in 1854, when the town was incorporated. Thereafter the post had virtually no functions, but he remained theoretically in office until his death on 2 January 1892; thereby serving as such for over 60 years.

His son of the same name was the architect who restored St. Nicholas's church in 1892, enlarged St. Peter's

church in 1896-1902 and built St. Martin's church, Lewes
Road, in 1875. The father had a lifelong connection with
St. Nicholas's church: he had been honorary secretary to
the restoration fund in 1853. In 1867 he presented to the
church an iron pulpit designed by his son and, later, a
stained glass window in memory of his friend the Vicar,
the Rev. H. M. Wagner, who died in 1870. Somers Clarke
also purchased the rectorial tithes in order to secure
control of the chancel for the parish.

The Accounts of the Parish Officers

Every year the accounts of the High Constable, of the
churchwardens and overseers of the poor and of the
Directors and Guardians of the Poor had to be passed by
the Vestry. The cost of the High Constable's annual
dinner was always a matter of some concern. In July 1824
it was resolved that this should not exceed 30 guineas.
In 1793 it had only cost four guineas.

There were often disputes about individual items. For
instance in October 1825 the sum of £29 2s. was disallowed by the Vestry. The officers appealed to the
magistrates in Petty Sessions and won their appeal. But
the parish then took their case to Quarter Sessions. The
verdict of this court was a compromise more in favour
of the officers than of the parish. Sums amounting to
£25 11s. were allowed, and others amounting to £3 6s.
disallowed.

On 27 October 1826 the Vestry disallowed from the
accounts of the Directors and Guardians of the Poor
the sum of £24 paid to G. Chasserau, the Assistant Overseer, for monies stolen by a pauper, on the grounds that
this was an illegal appropriation of public money. The
chairman of the meeting, Edmund Savage, refused to
sign the accounts as passed and left the chair. His conduct
in doing so was then voted 'highly censurable'. But on
3 May 1827 the payment of the sum previously struck
out of the accounts was in fact allowed.

The next dispute was with the Town Commissioners.
On 22 August 1827 the Vestry recorded that in 1825

they had allowed the scale of rating to be increased from one-ninth to one-sixth of the annual value of property for the specific purpose of widening Pool Lane (now Pool Valley), improving the market and removing the buildings which had 'so long been a Nuisance to His Majesty's Palace'. The Commissioners had, however, neglected to carry out these improvements, and had instead involved the town in 'other expensive Contracts without consulting the Inhabitants'. The Vestry therefore reduced the town rate to its previous level of 1825.

On 8 November 1827 a special rate of 9d. in the pound was levied to pay off the arrears of debts amounting to £326 16s. 8d. incurred by the Vestry. These arrears included money due to the parish clerk, John Pocock, whose salary had not been paid regularly for 12 years. John Pocock was a sawyer who, for some years after 1790, also kept the *Hen and Chickens* inn, later the *Running Horse*, in King Street. He was Clerk to the Chapel Royal from 1795-1808 and Clerk to the parish church from 1808 to 1846. He died on 13 June 1846 and was buried in St. Nicholas's churchyard. He tomb can still be seen in its original position to the right of the pathway leading up from Dyke Road.

On 11 October 1827 when the High Constable's accounts were presented, these included an amount of £105 for the arrears of the salaries of the Headboroughs for two quarters. This was passed, but the minutes of the meeting were followed by a protest written in the handwriting of the solicitor, Frederick Cooper, and signed by him and three other people to the effect that the payment of the police out of the poor-rate was illegal.

On 1 November a meeting was held to discuss the possibility of obtaining a further Act of Parliament to amend the existing regulations affecting the police. The meeting was evidently stormy. The High Constable, Edward Hill Creasy, attempted to 'usurp' the chair and thereby incurred the 'loud disapprobation of the Town'. A vote of thanks to the chairman, Johnson Lamprell, was recorded for his 'manly conduct in taking the Chair in opposition to the attempts of a base faction', with the additional rider: 'and may every future Chairman be elected as honourably and conduct himself as impartially as he has done'. The meeting did not favour a new Act because this would excite angry feelings and entail considerable expense, also because the existing powers were sufficient.

The disputed issue of the £105 was, without consulting the Vestry, referred to the magistrates, who ordered its payment. This was formally authorised by the Vestry on 16 January 1828. But nine days later the Vestry protested that the magistrates had no right to order this payment and decided to appeal to Quarter Sessions. They went on to say that they greatly regretted that the present High Constable had ever been appointed to that office and that the parish officers had neglected their duty to resist the misappropriation of parish funds.

The Vestry then proceeded to present memorials protesting against the local magistrates' action to Lord Egremont as Lord Lieutenant of Sussex, and to Lord Abergavenny as Lord of the Manor of the Hundred of Whalesbone, whose duty it was to supervise the election of the High Constable and Headboroughs. The memorial to Lord Egremont complained about the interference of the magistrates. Lord Egremont not unnaturally replied that he had no powers other than those of an individual vestryman and in any case would not think of interfering since the Vestry was appealing to Quarter Sessions.

The memorial to Lord Abergavenny stated that in recent years his steward had transmitted to the High Constable for the time being the mandate to summon the Leet jury of inhabitants which would elect his successor and that, as a result, certain persons had dictated to the High Constable who should be summoned. The jury had therefore been packed.

Lord Abergavenny replied through the mouth of Daniel Rowland, who had acted as judge of the Court Leet for the past 12 years. He stated that it had always been his custom to follow the practice of the Sheriffs in

summoning High Court juries, namely that he had directed
the High Constable to summon a meeting of about 40
substantial householders, from whom 23 had been chosen
by him indiscriminately to elect the High Constable.
For 10 years out of the 12 the then Vicar of Brighton,
subsequently Bishop of Chichester, had acted as foreman
of the jury. He was not conscious of any irregularity
having been committed by past High Constables, but he
saw no reason why magistrates should be excluded from
serving on the jury, as some local inhabitants had suggested. But in future he would require the High Constable
to present him with a list of at least 50 'of the most
respectable inhabitants'. These names he would make
public in advance and, if any of them were challenged, he
would exclude them from the list. Out of the remainder
he would select 23 names by ballot to form the jury.

When the committee who had prepared and presented
the memorials wished to report the replies to the Vestry
the parish officers refused to summon a meeting for the
purpose, and a meeting had to be specially requisitioned.

Quarter Sessions overruled the local magistrates and
decided that the sum of £105 paid for 'necessary aid and
assistance for securing Felons and Offenders' should be
disallowed. On 2 May 1828, therefore, the Vestry passed
another resolution in this sense because the Headboroughs
were bound by law to perform those services without
being paid for them. The sum seems, however, to have
already been disbursed. So at a meeting five days later
the existing officers were directed to obtain repayment
from their predecessors.

Two months later (23 July 1828) at a meeting when
the Director and Guardians' accounts were passed, seven
members of the Vestry signed a protest following the
minutes to the effect that these accounts contained
an illegal expenditure for services of the Headboroughs
but without more specifically mentioning its nature.

No further disagreement about money occurred until
1832 when, on 4 July, the Vestry recorded that, in their
opinion, the Town Commissioners had 'wantonly and

improvidently expended the funds of the Town entrusted to their care'. The Vestry appointed a committee to investigate the Commissioners' accounts and to report what steps should be taken to extricate the town from its difficulties without raising the rates. But nothing seems to have come of this.

Church Matters

Church matters occur fairly frequently. In 1814 a new table of fees was drawn up which remained in force until 1826.[1] In August 1814 a new treble bell was purchased, and in March 1818 two more bells were bought for the ringers at the cost of 62. 2d. a pound.

By 1818 the population of Brighton was 18,000. The two existing churches (St. Nicholas and the Chapel Royal) were therefore inadequate for this number. At a meeting held on 5 November 1818 with the Vicar, the Rev. Robert James Carr, in the chair, it was resolved to build another church, and a committee was formed to carry out the resolution. This led to the building of St. Peter's church.

Though the Vestry books do not mention it, a competition for the design of the church was organised, in which the winner was the young architect, Charles Barry, who had just returned from his grand tour of Europe and Asia. The runners-up in the competition were the local architects, Wilds and Busby, and the builder was William Ranger. The construction took from 1824 to 1828. The finished article is one of the best examples in England of an early Gothic revival church.

Finance eventually caused trouble between the parish and the architect, whose commission amounted to £1,150 13s. The parish refused to pay additional fees of £45 for designing the organ-case and of £13 for drawing of alterations to the west gallery. They also asked Barry to hand over to them the working drawings of the church,

1. In March 1791 the Vestry Clerk had been instructed to enquire whether the parish minister was entitled to claim a fee for breaking the ground on the burial of a parishioner. But no answer was recorded.

which he refused to do on the grounds that this was contrary to the usual custom.

But much greater trouble arose over the main finances of the church's construction. The parish decided not to obtain a private Act of Parliament but to proceed under the aegis of the Commissioners appointed by the Act of 1818 for the erection of additional churches. These Commissioners made a loan of £15,000 to the parish which was accepted as a charge upon the church rates and was to be repaid by annual instalments. Three thousand pounds a year was first suggested, but £1,500 was agreed by the Commissioners. Voluntary contributions were collected. Thomas Read Kemp, one of the lords of the manor, acted as honorary treasurer; Lord Egremont, Sir David Scott and the Vicar of Brighton as trustees. The remainder of the cost was defrayed by the parish.

In 1824 the parish applied to the Commissioners for further financial help. A grant of £3,000 was agreed and deducted from the £15,000 to be refunded. But there seems to have been some misunderstanding as, in 1833, the Commissioners claimed the sum back. The parish prepared to resist the Commissioners' claim in the law-courts if necessary. Presumably they were unsuccessful in so doing because in November 1836 the Commissioners issued a writ of mandamus against the parish. The Vestry then resolved to ask the Commissioners to remit the sum or, failing that, to allow it to be paid in two instalments. But there is no record of what transpired over this. The final figures are rather difficult to unravel because, when the accounts were published in 1828, showing a total cost of £20,365 5s., there were entries amounting to £4,700 in grants from the Commissioners, and the parish claimed that the amount taken from the parish funds did not exceed £15,000.

An application for a further grant had been refused in 1827. But the Commissioners for Building New Churches then consented to an arrangement whereby some of the pew-rents were to be used for the repayment of the debt incurred by the parish in building the church.

The building could seat 1,800 people. One-fifth of the sittings were set aside for the poor. The Minister or Perpetual Curate's stipend was fixed at £550 a year and the clerk's at £50. These were to be paid out of other pew-rents, and the remainder used for the repayment of the church debt. But in 1839 it was recorded that the maximum amount that these pew-rents had ever produced in one.year was £556. The Minister had never received more than £509 and sometimes as little as £364.

As originally designed by Barry, St. Peter's church was intended to have a spire surmounting the tower. This was never executed and there is nothing in the Vestry minutes to say why. A spire is never referred to. As late as 1841 Barry himself expressed regret that no spire had been erected and in fact designed another version.

In 1827 the parish voted a special sum of £1,500 for the internal fittings of the church including an external clock in the tower to be illuminated by gas. Beyond this the Vestry refused to go. The church plate had been presented by Lord Egremont in 1826. When the church-wardens showed a disposition to accept additional liability for inserting chandeliers in the church the Vestry reproved them for exceeding their instructions in view of the Vestry's repeated determination not to spend anything further on St. Peter's.

The minutes went on to say that the expenses attendant upon services were not legally chargeable on the parish. In 1835 this was taken still further when an attempt to levy a special church rate of 1d. in the pound for the purpose of paying the salaries of the organist, the sexton and the pew-openers was defeated on the grounds that this would be 'most unjust and oppressive towards the Dissenters'. Funds were raised by voluntary subscription for these salaries, and in 1836 it was resolved that all future legal liabilities with regard to the parish church which had hitherto been a charge upon the inhabitants generally should be defrayed by voluntary contributions.

In 1839 the Vestry was minded to object to paying the expense of lighting St. Peter's church for a third

Sunday service at 7 p.m., and took legal advice on the subject. But counsel's opinion did not encourage them to think that they could legally refuse to sanction this expenditure.

These were the first manifestations in the parish of the challenge by Nonconformity to the monopoly of the Established Church which became a marked feature of the Victorian period.

But the theme was to be a recurrent one in Brighton. In November 1836 a rate of 1½d. in the pound was proposed to defray the expenses of St. Nicholas's and St. Peter's churches. An amendment to adjourn the meeting for six months was carried on a show of hands. A poll was then demanded, at which the amendment was lost by 1,389 votes to 1,702, and the original motion carried. Similar incidents occurred in May 1839 and in March 1841. In October 1841 and December 1843 motions to levy a 1d. or 2d. rate respectively were even defeated on a poll.

Opposition to the payment of church rates was not confined to such local polls. In January 1843 the Vestry petitioned both Houses of Parliament against the levying of church rates in general as being 'unjust in principle, a violation of the rights of conscience and a continual source of division amongst the inhabitants'. A similar petition of April 1841 said that they were unjust to those 'who at their own expense provided places of worship and maintain that religious instruction which their own sincere and honest convictions approve'.

The next dispute related to St. Nicholas's churchyard. An extension north of Church Street had been opened in 1824. In March 1832 the parish had accepted from George Lowdell the gift of a portion of his garden to enlarge the original churchyard on the right-hand side of the pathway leading from North Street (now the lower section of Dyke Road). But by 1840 there was only room for about 100 more graves. A committee appointed to consider possibilities recommended the use of land adjoining the workhouse and the cattle market on the east side of Church Hill (now Dyke Road) which already belonged to the parish. But the Vestry decided to make a 3d. rate for the purchase of other land. This became the burial ground on the west side of Dyke Road which is entered through an archway with the date 1846 on its keystone. The first burial there took place in 1841. The land was laid out in an ornamental fashion with mounds, trees, plants, borders, walks, and a tank to the design of Amon Henry Wilds, for which he was paid a fee of £25. A print of the new extension exists showing an ornamental stepped pyramid and a terrace of catacombs as in Highgate cemetery, which were never built. However, despite this curtailment of the design, when the remainder of the work had been carried out in 1841 the lavish expenditure of £2,524 18s. 6d. incurred the extreme displeasure of a committee appointed to examine the churchwardens' accounts. A big row took place. A proposal to levy a church rate of 1d. was rejected and the churchwardens' accounts were not passed. Following the minutes of the meeting of 26 October 1841 a note was entered: 'Resolved that a vote of censure be passed against the Vicar for his improper conduct in the Chair and that the Vestry Clerk be ordered to enter such vote in the Parish Book immediately after the minutes of the meeting'.

Sergeant Talfourd, who was a local resident and magistrate was consulted and advised that the expenditure of parish funds on both the maintenance of an evening service at St. Peter's church and the embellishment of the new burial ground near St. Nicholas's was illegal. The parish had no obligation for either church other than the repair of its fabric. The items of expenditure involved were therefore disallowed from the churchwardens' accounts in November 1841. More members were urged to attend Vestry meetings to prevent decisions being taken by small majorities.

In March 1845 at the request of the churchwardens the path through the churchyard on Church Hill (Dyke Road) was paved with bricks at the expense of the Town Commissioners.

A year later a proposal was made to levy a church rate of 6d. in the pound for the purpose of enlarging St. Nicholas's church. But a poll was demanded and at this the proposal was defeated by 1,328 votes to 754. In the following year the Vestry was only asked to vote a church rate of 1½d. in the pound for current church expenses, but the suggestion was similarly defeated by 1,040 votes to 706. In May the churchwardens drew the attention of the Vestry to a recent decision by the House of Lords to the effect that the repair of a parish church was the legal responsibility of the parish and suggested a church rate of 1½d in the pound. This was nevertheless defeated by 1,227 votes to 1,030.

This matter came to a crisis in the following December, when the Archdeacon of Lewes issued a citation to the Vestry to hold a special meeting to fix a church rate. The Vicar of Brighton took the chair. On this occasion a church rate of only 1d. in the pound was suggested. But amendments were proposed, first that the St. Nicholas's and St. Peter's churches should be restored and maintained by voluntary contributions, and secondly that consideration of the proposed rate should be adjourned for six months. The Vicar declared both amendments illegal. On a show of hands the original motion was defeated by 90 votes to 47, but the Vicar declared the opposition to the motion to be illegal and that therefore the motion had been carried. The opposition then summoned another meeting at which a petition to the House of Commons was drawn up, stating that the compulsory imposition of church rates was 'contrary to the great principles of civil and religious liberty . . . and a source of bitterness and dissension in the community'. It urged the immediate abolition of this 'obnoxious impost'.

There the matter rested until September 1849 when the churchwardens' accounts were thrown out because much of the previous church rate remained uncollected. An attempt to levy another church rate of 1d. in the pound was defeated on a show of hands on the grounds that the churchwardens' accounts had not been passed.

The same procedure took place in December 1851 when another proposal for a church rate of 1d. was defeated on a show of hands by 143 to 32, on the grounds that it would be unjust to those who had already paid the previous rate 'now in course of litigation', whereas those who had not done so were by their 'legal position exempt from the liability'. This is somewhat difficult to understand. Not only was a poll requested in the usual way but also a scrutiny by written demand of one of the churchwardens, James Cordy. The chairman, who was the Vicar of Brighton, thereupon declared that the state of the poll was 'under protest from Mr. Cordy for the rate 1,120, against the rate and the clear, undoubted and established law of the land 1,244 and that the proceedings of the day were at an end'. The same occurred in May 1852 when the figures were 33 to 147 and on a show of hands, and 1,307 to 1,901 at the poll.

This rather ridiculous process of advance and retreat might perhaps have continued indefinitely until the church fell down, had not the Duke of Wellington most timely died on 14 September 1852. This gave the Vicar of Brighton a chance to put forward a brilliant suggestion. Before coming to Brighton in 1824 the Rev. H. M. Wagner had been tutor to the Duke's two sons for seven years. The Duke himself as a boy had been a pupil of Wagner's grandfather, the Rev. Henry Michell,[1] at the original Brighton vicarage in Nile Street and during that time had worshipped at St. Nicholas's church. When a meeting of gentlemen was called six days later after the Duke's death to consider the best means of testifying respect for his memory the Vicar suggested that no better form of doing so could be found than by restoring and enlarging the parish church where the Duke had worshipped as a boy. This idea was accepted and a committee was appointed to raise the necessary funds, Within a month £5,000 had been subscribed. The Vicar himself gave £1,000.

1. Henry Michell was Vicar of Brighton from 1750 to 1789.

The restoration was entrusted to R. C. Carpenter who was at the same time engaged in building St. Paul's church, West Street, for the Vicar's son, the Rev. A. D. Wagner. Carpenter was an excellent architect in original work, but unfortunately the restoration of St. Nicholas's church was carried out in the usual drastic fashion of all mid-Victorian work.[1] In 1853 the church presented somewhat the same picture as the parish church of Whitby, Yorkshire, does today; that it is to say it was an irregular Gothic edifice with the aisles of the chancel and nave of different heights and widths, and, inside, galleries on all four sides of the church, even over the chancel arch. These galleries were lit by dormer windows and entered by outside staircases which gave the building a most picturesque appearance. All these irregularities were swept away by Carpenter. The aisles were demolished and rebuilt to a uniform extra width of 15 feet. The arcade of the south chancel was altered from two arches to one. A new east window was inserted in the chancel. Inside, all the 18th-century fittings, which were so disliked by the Tractarians, such as box-pews and galleries were removed. The monuments were all moved to the west end of the nave, where they are now hidden from view in the darkest part of the church. New stained glass, designed by Hardman, was inserted. The only aesthetic gain was the erection of a monument to the Duke of Wellington, designed by R. C. Carpenter, and sculptured by Philip of Vauxhall, in the form of an Eleanor cross of hexagonal plan. This was first placed at the east end of the new south aisle. But in the 1920s, when things Victorian were greatly undervalued, it was removed to its present undignified position at the west end of the north aisle, where it cannot be seen, and where there is not even room for its finial to stand upright. It is high time that it was rescued from this oblivion, restored and removed to a more prominent position.

1. The church was still further altered and restored by Somers Clarke in 1892.

In the churchyard the avenue of trees lining the pathway up from Church Hill (Dyke Road) was planted. At this time it was clear that the churchyard, despite three extensions, would soon be unable to accommodate all the dead parishioners. In May 1853 the sexton reported that there was a vault in the new burial ground, west of Church Hill, that, if re-opened, would contain 100 coffins and that, if the chalk were removed, the burial ground would afford accommodation for another 12 months.

The introduction of new ideas about hygiene also gave rise to another interdiction. In February 1854 the parish received a communication from the Privy Council under the Burials Beyond the Metropolis Act, 1853, prohibiting any further burials after 1 June either in St. Nicholas's church, or any of its churchyards, or in any other church or chapel in Brighton, and directing that no other burial ground should be opened without the permission of the Home Secretary.

On further examination in May it was ascertained that the new burial ground contained space for 260 new graves, 20 vaults, and 25 steined graves, which would probably suffice for about four months. The Vestry therefore asked the Home Secretary, Lord Palmerston, to extend the time available for taking action under the Act until 1 October while they negotiated with the Extra Mural Cemetery Company. A deputation of five members of the Established Church and four Dissenters was chosen to wait on Lord Palmerston to discuss the matter. The assistance of the Brighton Members of Parliament was solicited in arranging the interview. Lord Palmerston replied, through Admiral Sir George Brooke Pechell, who was one of the Brighton Members, that he was prepared to extend the time available until 1 October.

The parish meanwhile approached the Extra Mural Cemetery to see whether they would be prepared to sell the land which the company owned, but received a negative reply. The next step was to enquire on what terms that company would undertake parish burials in their cemetery. The charge was 5s. for adult paupers and 3s. for children, both of whom had previously been buried free in the old churchyard, and £1 11s. 6d. for a common grave which had previously been 9s. in the churchyard. These higher charges and the fact that the Extra Mural Cemetery only contained 13 acres made the parish think that they must look elsewhere and should secure land of at least 40 acres in extent.

They therefore advertised in the local papers and approached nine landowners. Of those willing to sell, the choice lay between land belonging to W. C. Mabbott at Black Rock, adjoining the Gas Works; land belonging to the Marquess of Bristol, adjoining the Extra Mural Cemetery; land belonging to George Harrington, on the north-west side of Lewes Road opposite the *Bear* inn; land belonging to the Trustees of William Stanford at Goldstone Bottom on the Shoreham Road; and land belonging to Mrs. Ogle, between the railway and Dyke Road. On 15 August 1854 the parish therefore appointed a Burial Board of nine members, consisting of five members of the Established Church and four Dissenters, to negotiate the purchase of one of these pieces of land, and requested the Home Secretary to allow them a further extension of time for the purpose, until 1 January 1855.

At a further meeting on 29 August the Burial Board reported that the directors of the Extra Mural Cemetery were, after all, prepared to sell their land for £25,000, but that they did not recommend purchase, particularly as the Vicar of Brighton would have to be compensated for the loss of burial fees. Meanwhile the proprietors of Kemp Town had protested against the use of W. C. Mabbott's land at Black Rock, and the Board thought this protest was 'justly entitled to attention'. The choice was, therefore, between George Harrington's land and Mrs. Ogle's land, both of which could be obtained for approximately £10,000.

Lord Palmerston refused the request for extension of time beyond 1 October. When the Vestry met on 26 September the Burial Board recommended the purchase of part of George Harrington's lands at the cost of approximately £7,500. This would comprise 30 acres in the western part of the land which would enable it to be approached from the London Road and Preston Drove and would avoid the steep approach from Ditchling Road. But despite the fact that authority to use the existing churchyard of St. Nicholas expired in a week's time the Vestry passed an amendment to the effect that the matter should be adjourned and the appointment of the Burial Board be not confirmed. A show of hands to this effect was confirmed on a poll by a vote of 1,308 to 1,267.

The minutes are silent as to what ensued on 1 October, and the matter was not mentioned again until early in 1856. In the interval, however, the Marquess of Bristol came forward and offered the parish free of charge 20 acres of his land immediately to the south of the Extra Mural Cemetery, and, like it, approached from Lewes Road. He had previously been reluctant to provide the land because it had been leased for 99 years to William Hallett, who was then Mayor of Brighton. The Mayor had, however, agreed to surrender his interest, which made the gift possible. On 9 April 1856 the Vestry grate-fully accepted this gift and expressed the opinion that a memorial should be placed at the entrance to the ground recording Lord Bristol's generosity. It was further sug-gested that a deputation should wait upon Lord Bristol in London to express the thanks of the parish, but this he declined.

A committee was appointed to consider the best way to lay out the grounds. This committee reported that it would only be necessary to use part of the ground as a cemetery for the time being and that the remainder could be let. Part of the land would have to be consecrated for use for Church of England burials and part unconsecrated for use by Dissenters. The Vicar, clerk and sexton would be entitled either to the same fees for burials in the conse-crated ground as had been paid in the old churchyard or to compensation in lieu. The Vicar received £100 a year from the Extra Mural Cemetery Company and had agreed that this sum should be taken into account in deciding the amount of the revised fees to be paid to him. The committee therefore recommended that he should be paid £100 a year for three years and thereafter an additional sum of £25 a year up to a maximum of £200; that the clerk should similarly be paid £45 a year, rising by increments of £11 5s. to a maximum of £90; and that the sexton should be paid a separate fee for each grave dug. Similar arrangements ought to be made with a Dissenting minister in relation to burials in the unconsecrated part of the cemetery. But when the Vestry met on 7 May 1856 they did not confirm this arrangement. It was instead resolved that all remuneration for burials in the consecrated part of the cemetery should be by way of fees and not by salary. They did, however, agree to appoint a new Burial Board. This action was reported to the Home Secretary, who sent down an inspector to inspect the land provided for the new cemetery.

The Workhouse and the Poor

The Brighton Act of 1810 put the collection of the poor-rate and the administration of the workhouse on a more efficient basis. It provided for the appointment by the Town Commissioners of Directors and Guardians of the Poor and for the engagement of a paid Assistant Overseer of the poor who received a salary of £200 a year. The first two occupants of that office were Grenville and White. The successor to John Sickelmore as Master of the workhouse was named Bailey.

The whereabouts of the minutes of the Directors and Guardians of the Poor, if they survive, are not known. But there is in existence a report made by them to the Town Commissioners within a year of their assuming responsibility for the workhouse. This is actually entered in the minutes of the Town Commissioners, since it was the latter who actually chose the Directors and Guardians. But it may be convenient to consider it here as most of the dealings with the workhouse and the poor normally come under the heading of the Vestry. The report is dated 17 April 1811.

On taking over the workhouse the Directors and
Guardians found that the number of inmates which it
contained was approximately a hundred. This number
they had reduced to 82 on the principle that 'it should
be a *Workhouse* and not a *playhouse*'. Similarly, outdoor
relief was not given without work being entailed, and the
Directors found that 'many who applied for parochial
aid, when found that they must work if they received it,
then found that they could do without it and have never
renewed their application'. They added: 'It is well known
how many of the Fishery in this Town are idle and
drunken. They can get enough in the Summer nearly to
maintain themselves and families thro' the Winter. But
idleness and drinking consumes that which ought to be
laid up for a rainy day'. No relief, therefore, was given
to any fisherman who 'could not braid and who refused
to learn'. Spinning wheels were bought for the use of
women and children in the workhouse who were thereby
enabled to earn 6d. and more a day.

As the town was in debt and 'many at the present
distressing Period are called to pay parochial and other
taxes who have hardly Bread for themselves and children'
the Directors and Guardians felt a strong urge for
economy. Some of them had 'turned their minds much
to the writings of Count Romford respecting food and
the most economical method of cooking it'. They felt
that 'improvements' could be made in the diet of the
workhouse which would be 'full as or more nutritious
than the mode of diet which had formerly obtained
and which will produce to the Parish a saving of from
three to four hundred a year'. This plan was adopted,
and the Directors claimed that after nine months the
surgeon declared that he 'never knew the House so
healthy'. It is a pity that we have no comment from
the inhabitants of the 'House' on these 'improvements'.

The Directors and Guardians finally added the smug
comment that they wished to pursue the same plan of
economy concerning themselves as they had followed
for others. 'They have neither tasted a bit of Bread or

drank a glass of Wine at the Parish expense and without wishing to take any merit to themselves or meaning the smallest reflection on the Gentlemen who preceded them each Director can lay his hand on his Heart and conscientiously say that he has not cost the Parish a single farthing'. Virtue could hardly go farther! The comment is chiefly interesting in view of the situation in the workhouse which was found to exist 25 years later.

At about this time the average number of inmates in the poor-house was said by Erredge to be about 150.

The master was then named Hayward, the matron Mrs. Harriet Dennett, the surgeon a Dr. Baldey, and the Assistant Overseer of the Poor G. Chassereau. Erredge records that at this time the inhabitants were farmed for their board to a Mr. Price at a contract price of 4s. a week per head. In 1820 Brighton contained 24,000 inhabitants and 4,000 inhabited houses. As the old workhouse had existed in Bartholomews since the early 18th century, though it had been enlarged at different periods, it was obvious that it could not supply the needs of the parish for much longer. In November 1818 the Directors and Guardians of the Poor therefore offered to sell the workhouse to the Town Commissioners, preparatory to building a larger house elsewhere. A committee of Town Commissioners was appointed to examine the matter but never reported. However, agreement was eventually reached to sell the building for £4,333 6s. 8d., and this was eventually confirmed by the Brighton Act of 1825. The Directors and Guardians then decided to build a new workhouse on the east side of Church Hill immediately above the extension of St. Nicholas's churchyard which lies to the north of Church Street. The site cost £1,400, and the total cost of the building was £10,000. The architect was William Mackie of Charlotte Street, Blackfriars, London, and the builder John Cheeseman. One hundred of the inhabitants from Bartholomews were transferred to the new building between 12 and 24 September 1822. Hayward, the Master of the old house, absconded after a few days in the new premises. His successor, named

Nuttall, did not do much better and was dismissed by the Directors and Guardians on 5 November. The third nominee, Samuel Thorncroft, lasted until April 1834, when he was promoted to be Assistant Overseer.

The Brighton Act of 1825 had increased the assistant overseer's salary to £300 a year. Samuel Thorncroft was still in office not only at the time of incorporation in 1854 but when Erredge wrote his *History of Brighton* in 1862. His successor as Governor of the workhouse was named Collington. Mrs. Dennett, the Matron of the old house, followed her charges up the hill and remained there for five years. In 1827 she was succeeded by Mrs. Alice Pickstock, then from 1843 onwards it became customary to appoint a husband and wife as Governor and Matron. In 1836 Bartlett had succeeded Collington. Mrs. Bartlett became matron in 1843. She and her husband were followed in 1848 by Mr. and Mrs. Cuzens, by Mr. and Mrs. Hodges in 1849, by Mr. and Mrs. C. J. King in 1850, and by Mr. and Mrs. Passmore in 1854.

Despite the high moral tone of the report by the Directors and Guardians of the Poor in 1811, nevertheless a number of scandals occurred in the history of the workhouse, which substantiate Dickens's strictures on the poor law as it then stood. The first was in 1824 when the Directors and Guardians were severely criticised and a committee of the Vestry was appointed to examine their conduct. This committee reported that about 13 per cent. of the poor-rate assessed remained uncollected, which the Assistant Overseer considered inevitable. Due economy had not been observed concerning the prices of some articles supplied to the workhouse, principally on account of the fact that articles were not supplied under contract and payment was often dilatory and made by instalments. The chief irregularity, however, was that in some cases officers of the parish had themselves supplied articles to the workhouse, had benefited from such transactions and had themselves subsequently passed the accounts. No names were mentioned, but the Vestry recorded its deep regret and unqualified censure of these illegalities and hoped the expression of this opinion would be sufficient to prevent their reoccurence in future.

In 1834 the whole position of the poor and workhouses throughout the country was greatly altered by the passing of the Poor Law Amendment Act of that year. This set up a board of three commissioners for the control of the whole administration of poor law relief. The parish considered that these commissioners would have arbitrary power over local Directors and Guardians of the Poor throughout the country. They could direct the erection of workhouses or order the union of several parishes for the purpose. As Brighton had at considerable expense erected a new workhouse only 12 years before, the Vestry was afraid that the new commissioners might direct that other parishes might be united with Brighton without payment on their part. They felt that under the existing laws a saving of over £8,000, which was one-fourth of the total annual outlay on the poor, had been effected by alterations in management and new arrangement for relief 'without any oppression' to the poor. Moreover, under the Act the new Directors and Guardians of the Poor would need no qualification to act as such and would have no control over the arrangements for the parish. They therefore petitioned Parliament against the Bill on 15 May 1834.

The Act, however, was passed, and a year later (17 March 1836) the Vestry presented a memorial to the new Poor Law Commissioners. This stated that 'the owners of property, the Rate payers and the Poor themselves are all well satisfied with the present management of the affairs of this Parish'. As the parishes adjoining Brighton had been united for poor-law purposes, but Brighton had not been affected, and as the arrangements in force in the parish were very similar to those prescribed by the new Act, they requested that these arrangements should not be disturbed.

A year later, in December 1837, the Vestry objected to the appointment of an assessor by the Poor Law Commissioners and instructed the Directors and Guardians of the Poor to disregard the order sent to them and to proceed to appoint an Assistant Overseer as they had always done before under the local Acts of Parliament.

In February 1841, when it was proposed to continue and extend the provisions of the Poor Law Amendment Act, 1834, the parish petitioned Parliament against this. They urged that by the rigid administration of the Act in many places the poor had been caused great hardships and suffering. In December the Vestry again repeated its opposition to the Poor Law Commissioners interfering with the 'local jurisdiction of the Inhabitants over their own Poor'. The Members of Parliament for Brighton, Captain Pechell[1] and Lord Alfred Hervey, were asked to vote against the continuance of this 'oppressive and inhuman ' Bill. In May 1842 both Members attended a meeting of the Vestry in which another petition was drafted for presentation to the House of Commons in a similar sense. Captain Pechell did vote against the second reading of the Bill in June, but Lord Alfred Hervey, and the two Members for East Sussex all voted for it, to the high dudgeon of the Vestry.

Despite the opposition of the parish to these general poor-law measures and their consciousness of their own moral superiority two more grave scandals in the workhouse occurred which were worse than that of 1824. Towards the end of 1836 considerable irregularities were discovered in the accounts of the Directors and Guardians of the Poor. Their Clerk, Frederick Cooper, was being paid at the rate of £500 a year, whereas the Vestry had only voted him the salary of £300 a year, and the two Surgeons of the workhouse were receiving £125 a year instead of £100. Payment had also been made of Frederick Cooper's legal fees of £69 1s. which were incurred in resisting, on behalf of the parish officers, an appeal against an assessment to the poor-rate which was contrary to the express instructions of the Vestry. Moreover, in the two preceding

1. Later Admiral Sir George Brooke Pechell of Castle Coring, who represented Brighton in Parliament from 1835 until his death in 1860.

quarters the sums of £34 3s. and £22 7s. respectively had spent on brandy, gin, port and sherry which the Vestry concluded had been 'consumed otherwise than for the sustenance of the Poor to which alone it appears to them that it should be applied'. The poor souls no doubt never tasted a mouthful of these wines and spirits.

A worse case occurred in 1838. In February another committee of the Vestry was appointed to investigate affairs at the workhouse and reported that some of the Directors and Guardians of the Poor were accustomed to dine twice a week at the workhouse at the expense of the parish, and ordered expensive dishes of fish and other articles for the purpose, as well as dish-covers for their table. A summerhouse in the garden had been fitted up for these repasts. Wines were sent in from outside at the expense of the Directors and Guardians, but in addition 'a considerable quantity of brandy', as well as tea and coffee 'in which brandy was infused', and cigars, were consumed at the expense of the parish. 'Some of the members of the body became affected by the Spiritous liquors consumed by them.' The expenditure involved amounted to £139 3s. 1d. Bartlett, the Governor of the workhouse only gave evidence to the committee reluctantly for fear of victimisation, but what he said was confirmed by other employees. The commitee roundly condemned the whole practice but did not try to enforce restitution of the money spent as they admitted that the practice did not originate with the existing body of Directors and Guardians. They were of opinion that the evils resulted from the removal of the relief of the poor from the Town Hall to the workhouse, which was far away up Church Hill.

These scandals of 1836-8 were remembered as long afterwards as 1862 when Erredge wrote his *History of Brighton*. He even gives more details than the Vestry books provide. He says that the Guardians 'pampered their appetites with john-dorees, salmon, lobsters, Norfolk squab pie and joints in profusion; red and white wines by the dozen and spirits by the gallon; cigars by the box,

and snuff by the pound; with a handsome snuff-box too'.
Blacking was also ordered and a Guardian whom he named
as Paul Hewitt—presumably by then dead—sent his boots
to the workhouse to be cleaned. Another named Storrer
sent his dog to be kept there when it was inconvenient
to have it at home.

Erredge went on to record that 25 years before the
time when he was writing the poor of the parish were
employed in scavenging and watering the streets, 'har-
nessed by means of ropes to the muck-trucks and barrel-
constructed water-carts'. When the officers of the parish
were shamed out of this system they substituted the
corveé of wheeling barrels of shingle from the beach to
the workhouse (which was uphill all the way) until one
of the unhappy creatures died of 'disease of the heart'
under the burden.

In July 1841 grounds for another dispute at the
workhouse arose, when the Vestry recorded that the new
works in progress there were illegal. The exact nature of
the work was not specified. A committee was appointed
to consult with the Directors and Guardians of the Poor.
This achieved an amicable settlement because, after
consultation, the Guardians rescinded their resolution for
the work to be done.

In 1848 the workhouse, which could house 600
inmates, was found too small for the calls upon it. In
particular it was impossible to provide adequate accommodation and training for the children 'without bringing
them into contact indiscrimately with the other inmates
and exposing them to bad examples from persons of
more mature age and likely to exercise a baneful influence
over their minds'. The boys at that time were employed
in shoe-making, tailoring, gardening, and picking feathers
and wool. The elder girls were employed in cleaning rooms
and some needlework, but more instruction for them in
cooking, washing, ironing, and household duties was
needed. A committee appointed by the Directors and
Guardians of the Poor therefore recommended that the
existing workhouse should be extended, at a cost of

£1,749 12s. in order to accommodate 300 more people and that a separate industrial school should be built, at a cost of £8,354, to house 250 children. The report was received and entered at the foot of the minutes, but there is no record of any action being taken on it, and the the industrial school at Warren Farm (now Woodingdean) was not in fact built until 1856. The workhouse was eventually moved to its third and final site at the top of Elm Grove in 1866.

The affairs of the workhouse in Church Hill also gave rise to hostility between the Established Church and Non-conformity. In 1836 the Directors and Guardians appointed the Rev. Henry Mortlock, of 30 Oriental Place, chaplain to the workhouse at a salary of £100 a year. This step was considered objectionable on two grounds: to Nonconformists as being a contribution to Church of England expenses, and to critics of the Vicar of Brighton, the Rev. H. M. Wagner, who, as a high tory, was very unpopular in zealous whig circles. The Rev. John Nelson Goulty and the Rev. James Edwards, who were prominent Nonconformist ministers in the town, made representations that this was an unnecessary expense and offered their own services on an honorary basis. This induced the Vestry to declare on 25 August that, in their opinion, 'the Vicar and Clergy of the Parish are the proper parties to supply the spiritual wants of the poor and the meeting feel no doubt on proper representations in that quarter such wants will be cheerfully supplied'.

This wording was, however, ironical because at a subsequent meeting on 22 September the committee appointed to consider the matter expressed the view that 'the poor in the Workhouse require regular religious instruction which your Committee are led to believe has not hitherto been bestowed upon them'. They represented that 'it is the imperative duty of the Vicar as the legal pastor of this Parish to provide either by his own personal attention or out of the large income which he derives from the Parish the religious instruction necessary for the purpose'.

The Vestry Clerk advised that the chaplain's appointment was illegal. The Directors and Guardians were
therefore asked to rescind it. They insisted on first
consulting counsel, but when the Attorney General
confirmed the Clerk's opinion they were forced to take
the required step.

However, another chaplain, the Rev. W. Drummond,
seems to have been appointed all the same, for in August
1838, February 1839 and May 1839 sums of £100, £25
and £25 respectively for his salary were disallowed by
the Vestry from the accounts of the Directors and
Guardians, and on the last occasion the Directors and
Guardians were told to pay him no further salary.

Even outside the workhouse the poor were often a
severe problem to both the Vestry and the Town Commissioners. In February 1811, for instance, the Commissioners instructed their Street-keeper to employ all such
poor persons as should apply to the Directors and
Guardians of the Poor for relief and who were recommended to them by the latter for employment. The wage
paid to labourers was to be not more than 2s. a day,
and to carpenters and bricklayers not more than 2s. 9d.
a day. The same occurred in December 1814, when
the rate for labourers was only 1s. 6d. a day.

In September 1819 it was reported that begging had
greatly increased in the town. The Directors and
Guardians of the Poor had decided to station a person
'at each avenue of the town' to prevent this. The Town
Commissioners confirmed this action by appointing six
nominees of the Guardians as 'Officers for preventing
Mendicity and acts of Vagrancy' with power to apprehend
all those found wandering or begging.

It was not until 10 years later than a more charitable
note was struck. From December 1829 a committee was
formed to open a soup kitchen. Seven years later, owing
to the 'extreme inclemency of the weather', another
committee came into existence for the same purpose.
Soup at a price of 1d. a quart was distributed to the poor.
This measure, with the addition of coal, was repeated in

January 1838, and the distribution was effected from premises in Spring Gardens lent to the committee by Isaac Bass, a Quaker, who acted as honorary treasurer of the committee.

A year later the Vestry came to the conclusion that the high price of corn and considerable unemployment necessitated the establishment of permanent soup kitchens. Two were established in Ship Street and Mighell Street. In the following month the charity of the parish was extended slightly further afield as a fund was raised for the relief of misery and destitution in Ireland, following a hurricane.

In January 1840 the committee appointed to carry out local relief reported that they had established three permanent soup kitchens, the third one being in Vine Street. The sum of £754 11s. 1d. had been collected, and with this money 40,989 quarts of soup had been distributed from Ship Street, 25,080 quarts from Mighell Street. and 13,105 quarts from Vine Street, making a total of 79,174 quarts.

In the year following the kitchen at Vine Street was apparently not used. But a further sum of £477 7s. was raised, and 69,041 quarts of soup distributed from the other two kitchens at 1d. a quart. During 1841 £944 7s. 10d. was raised and 126,493 quarts were distributed. The third kitchen in Vine Street was again in use. By January 1843 a fourth kitchen had been established at Cross Street, Hove, £610 12s. 5d. being raised during the year and 60,532 quarts of soup distributed. There was no equivalent entry in the minutes a year later. But subscriptions amounting to £434 16s. 8d. were collected during the winter of 1844/5, and 72,452 quarts of soup were distributed. The following winter was so mild that no distribution was made. The winter of 1846/7 brought subscriptions of £715 2s. 8d, and 79,382 quarts of soup were dispensed. The Vine Street kitchen was replaced by one in Trafalgar Street. Action was late in the following winter and did not come till the end of January 1848. But it was repeated in January

1849 and January 1850, though no details were given of the quantities of soup supplied. The Ship Street kitchen was apparently replaced by one in Spring Gardens. The last reference to the General Relief Committee in the Vestry books occured in December 1853, when a newspaper cutting was pasted into the book. This showed that in 1852/3 only £236 18s. 6d. was subscribed. The kitchens were in Trafalgar Street, Essex Street, near Upper St. James's Street, and Regent Row, North Street. The committee stated that, owing to severe weather and the high price of coal and food, they had seldom found it necessary to make their appeal so early. During this whole period from 1836 to 1853 the Vestry Clerk, Somers Clarke, acted as honorary secretary of the relief committee, and Isaac Bass, of Brighton Place, as its honorary treasurer.

Transport

The alteration of turnpike roads was a matter which occasionally concerned the Vestry. In 1816 it was decided not to oppose a Bill introduced by the trustees of the Henfield turnpike road authorising them to increase the rolls levied on this road, provided that the toll-house at the southern end of the road was moved to Saddlescombe and the portion of the road between there and Brighton was free from tolls.

In the spring of 1824 there were two turnpike cases which gave trouble. Both the Vestry and the Town Commissioners opposed the removal by the trustees of the Ditchling turnpike road of the toll-house at Pillingsworth Manor to a position nearer Brighton. At the same time a Bill was promoted in Parliament for the construction of a turnpike road to Newhaven. The Commissioners were at first disposed to oppose this Bill unless the toll-gate was at least two miles from Brighton. But they abandoned their opposition when an undertaking was given not to place the toll-house nearer than Roedean Bottom.

In April 1839 the Vestry protested at the action of the trustees of the Shoreham turnpike road in erecting a gate or side-bar across Hove Street which had been moved from Aldrington. This was held to be illegal under the Act establishing the turnpike, and a deputation was instructed to wait upon the trustees, the local magistrates and Captain Pechell, M.P., about this. When the trustees of the same turnpike proposed two years later to promote a Bill in Parliament to enable them to increase their charges on the road the Vestry opposed this.

Three years later the Vestry welcomed the proposal of the trustees of the Cuckfield turnpike to remove their gate to the northern boundary of the parish of Preston, which would give access to the Downs to the east and west. The same road came under lengthy consideration in 1854. On 9 February the Vestry passed a resolution to the effect that it was in the interests of the town to secure the removal of the toll-house to a position not less than 100 yards beyond the north wall of Patcham Place for the benefit of residents and visitors in 'taking carriage and horse recreation'. Unless this removal could be secured the Bill to renew and extend the powers of the trustees of the road should be opposed. The trustees were unwilling to comply with the Vestry's request for the removal of the gate. Therefore subscriptions were collected and a petition presented to the House of Commons. The Brighton Members of Parliament were asked to support the petition, and prominent local residents like the Marquess of Bristol were requested to give evidence in its favour before a committee of the House of Commons. It is not stated in the minute books of either the Vestry or of its committees what was the result of the petition, but it was presumably successful. The cost of the Vestry's action in Parliament was £301 19s. 5d. This amounted to £115 12s. 5d. more than had been collected. Appeals were therefore made to Patcham residents to subscribe towards this. The eventual deficit presumably had to be paid by the Town Council after Brighton was incorporated because, as late as March 1858, there is an entry in the minutes of the Vestry committees to the effect that the accounts should be presented to the council.

The construction of a railway from London was frequently considered by the Vestry, but it was not until 1835 that any practical steps were really taken. On 27 July of that year it was resolved that the establishment of a railroad to London was highly expedient, and a committee was appointed to examine the plans of the six companies which desired to promote a Bill in Parliament for a London to Brighton line.

The project which at first received most support was Stephenson's line, designed by Robert Stephenson, whose father, George Stephenson, was the father of English railways. The London terminus of this line was to be at Nine Elms, Vauxhall. From there the line would follow the London to Southampton line as far as Wimbledon Common. Thence it would proceed, via two tunnels, to Capel, Horsham, Henfield and Shoreham. The Brighton terminus was to be north of Western Road opposite Waterloo Street. Its supporters referred to it as the natural line.

The strongest competitor to this line was Sir John Rennie's, or the direct line, as it came to be called. This was to start at London Bridge and to follow the London to Greenwich line as far as Croydon. Then it proceeded to Merstham and, by way of two tunnels at Balcombe and Clayton respectively, to a terminus in Brighton which was near to the site of Park Crescent. The Merstham and Clayton tunnels were not at first included in the plans of this line but were added later. Similarly the Brighton terminus was later shifted southwards to its present site.

The third main competitor was Gibb's line, which was a mixture of the two previous ones. It followed the direct line to Merstham and then made a detour to Horsham and Henfield, finally reaching Brighton via a tunnel through the Devil's Dyke hill. This tunnel was later omitted so that the line could call at Shoreham. The Brighton terminus was to be near Market Street.

Nicholas Wilcox Cundy's line was a less serious competitor. Its London terminus was to be at Kennington Oval, its Brighton terminus near Brooker's Chapel, which was a little to the north of Rennie's original terminus. It took a western route, but its chief distinction was that alone among the six lines, it did not propose a single tunnel. So it came to be called the Brighton and London railway without a tunnel.

The fifth, or Palmer's line, took a quite different route, and for that reason was sometimes called the south-eastern line. From London Bridge it followed the London to Dover line as far as Oxted. It nearly touched Lewes, from where a branch line was to run from Falmer, and would have ended on Carlton Hill at Brighton. It constituted the chief contrast to Cundy's line, as it would have had no less than seven tunnels.

The sixth, or Vignolles's line from the Elephant and Castle was hardly a serious competitor.

The Vestry committee met on 16 September and reported that there were insuperable engineering difficulties in the way of Sir John Rennie's line. They favoured Robert Stephenson's Brighton terminus in Western Road and Gibbs's London terminus at London Bridge. In view of this report the Vestry expressed itself as being in favour of one of the western lines through Horsham but recommended the amalgamation of the various competing companies.

When it was subsequently discovered that the engineering difficulties of the direct line were not insuperable the Vestry petitioned the House of Commons on 18 February 1836 in favour of this line, not only on account of its directness, but because, south of Merstham, it could well lead to a series of branch lines in Kent and Sussex. The Town Commissioners then took a hand in the matter. In March 1836 Henry Faithful presented to them particulars of the direct line, and Somers Clarke presented particulars of the western line. The Commissioners decided to support the direct line, but two months later this decision was rescinded. Thereafter they seem to have left the matter in the hands of the Vestry.

By this stage five private Bills were being considered by a committee of the House of Commons under the chairmanship of Lord George Lennox. Sir John Rennie's cross-examination lasted seven days. The Brighton and London railway without a tunnel failed to make out its case. The south eastern line was withdrawn because its promoters were then concentrating on a railway line to Dover. Stephenson's and Gibbs's companies amalgamated their projects. The committee of the House resolved that Stephenson's line was the most capable of being carried into execution advantageously as its gradients were were superior and its tunnels shorter than those of the direct line.

This recommendation did not please the inhabitants of Brighton. The residents of Brunswick Square in particular were appalled at the thoughts of having a railway terminus so near to their houses 'of the first class', as they were then called. A public meeting was held on 18 June 1836 at which the advantages of the direct line were again stressed. Its Brighton terminus would annoy no local residents. Its London terminus at London Bridge was far preferable to Vauxhall. It was 10 miles shorter than Stephenson's line, which would entail a saving of £35,000, and 52,560 miles a year. Its gradients were fair gradients. It afforded facilities for branch lines to Lewes and Newhaven, which Stephenson's line did not. It could be completed in three years at a cost of £900,000. The meeting therefore petitioned Parliament not to pass any Bill in the present session without further investigation.

All five Bills were re-presented to Parliament in the following year. By this time the direct line had been much improved. John Urpath Rastrick was associated with Sir John Rennie in its design, and in fact was the engineer who actually put it into execution. At a Vestry meeting on 25 January 1837 spokesmen of all five lines expounded the merits of each. But the Vestry came down firmly in favour of the direct line and requested the two Brighton Members of Parliament, Captain Pechell and Isaac Newton Wigney to inform the House of Commons that they considered the direct line to be 'of the utmost importance to the Town and at the same time productive of great national benefit'.

By April the Vestry was afraid that, owing to the multiplicity of lines before Parliament, no Bill might pass that session. They therefore recorded that, while still in favour of the direct line, if this line was rejected by the committee of the House of Commons, they would prefer some other line to be adopted rather than no line at all.

The committee of the House duly found in favour of the direct line. But a last-minute attempt at reconsideration was made by the Members of Parliament for West Sussex, who naturally favoured Stephenson's line because of its connection with Capel and Horsham. The Government therefore intervened and proposed that a military engineer of the Ordnance Department should report on all five lines. This step distressed the Vestry as they thought that it would delay a decision. They again petitioned Parliament against hesitation and urged the Government to withdraw its opposition to the direct line.

To assist matters Sir Samuel Whalley, who was M.P. for Marylebone and a prominent supporter of the direct line, called a meeting of representatives of the competing companies and urged them to amalgamate in order to be sure of securing an Act that session. An agreement was reached for a joint line to Merstham from both London termini of London Bridge and Vauxhall. From Merstham the line would run to Capel and Henfield, as in Stephenson's line, but would adopt Rennie's Brighton terminus. The Vestry accepted this compromise as a second-best proposal if the direct line was rejected.

However, the Government engineer, Captain Ralph Carr Alderson, came to their rescue. His report was published in June 1837. This admitted that Stephenson's line was preferable from the engineering point of view but declared that the deciding factors were the superior convenience of both Rennie's termini and the possibility for branch lines which it offered. The latter would avoid

the necessity for more than one southern trunk line. He
therefore found for the direct line, which passed through
the House without further opposition.

Work on the London line began in the spring of 1838
and on the Shoreham branch line in July. The latter was
completed in just under two years. The first train holding
a select company of 230 people left Brighton Station for
Shoreham on 11 May 1840 at 3 p.m. The band of the
12th Lancers played them off to the tune of 'Off, off,
said the stranger'. But at first the engine, with full steam
up, failed to move. It was found that the brake of the
second carriage was locked. When this was adjusted
the train moved out of the station 11 minutes later
accompanied by a push from behind from the engine
known as the Eagle. The journey of 5 miles took 12
minutes, to the repeated hurrahs of the spectators along
the line. Next day 1,750 people made the journey. There
were seven trains a day. The fare was 1s. first class, 9d.
second class, and 6d. third class. Omnibuses left Castle
Square and Kemp Town half an hour and a quarter of an
hour before the departure of each train.

The completion of the main line took another 18
months. By 11 July 1841 it had been opened to the public
as far as Haywards Heath. The rest of the journey was
made by coach. The southernmost section took another
two months to complete. Brighton station, which was
designed by David Mocatta, was then a very handsome
building with a colonnade in front of it. It was built
between October 1840 and August 1841. The great day
of the opening of the line was 19 September 1841. The
first up-train left Brighton at 7 a.m. and was soon lost in
thick mist. The first down-train, containing the directors
of the line, reached Brighton at 2 p.m. The band of the
Scots Greys played 'God save the Queen', and a peal of
bells was rung from St. Nicholas's church. In the evening
the inhabitants of Brighton entertained the directors of
the line to dinner at the *Old Ship* hotel. Messrs. Cuff and
Strachan supplied the meal at a cost of £1 11s. 6d. per
head, to include 'venison and desert and champagne,

claret, moselle and wines of lesser quality without limit
as to quantity'. The band of the Scots Greys provided
the music, apart from the singing, which cost £10.

The fares to London at first were 14s. 6d. first class
and 9s. 6d. second class; the day returns were 20s. and 15s.
respectively. There do not seem to have been any third
class coaches on the main line at first. There were six
trains in each direction daily, and the journey took one
and three quarter hours at a maximum speed of 20 miles
an hour.

Two years after the opening of the London to Brighton
railway line the Vestry protested to the directors about
the increase of fares and at alterations in the time-table.
They claimed that fares on the Brighton line were greater
than those on any other line leading out of London. A
deputation was appointed to confer with the directors
on the subject. This deputation at first had no success,
but after they had advertised their views in the *Railway
Times* and the *Railway Magazine* they were again received
by the directors who announced alterations in the fares.
These were considered satisfactory.

In March 1844 the Vestry petitioned the House of
Commons in favour of the Bill then before it to provide
branch lines from Brighton to Lewes and Hastings and
from Shoreham to Chichester. When the Bill was passed,
the Vestry presented a further petition in April 1845 for
the continuation of the Chichester line to Portsmouth,
with a branch line to Fareham. They considered that it
was of the utmost importance that the railway line from
Dover to Portsmouth should be continuous and not under
the control of the 'south-western or any other Company
interested in obstructing the coast line and diverting the
traffic to other lines in which they are more interested'.
Both the lines to Hastings and Chichester were built in 1846
and the latter was extended to Portsmouth in 1847. But as
no coast line ever proceeded beyond Hastings it looks as if
the companies 'interested in obstructing' had their way.

In May 1848 the Vestry protested to the directors of
the London, Brighton and South Coast Railway at the

increase in fares and the limitation of accommodation, particularly the reduction in the number of third class trains. They thought that the charges for the carriage of small parcels and merchandise exorbitant. They reminded the directors that 'Property has its duties as well as its rights and that in the adjustment of these principles the labouring and poorer classes of Society have a right to be considered especially in the management of Monopolies regulated by Act of Parliament'. Moreover, 'the interests of the Public and of the Railway Proprietors are identical' and 'these great commercial undertakings can only remain prosperous by acting in accordance with the exigencies of the population supplying the Traffic and that more accommodation and still lower fares would promote the interests of the Shareholders themselves'. The directors replied that third class trains had been 'found to be used by a class of person for whom they were not intended which led to a diminution of their number'. They contended that 'abstract propositions, however true in themselves, are generally used to suit the interest of parties on one side of the question' and in their view the benefits arising from the railway to their own proprietors had been very small, whereas those derived by the town as a whole had been very great. The directors' reply was considered unsatisfactory, and the whole proceedings between the two bodies were then printed. The Vestry's arguments are still as valid today after the nationalisation of the railways as they were in 1848 and the replies of British Railways are still equally unsatisfactory!

When the railway from London reached Brighton both the Vestry and the Town Commissioneers were looking further ahead to communications with France. At that time the only vessel plying between Brighton and Dieppe was the steam-packet *Belfast,* which made the journey twice a week from the Chain Pier. In the Commissioners' opinion this was not adequate to the importance of Brighton or to the shortest route between London and Paris with a railway from London under construction and improved roads in France. They urged the directors of the Steam Navigation Company to put on to the station one or more vessels 'in power, strength and elegance such as the great importance of Brighton as a station justly demands'. The directors at first replied that the *Belfast* was a perfectly sound and seaworthy ship and equal to any other that had served on the station. Moreover they had kept the communications open for several years at a considerable loss. If the Commissioners desired to have a better service then they must contribute to this. They even threatened to send the *Brocklebank,* instead of the *Belfast*, which was an even inferior vessel. The Commissioners had no power under their Act to make contributions for sea transport, but they in their turn threatened that Brighton, 'if left to itself', would provide adequate alternative vessels, since the Steam Pleasure Yacht Company was in the course of formation at the time. This threat seems to have brought the company to heel and they sent down a vessel superior to the *Belfast,* named the *Dark.*

The railway from Paris to Dieppe was then under construction, though it only reached Rouen two years later. The Vestry thought that the exposed state of the south coast rendered a harbour at Brighton 'of great national interest' as there were frequent wrecks on the coast. In the winter of 1840/1 there had been as many as three at one time.

In August 1841 Captain I. N. Taylor, C.B., R.N., exhibited to the Vestry a model of his invention of a floating breakwater which would, if attached to the Chain Pier, produce the effect of a harbour far more cheaply than if a fixed stone breakwater were built. A most attractive print of this project exists, though the designer of it is given as William Henry Smith, C.E. This shows a circular basin with a charming little Italianate building on the shore. The eastern arm, attached to the Chain Pier, terminated in a lighthouse. The longer western arm was to be wide enough for wheeled traffic to convey fish, water and provisions to and from the circular fortification and revenue station at its head.

The Vestry thought that the size of Brighton offered 'a strong reason for the establishment of such a harbour' and recommended that seven sections of the floating breakwater should be laid down as a test and that ways and means of financing the harbour should be investigated. The Chain Pier Company at this point offered £500 towards the cost. Captain Taylor offered to lay one section at his own expense if at least two others were built at the cost of the town. He estimated that the cost of each section would be £500. The Vestry enlisted the aid of one of the Members of Parliament for Brighton, Captain Pechell, R.N., who applied to the Admiralty for the loan of the anchors and chains required for the moorings. The Admiralty replied by letter the following day agreeing to lend such stores. What promptitude for a Government Department! The Vestry calculated that this would involve a saving of £1,687 7s. in the total cost of the seven sections. They therefore asked Captain Taylor to deduct this amount from his estimate, but he replied that his figures had always been based on the assumption that the moorings would be lent free of cost by the Admiralty. He suggested that the town should take over the whole undertaking, provided that it were carried out under the supervision of a foreman appointed by him. This produced the cryptic reply that 'the Committee cannot depart from the arrangement of £10 section but they will be built by contract specifying the time'. They did, however, obtain an estimate of the cost of each section. This was found to be £878. The Vestry thought that the Treasury ought to give a 'drawback' of the duty on the timber involved.

Nothing was actually done for three years. But in September 1844 Captain Taylor reported that he had three sections nearly ready and, if approximately £1,000 was forthcoming from other sources, he was prepared to moor these sections by mid-October so that they could undergo the test of being exposed to the impending winter.[1]

The Vestry felt that the creation of such a harbour was of so much interest to the London to Brighton

1. The Directors of the Chain Pier agreed to provide £300.

Railway Company that the latter ought also to contribute £300, and the directors in fact agreed to do this. The Shoreham Navigation Company gave £100, and £220 was raised by private subscriptions. Sir Samuel Brown, on behalf of the Chain Pier Company, gave permission for the three sections to be moored south-south-east of the pier, and on 23 December 1844 Captain Taylor reported that they had been so erected. Nothing further about them was recorded in the Commissioner's minutes, but in fact they were left in the sea for 12 months and were then towed away to Shoreham harbour, except for one section which broke loose during the process and was washed up on Brighton beach.

In December 1846 Captain Sir Samuel Brown, the designer of the Chain Pier, demonstrated to the Vestry on behalf of the directors of the Chain Pier a model of a fixed breakwater for the facilitation of embarkation and disembarkation which the company was intending to construct. The Vestry considered this to be 'highly conducive to the interests of the town' since it would augment the traffic between England and France and 'bring into full operation the shortest and best route by Sea and Railway between London and Paris'. This breakwater again seems never to have been erected. In December 1850 the minutes of the Vestry committee recorded that the parish officers could not comply with a resolution to convene a meeting on the subject of a proposed breakwater as parish funds could not be expended for that purpose, but they nevertheless expressed the opinion that the formation of such a breakwater was highly desirable for the town.

Miscellaneous Local Matters

There are a number of miscellaneous entries of general interest in the Vestry books after 1810 which cannot be classified. For instance, on 3 June 1811 the Vestry approved a resolution of the Town Commissioners authorising a Mr. Francis to take down a house in Great East Street and build two dwellings on the site upon paying £5 compensation to a neighbour for a slight adjustment of land.

In January 1813 the parish authorised the churchwardens and overseers of the poor to raise 58 men for the local militia by paying a bounty of two guineas each out of the poor-rate.

In March 1819 it was recorded that the provisions of the Insolvent Debtors Act which provided for the imprisonment of debtors for a period of three months did not ensure the payment of the debts due and was an infringement of the liberty of the subject without trial by jury. A petition was presented to Parliament for the repeal of the Act.

On 5 June 1827 it was resolved that Mr. Vallance's invention for the conveyance by atmospheric pressure of goods from Shoreham harbour and of passengers from London would be beneficial to Brighton. Claims were made that this could travel at the rate of 100 miles an hour, but nothing came of the proposal.

A year later (13 May 1828) a quite different activity was also thought beneficial to the town. This was the permanent establishment of races, which had first been held in 1783. The inhabitants were urged to collect the necessary funds, and a committee was formed for the purpose. This same view was expressed in 1840, when the committee was thanked for their activities.

On 10 December 1829 the Vestry expressed itself in favour of the erection of a new bridge leading from Shoreham to South Lancing, which would save a detour of two miles imposed by the bridge further north.

On 18 March 1830 the Vestry petitioned the House of Commons against the enforcement of a demand made by the postmaster of Brighton for payment of an extra penny above the normal postage rate for the delivery of letters and newspapers beyond the area of Charlotte Street on the east, Canon Place on the west, and Sussex Street on the north. The outer area was called 'off the stones'. The petition was not successful as in 1839 the position was roughly the same except that the privileged area had been extended northwards as far as 69 London Road. The Vestry remained concerned about the high cost of postage in general. In their view this amounted to a total prevention of communication between the members of the poorer classes. In 1839 a committee of the House of Commons was examining the matter and had reported that the high charges led to notorious evasion of the dues payable. The Vestry therefore petitioned both Houses of Parliament to adopt the committee's recommendation in favour of a charge of 1d. per half-ounce for distances not exceeding 15 miles and 2d. a half-ounce for greater distances. Penny postage was in fact adopted by the budget of that year at the instigation of Rowland Hill. In view of this it is interesting to note that Rowland Hill himself lived in Brighton, though not at this exact date. He occupied 11 Hanover Crescent from 1844 to 1846. In November 1844 a committee of the Vestry was appointed to raise subscriptions for a presentation to him in acknowledgment of his service in introducing the 1d. postage.

In October 1833 one of the many great gales of Brighton's history seriously damaged the Chain Pier. The Vestry, being anxious to preserve 'so great and elegant a Convenience' in 'this highly favoured Place of Fashionable resort' (17 October 1833), appointed a committee to raise funds for its repair.

On 29 May 1835 the Vestry expressed the opinion that it would promote the interest of the town if the spring Assizes, which were formerly held at Horsham, could be transferred to Brighton. The Town Commissioners were asked to take steps to have this brought about. This desired result was never accomplished.

During that winter season of 1836/7 the local hunt, the Brighton Union, which hunted hares, not foxes, showed a deficit of £65 8s. and the question of its continued existence arose. A committee appointed by the Vestry to consider the circumstances affecting it advised that it was of importance to the town as 200 families annually frequented Brighton on its account and more than 500 horses were kept there in the season. The Vestry therefore recorded that 'the continuance of the Brighton Union Hunt is essential for the best interests and prosperity of the Inhabitants of this Town'. A larger committee was formed to raise subscriptions in order to keep the hunt going.

In July 1838 the Vestry passed a vote of thanks to Sir Edward Sugden for opposing and securing the rejection of the General Enclosures Bill in the House of Commons. The Vestry was indignant about the numerous obstructions and encroachments that had lately been made upon the open tenantry downs and other commons in and near Brighton, which curtailed the privileges of the inhabitants and deprived visitors of their customary rides and walks. They appointed a committee to investigate the circumstances of these encroachments and to try and secure their removal.

These tenantry downs were not mentioned again in the minutes for 10 years. They were all that remained of the medieval land tenure of Brighton. The arable land surrounding the town had originally been divided into five large fields known as 'tenantry laines' (as distinct from the lanes or narrow streets of the old town). These were called West, North, Hilly, Little, and East Laines. Beyond these were the sheep tenantry downs, over which the owners of land in the laines had rights of pasture in common. By a deed of 1822 the remaining tenantry downs which had not been converted into arable land were divided between the owners of the land in the laines in proportion to their arable holdings, and the only land still held in common for the benefit of the parish comprised the Old Steine; the two pieces of land to the north of this which are now known as the Valley Gardens but were then called the North Steine Enclosures; Richmond Green, which was later conveyed to the ecclesiastical authorities for the erection of St. Peter's church; the Level or cricket ground; and the race-ground and racestand in the East Tenantry Down.

By the deed of 1822 seven managers had been appointed to make rules for the control of these open spaces. But no rules were actually made, and the number of managers was not maintained at a total of seven when deaths occurred, as it should have been under the deed. By 1846 the only surviving managers were Thomas Attree of the Attree Villa, Queen's Park, and Charles Scrase Dickens, who was one of the lords of the manor. The committee appointed by the Vestry to ascertain the rights of the inhabitants over the tenantry down found that no action had ever been taken under the deed of 1822. Old Steine and the Level had been neglected by the managers and so had been supervised by the Town Commissioners for many years. The North Steine enclosures had remained under the control of Thomas Attree. He claimed that this was under a grant of part of the wastes of the manor to Sir Benjamin Bloomfield and Messrs. Hart and Vallance by the lords of the manor. But the committee contended that, as these three people and the lords of the manor all joined in the deed of 1822, this deed superseded the grant of 1818. These lands produced a revenue, but the committee had been unable to obtain particulars of this from Thomas Attree.

The committee found that a portion of the race-ground had been enclosed by William Hallett, who claimed it as his own and said that the public had no rights over it. He was, however, willing to sell land to the parish for a road over it at a moderate price. The pasturage was vested in the Marquess of Bristol, who had acquired it from Thomas Read Kemp. But the committee held that the public had, for at least 60 years, had rights to erect booths and stalls on this land during the races. Interference with these rights had occurred without Lord Bristol's knowledge. The committee recommended that the matter should be brought to Lord Bristol's attention.

The racestand, like the North Steine enclosures, remained under the control of Thomas Attree. He claimed to represent the shareholders who, in 1796, had raised £400 for the erection of the stand and had been granted a lease of it for 99 years at a rent of one guinea a year. All the inhabitants named in this lease as tenants were

dead and the original deed had been lost. But Thomas
Attree retained a copy of it and himself held nine of the
total 18 shares. He distributed the proceeds arising from
the racestand to the other shareholders entitled to it,
but admitted that no rent had been paid for 40 years.
The sum of £400 raised for the construction of the
stand remained a charge upon it, and he was willing to
sell the stand to the parish for that amount. There were
no other legal interests in the stand known to him. The
committee contended that there was no reference to this
lease in the deed of 1822, to which Attree himself had
been a party, or to the sum of £400 being a charge upon
the stand. This charge ought long since to have been
liquidated out of the revenue from the stand since 1796,
and the inhabitants were therefore beneficially interested
in the stand, free from any charge.

The committee also found that various roads had
been encroached upon, particularly Black Rock road
(now Roedean Hill) which was barred by gates 'about
1,162 feet from the north west corner of Hospital Hall'.

In their report the committee recommended that
seven new managers of the tenantry down land should
be appointed out of 20 people nominated by Thomas
Attree and Charles Scrase Dickens. These were William
Catt junior, James Cordy, Thomas Cooper, Henry
Faithful, D. M. Folkard, Thomas Freeman, and William
Lambert. They said that in the course of negotiations
Attree and Scrase Dickens had agreed to appoint these
people. But when the committee's report appeared in
May 1847 Attree and Scrase Dickens had retracted this
agreement as Thomas Attree claimed that the report
contained several erroneous conclusions. He contended
that it was injurious to private individuals who had, for
instance, enjoyed rights over the North Steine enclosures
since 1818 which were incompatible with public use, as
well as injurious to the rights over the racestand already
mentioned. The committee replied that it would be part
of the new managers' functions to investigate these
claims. When they made their final report to the Vestry

in June 1848 a further committee was appointed to ascertain from the Town Commissioners what steps the latter intended to take to enforce the public's rights.

The Commissioners, however, did not make any better progress. Attree and Scrase Dickens seem to have expressed their willingness to appoint as additional trustees D. M. Folkard and John Colbatch, who were members of the Tenantry Down committee of the Commissioners, together with William Furner, Bright Smith, and William Catt junior. But no reply had been received to this offer when, on 28 July 1848, some members of the Tenantry Down committee took forcible possession of the racestand and retained the income therefrom. Attree and Scrase Dickens thereupon brought an action against John Colbatch, who was Clerk to the magistrates, Charles Sharood, who was afterwards the first Town Clerk of Brighton, F. Glading, George Cobb, D. M. Folkard, and Thomas Pocock, for illegal tresspass and suspended any action over the appointment of new trustees until this litigation was settled. The Town Commissioners recorded that the committee had no authority from them to take possession of the racestand and disavowed their action. But they appointed another committee to investigate the whole matter further.

The matter was eventually settled in 1849. A new race committee was formed which purchased the stand from Thomas Attree, H. Blackman, and a third trustee named Tamplin for £360. The directors of the London to Brighton and South Coast Railway contributed £100 towards this sum. The old wooden building was demolished in 1851 and replaced by a new one designed by Richard Allan Stickney, the Surveyor to the Town Commissioners. Eventually, in 1884, Brighton Corporation acquired all the rights vested in the racestand trustees under the Brighton Corporation Improvement Act of that year.

In November 1839 the Vestry, in a petition to the House of Commons, drew the attention of the House to the fact that considerable trade existed between

Brighton and the port of New Shoreham which gave rise to the contraction of small debts. They asked leave to bring in a Bill for the establishment in Brighton of a local court of requests equivalent to a modern County Court for the recovery of debts up to but not exceeding £15, which had been incurred in Brighton, Shoreham or the parishes between the two places.

In 1842 a considerable sensation was caused locally by the failure of the bank of Wigney and Co. in Great East Street, and the bankruptcy of its partners, Isaac Newton Wigney and Clement Wigney. The Vestry held a special meeting in March to express their confidence in the two remaining local banks, Messrs. Hall, West and Borrer and the London County Bank.

National Affairs: (a) The Royal Family
The close connection between the town and the Royal Family persisted and is reflected in the Vestry books throughout the period. On 26 October 1820 the Vestry drew up and presented to George IV a loyal address on the occasion of his first visit to the town as King. On 17 January 1827 an address of condolence with the King on the death of the Duke of York was passed, which was to be presented by the High Constable to the Home Secretary. This described the Duke with somewhat more loyalty than truth as 'one of its [the country's] brightest ornaments and most faithful adherents to the principles of the British constitution in Church and state'.

On 13 October 1828 a committee was appointed to make arrangements for a public dinner to commemorate the erection of the statue of George IV which originally stood on the site of the First World War memorial in Old Steine. Its sculptor, Sir Francis Chantrey, was invited to this dinner 'in order that the inhabitants may have the pleasure of personally expressing to him the high sense they entertain of the Zeal and talent with which he has executed his work'.

Though they naturally cannot have been aware of it at the time, George IV was not subsequently to visit

Brighton. When he died on 26 June 1830 the Vestry passed a resolution of condolence with the new King which expressed its gratitude 'for the many very important benefits which we [the inhabitants of Brighton] derived from the long residence of his late Majesty amongst us'. They were on rather less safe ground in attributing the 'glorious termination' of the Napoleonic wars to 'the Wisdom and energy of His late Majesty's councils'.

This resolution was presented by the High Constable, J. G. Sarel, to the new King personally, who, in his breezy nautical fashion, replied, 'Tell the Inhabitants of Brighton that I shall soon be with them'. On 29 June a procession of the parish officers and inhabitants, escorted by two divisions of the 14th Light Dragoons, proclaimed the new King's accession at Ship Street, West Street, North Street, St. Peter's church, New Steine, Grand Junction Road, and Black Lion Street.

William IV was as good as his word and arrived at the Royal Pavilion on 30 August. A committee had been appointed to welcome him and to arrange for the illumination of the town. With the permission of the Commissioners, an evergreen arch of welcome was erected at Marlborough Place. The committee, who had all been requested to wear purple sashes, duly presented an address to the King in which it was stated that 'Brighthelmston almost owed its birth to the patronage of King George IV' and now contained 40,000 inhabitants. The Commissioners were also in attendance as a body. The King was accompanied by Queen Adelaide, to whom a separate address was presented. This unconsciously emphasised the weaknesses of the late sovereign in this connection by stressing the pleasure of the inhabitants 'upon welcoming the entrance of a Queen into this Palace where the splendours of Royalty are chastened by the calm and peaceful virtues which constitute at once the ornament and happiness of domestic life'. No-one could have said that of George IV. The King replied that he had 'long felt very partial to Brighthelmston' and had watched its increasing prosperity with satisfaction.

Three days later the schoolchildren of the town were entertained to roast and boiled beef and plum pudding on the Steine enclosure. The King and Queen, accompanied by the Landgravine of Hesse Homburg (Princess Elizabeth) and the Duke of Cambridge walked over from the Royal Pavilion to see the festivities. Sixty thousand other people are said by Erredge to have been present.

During the heat of the Reform Bill crisis a slight shadow fell across the local image of the new King when he manifested some reluctance to create enough peers to secure the passing of the Bill by the House of Lords. The Vestry minute of 14 May 1832 recorded that 'the Answer given by His Majesty to His ministers on their advising him to Create Peers for the purpose of ensuring the safety [*sic*] of the Reform Bill in the House of Lords is considered by this Meeting to have caused a strong suspicion in the minds of the people that the determination of that illustrious personage is prejudicial to the Cause of Reform and therefore to the best interests of the Nation'. However, this was forgotten when the King did eventually give his consent to the creation of sufficient peers to pass the bill, and it was in fact passed. Almost immediately after the Vestry meeting which arranged for public rejoicing at this satisfactory conclusion a further address was passed for presentation to the King congratulating him upon his late escape from an attempted assassination.

On 17 May 1837 the Vestry drew up an address of congratulation to Princess Victoria on attaining her 18th birthday a week later. A committee was appointed to arrange for the school children to have a holiday and a display of fireworks and also to erect some public ornament, such as a fountain.

On William IV's death a month later the new Queen's accession was proclaimed from the balcony of the Town Hall, and by a procession of the parish officers and professional men of the town, escorted by the 6th Royal Dragoon Guards or Carabineers, at the Battery on King's Road, at the corner of New Road, opposite St. Peter's church and at the top of New Steine. Five days later addresses of condolence on the death of the late King were prepared for presentation to the Queen and the Queen Dowager.

When Queen Victoria made her first visit to Brighton on 4 October 1837 a similar committee was appointed as had been formed to welcome William IV and Queen Adelaide in 1830. This body raised £613 7s. in subscriptions. Of this £350 was spent on an amphitheatre,[1] designed by a Mr. Fabian, the seats in which sold for £289. A rural arch, designed by the builder, George Cheesman, cost £90. The town was illuminated, and a public dinner was held. After paying all the expenses a balance of £119 remained in hand. Twenty-five guineas out of this was spent on a gold snuffbox for presentation to the Vestry Clerk, Somers Clarke, who had acted as honorary secretary of the committee of welcome. The remainder was given to the Sussex County Hospital in aid of the fund to build a new wing. At the same time the committee appointed to celebrate the Queen's 18th birthday reported that that they had raised £298, but did not favour the erection of a fountain. They recommended instead the erection of a permanent ornamental arch or similar object. No such arch was however built, and the Victoria Fountain in Old Steine was not erected until 1846.

The address presented to the Queen referred to the 'fostering munificence and protection' of her predecessors, to which Brighton owed its 'present eminence and distinction'.

A year later, in June 1838, a committee was appointed to celebrate the Queen's coronation day as a gala day, but without illuminations on account of the danger of fire. On the occasion of the Queen's second visit to the town, on 18 December 1838, the public were requested to congregate at the Royal Pavilion gates, and a display of fireworks was given on Old Steine in the evening.

On 11 February 1840 the Vestry prepared addresses of congratulation to the Queen and Prince Albert on their forthcoming marriage. That June occurred the first of

1. This was attached to the North Gate of the Royal Pavilion.

several attempts to assassinate the Queen. The Vestry
passed a resolution of abhorrence at the deed and
presented addresses of congratulations at the Queen's
escape to the Queen, Prince Albert and the Duchess of
Kent. Similar steps were taken after another attempt
on the Queen's life in June 1842. On the birth of the
Queen's eldest child, the Princess Royal, in November
1840, three such addresses of congratulation were again
presented by the Vestry. The same step was taken on the
occasion of the birth of the Prince of Wales in 1841, but
not on the birth of the Queen's later children.

The Queen's third visit to Brighton occurred in February 1842, when she was again welcomed with illuminations and fireworks. On her fourth visit, in September
1843, she and Prince Albert landed at the Chain Pier
after visiting Louis Philippe in France. No illuminations
seem to have been arranged, but a picture of the landing
was painted by the marine artist, Richard Henry Nibbs
(1815-93). This was purchased by private subscriptions
amounting to £54 18s. 6d. and was presented to the
Brighton Commissioners in 1845. The Chain Pier Company
contributed five guineas, Captain Pechell and Lord Alfred
Hervey, the two Brighton Members of Parliament, two
guineas each, and Somers Clarke, Lewis Slight and Thomas
Attree, amongst others, a guinea each.

In April 1843 the Duke of Sussex died. He was the
only son of George III, who entertained genuine liberal
convictions. He was therefore likely to have appealed
specially to the people of Brighton who then held such
advanced whig opinions. The Vestry presented addresses
of condolence, not only to the Queen, but to the Duke's
morganatic wife, Lady Cecilia Buggin, whom the Queen
had created Duchess of Inverness. These addresses
referred to him as one of the country's most distinguished
ornaments and one of the most liberal patrons of science
and literature.

On the Duke of Wellington's death in November 1852
the Vestry recorded their sympathy with the Queen and
the nation at large at his loss and recommended the

suspension of business on the day of his funeral as 'an expression of the Veneration of the Inhabitants for His Grace's memory'.

National Affairs: (b) Politics

National politics are reflected in the Vestry books more frequently after 1825 than before. In contrast to the position in the 20th century, Brighton was then a town of strongly whig sympathies. It had been of this persuasion at the time when its development began under the influence of the Prince of Wales, then a whig, and had not changed its allegiance when he, as Prince Regent, turned to the tories. These whig sympathies were never better shown than in an entry of 1830. At that time Sir Robert Peel, as Home Secretary in the Duke of Wellington's government, was engaged in reforming the criminal law by relaxing its harshest penalties and, in particular, by abolishing the death penalty for more than 100 offences.

A resolution of 1 June 1830 expressed the view that 'the great objects of the punishment of crime are the preservation of the property and the peace of the subject and the reformation of the Criminal. These objects are most likely to be attained by an adaptation of the punishment to the nature of the Offence and are frustrated in proportion as the infliction is severe and sanguinary by exciting pity for the Culprit rather than indignation at his crime. The punishment of death for crimes affecting property is abhorrent to the feelings of humanity—inconsistent with the mild and beneficent Character of the British Government—ineffectual of the great objects of legislation; deteriorating to the Character of the People—injurious to the interest of the commonwealth and opposed to the genius and spirit of Christianity'. The Vestry therefore petitioned the House of Commons to amend the Bill then before them so that the death penalty for crimes against property should be replaced by some other form of punishment. These sentiments were very advanced for the period, and many people did not then, in the words of the Vestry resolution just quoted, find the death penalty for relative minor offences 'abhorrent to the feelings of humanity'.

On 18 February 1834 the Vestry presented another petition to Parliament. In view of the 'universal distress unparallelled in the History of this Country under which the industrious classes have for a long time been suffering' the Vestry felt that the 'evils which threaten to disorganise Society' could only be averted by a great reduction of taxes; that the latter could only be effected by a reduction of the interest of the National Debt; that this reduction could only be effected if 'all unmerited sinecures and pensions and all useless offices shall have been abolished, the salaries of all necessary Officers considerably curtailed, the Army lessened, and a large portion of that species of public property called Church property applied towards the exigencies of the State'. They went on to say that they had no confidence that any such step would be taken unless the people were fairly represented in Parliament. A further demand was therefore made for the curtailment of the duration of Parliaments—then governed by the Septennial Act—and the enfranchisement by ballot of every householder paying scot and lot.

This resolution and petition was an introduction to the subject of the Reform Bill which was followed by the Vestry with the keenest interest throughout all its phases, and supported in both setbacks and successes by petitions to the King and Parliament. At the very next meeting, held on 14 March 1831, the Vestry recorded its pleasure and gratitude to the King and his ministers for having introduced a measure of parliamentary reform and pledged their support of this action 'by every Constitutional means in our power'.

On 16 April, when it was discovered that the Bill before Parliament would be more favourable to the county voters than to those in towns and would therefore greatly increase the already predominant landed interest, the Vestry presented another petition to the House of Commons urging that Brighton, whose population exceeded

40,000 inhabitants, and other similar towns, should be amongst the boroughs to be enfranchised by the Bill and that their freeholders should also retain the right to vote for the county members.

When Parliament was dissolved on 22 April after a motion had been carried against the Government, the Brighton Vestry three days later passed a resolution congratulating the King on having taken this step. When the second Reform Bill passed the House of Commons in September the Vestry passed a resolution congratulating the House on its 'glorious struggle and triumphant success in obtaining for the people of England a free and perfect representation of the people in the Commons department of the Government'. The Vestry then petitioned the House of Lords to pass the Bill similarly.

The Lords of course did not do so, and riots ensued all over England. None are recorded in Brighton, but apprehension was not wanting because the Vestry recorded three days after the Lords rejected the Bill that nothing but the passing of another Bill with similar provisions 'will prevent the most fearful National Commotions'. The Vestry congratulated those members of the House of Lords who supported the Bill and begged the Government 'not to desert His Majesty's counsels'. A committee was appointed to watch future progress of any new measure introduced and to take whatever action was appropriate.

When the House of Lords threw out the Bill a second time in May 1832 the Brighton Vestry, moved by 'combined feelings of acute anguish and irrepressible indignation' at 'this factious vote of their Lordships', petitioned the King to create sufficient peers to secure the passing of 'the Nation's Bill of Reform'. The King at first refused to agree to this. Lord Grey resigned, and the King turned to the Duke of Wellington. This step moved the Brighton Vestry almost to hysteria. On 14 May they resolved that the rights and liberties of the people had been 'laid prostrate at the feet of an Odious Oligarchy', and if the House of Commons did not stand firm they saw no prospect before them but 'Absolute Submission to their Oppressors on the one hand or Confusion, Anarchy and Civil Commotion on the other'. A 'once contented, happy and prosperous country' had been reduced to grievous distress. 'Almost the whole of the industrious population comprising the Commercial, the Manufacturing, the trading and the agricultural Classes of the Community are on the brink of ruin and consequently the labouring millions dependent on them for support are reduced to a state of privation bordering on famine'. The Vestry went on to express complete lack of confidence in the Duke of Wellington and his associates and to petition the King to recall Lord Grey to his counsels.

When the Bill was actually passed in June 1832 the committee of the Vestry which had been appointed to watch its progress through Parliament reported to a special meeting which resolved that 27 June, as the anniversary of the signing of Magna Carta, should be appointed as a day of public rejoicing for the passing of the Bill, and tables should be placed in Old Steine for the purpose of serving dinners of roast beef and plum pudding. It is not stated in the minutes at whose cost these dinners were to be served, but the expenses of collecting signatures to all previous petitions and forwarding them to their destination were paid for out of parish funds. One wonders what the tory members of the local population thought of such proceedings.

Soon after the passing of the Reform Act it was made clear in the Vestry books that the sentiments of Brighton inhabitants in favour of parliamentary reform were not perhaps quite so disinterested as the language of their resolutions and petitions might have suggested. In August 1831, at the height of the Reform Bill crisis, a reassessment was made by the Government assessors in connection with the inhabited houses and window taxes. The Vestry, therefore, petitioned the Lords Commissioners of the Treasury for relief from this measure on the grounds of the 'precarious values of the property in Brighton, a considerable portion of which consists of Lodging Houses let only for portions of the year'.

The Vestry considered that one of the first duties of the first reformed Parliament was therefore the abolition of the inhabited houses and window taxes. It had in fact petitioned Parliament against them in March 1825. The claim was made that these taxes had been initiated as war taxes, but were still in force after 18 years of peace.[1] They had recently been made more burdensome by reassessment. They were 'unequal in as much as they press with greatest severity upon the middling and industrious classes of society And unjust as in as much as they are Taxes which in their operation affect the comfort, conveniences and health of the community at large'. The Vestry therefore petitioned the House of Commons to repeal them.

When the Government and the House of Commons refused to take this step the fury and disillusionment of the Vestry knew no bounds. On 29 May 1833 they resolved that the Government and the reformed House of Commons had 'disappointed the just expectations and shaken the confidence of the King's most grievously burdened but hitherto patient and loyal subjects'. The loss of revenue from these taxes would not be felt if large salaries were cut, costly and useless establishments terminated, and sinecures and unmerited pensions abolished. As the 'reasonable petitions of the people' had been disregarded by the House of Commons, they therefore petitioned the King to dissolve Parliament and thereby give the country an opportunity of electing another House which 'will attend to the petitions and relieve the sufferings of your Majesty's loyal subjects'. This was little more than two years after the Vestry had anticipated that the Reform Bill would provide a 'free and perfect representation of the people in the Commons department of the Government' (Vestry minutes, 22 April 1831).

1. They had actually been initiated in 1778.

On 30 March 1835 the Vestry recorded that bribery and intimidation at elections still continued to exist since the passing of the Reform Act and would continue to do so unless vote by ballot was adopted. It therefore petitioned the House of Commons to introduce this measure without delay.

Three years later (7 March 1836) another tax—the newspaper tax—excited the extreme ire of the Vestry. They considered this was 'degrading to the industrious wealth producing classes and evinces a desire to perpetuate Ignorance, to alienate the affections of the people, to render them passive under oppression and to annihilate those feelings of respect which at all times should exist between the government and themselves'. They therefore petitioned the House of Commons, not only to abolish this mischievous tax on knowledge, but also to introduce vote by ballot in order to prevent 'Arbitrary Acts of Influence and Intimidation on the part of the wealthy and Powerful over the conscientious and honest constituents'.

They went on to say that the enactment of the Septennial Act was 'the most gross act of usurpation recorded in the History of any Nation' and that every hour of the continuance of that Act was a 'crime against the constituent body of this nation'. They therefore petitioned that this Act should be repealed and that triennial parliaments should be restored in accordance with the practice claimed—on rather shaky grounds—to have been in force from the reign of Edward III to that of George I.

The petition ended with complaints about the disenfranchisement under the Reform Act of the owners of certain houses whose occupiers were voters and of the practice of the overseer of the poor-rate in making a double assessment in certain cases.

In March 1837 a further petition was presented to Parliament in favour of the extension of the franchise, vote by ballot, and triennial parliaments. But this was not the limit of the Vestry's radical sentiments. In 1838 the London Working Men's Association drew up the famous People's Charter advocating manhood suffrage, vote by ballot, annual parliaments, equal electoral districts, the abolition of the property qualification for Members of Parliament and the payment of Members. On 22 September the Brighton Vestry adopted the Charter and appointed a delegate to watch the proceedings of the presentation of a petition for the Charter by the Birmingham Political Union. The meeting felt that the cause of the misery affecting the working classes was 'our representative system which is based upon exclusive and unjust privileges and not on the rights of the people'. In January 1839 a committee was appointed to collect subscriptions for the promotion of the Charter.

This was followed in May 1839 by a petition to the Queen to dismiss Melbourne's Government and replace it by a government which had the confidence of the people. This petition was a truly wonderful document. It began by saying that 'neither of the aristocratic factions which have for centuries usurped the executive power by corrupting and controlling the legislature of this deluded, oppressed and degraded country do now possess the confidence and support of any large class of the people'. It acknowledged the attempt made by the Reform Act to extend power to the middle classes but thought that 'the results of middle class legislation have only rendered the actual existence of despotism more obvious' by 'substituting palpable falsehood and barefaced fraud for the covert manoeuvres and intrigues by which oligarchical despotism had been clothed in the garb of constitutional law'. The working class with whom they alleged 'all useful reforms have originated' were 'kept in subjection by a military force which it is no longer concealed is kept up not for defence but for the subjugation of those [from] whose industry is wrung the means of maintaining it'. But later on in the petition the rather illogical complaint was made that the country was without sufficient means of defence against states which were anxious to 'destroy the last remains of our once boasted wealth and power'.

On 14 September 1841 the Vestry again recorded the view that the evils of the pre-1832 corrupt electoral· system had been 'not only perpetuated but actually increased' by the Reform Act. They therefore presented another petition in favour of vote by ballot and the extension of the franchise 'to the greatest practicable limit'.

Two months later the People's Charter was again adopted by the Vestry, and following a meeting of 15 November, at which the two Members of Parliament for Brighton, Captain Pechell and Isaac Newton Wigney, were present, a copy of the National Petition, as it was called, was pasted in the Vestry book. This enumerated all sorts of grievances. Only 900,000 out of 26 million inhabitants could vote. Nine million pounds was devoted to the maintenance of the Established Church. The Queen received £164 17s. 10d. a day for her private purse, Prince Albert £104 2s., and the King of Hanover £57 10s.; while many families had only between 2¾d and 3¾d a head to live on. The hours of factory workers were protracted beyond the limits of human endurance. Agricultural labourers earned only starvation wages. Thousands of people were dying from actual want. Meanwhile the country was kept in subjection by an enormous army, an unconstitutional police force, the tyranny of the poor law and its bastilles.

But in 1843 when a Bill was before the House of Commons for the regulation of the employment of children in factories and for the better education of such children the Vestry petitioned against those clauses which would deprive parents of the responsibility for the religious training of their children and make this a further ecclesiastical encroachment upon the poor-rate.

In January 1846 the Vestry presented a petition to the House of Commons urging the repeal of the corn laws which were 'unjust in principle, oppressive in their operation, and injurious to the best interests of the Community'. The necessity for the repeal sprang from the deep distress of the people owing to a bad harvest and a blight affecting the potato crop, 'an esculent on which your Petitioners regret to say a large portion of the labouring population are compelled to subsist owing to restrictive commercial enactments' such as the corn laws.

The following year (January 1847) brought another petition in favour of the People's Charter. In their supporting arguments the Vestry said that men's deprivation of other men's right to vote was 'an act which, if tolerated, evidences the existence of tyranny and injustice on the one hand, and servility and degradation upon the other'. The Reform Act of 1832 'renders seven men subservient to the will, caprice and dominance of one' since it restricted the franchise to a seventh of the adult male population. Seven-year Parliaments were too long as such a period 'affords an opportunity to venal and time-serving men to promote their selfish interests at the expense of those whose welfare should be the ultimate aim of all their labours'.

In May 1849 the Vestry presented another petition to the same effect since 'the Reform Bill has utterly failed to accomplish the objects of its promoters as it has proved inefficient to relieve the National Distress and reduce taxation'.

The last word was perhaps the dominant one in the Vestry's consideration. In the preceding year (February 1848) when the Government proposed to increase the income tax from 7d. in the pound to 1s. the Vestry had recorded that, while approving direct taxation, 'it is unjust to levy any tax in the same proportion on precarious and uncertain incomes arising from trades and professions as from landed, funded or other accumulated property'. They recommended the extension of the probate and legacy duties to land as a more just system of taxation than 'the taxation of labour'. As 'the inquisitorial character of an income tax renders it at all times peculiarly obnoxious' the House of Commons should review the whole unjust and unequal system of taxation. This amounts to little more than a repetition of the maxim that is universal to all classes and periods, namely that just taxation is always taxation of other people.

In July 1850 a proposition was made to the Vestry to petition Parliament against the Postmaster General's recent prohibition of the delivery of letters on Sunday, but on a show of hands the resolution was defeated by 90 votes to sixty-nine.

The year 1850 brought the so-called papal aggression when the Pope divided England and Wales into Roman Catholic dioceses. This measure induced outbursts of Protestant hysteria throughout the country. The Vestry thought that this 'obviously contemplates the extension of Popery with all its vital errors in our Protestant Kingdom and it is further an Act based on the arrogant assumption that neither the sovereign of this mighty empire nor any other individual among the many millions of Protestant subjects has any right to be accounted a Member of the true Church of Christ or any inheritor of His Heavenly Kingdom! A more audacious attempt to bind under the chains of an unlawful thraldom the dearest spiritual birthrights of the people of this land has not been made since those chains were broken asunder at the reformation'.

They went on to say that they regretted the defection of some Anglican clergymen to Rome and 'the continual and unanswerable tampering with Romish Practices by Others'. The Vestry felt it difficult to suppose that there was no power under existing law to 'resist this insolent aggression' but, if such was lacking, they petitioned the Queen for the enactment of a provision which, while 'leaving to the adherents of the Church and Court of Rome the liberty now enjoyed by them of exercising with the most perfect freedom their own religious worship, shall teach them to respect the rights of others and preserve Your Majesty's United Kingdom and Your Gracious Colonies from any real or nominal subjection to the Pope and his Cardinals'. The lead in this furious Protestant trumpeting was taken by the Rev. Henry Venn Elliott, the Perpetual Curate of St. Mary's church and the founder of St. Mary's Hall, and by the Rev. J. N. Goulty, the Minister of Union Chapel, Union Street, the oldest Nonconformist chapel in the town. But a special vote of thanks was recorded to the Vicar of Brighton for concurring in the convening of the meeting 'and for his courteous, able and impartial conduct in the Chair'. The word 'impartial' presumably has a strictly local and personal meaning as the Vicar's own son, the Rev. A. D. Wagner, had just begun his ministry in the church as the Perpetual Curate of St. Paul's church, West Street, and was one of the earliest members of the Anglican High Church movement. His father could hardly have been praised for impartiality towards the Roman Catholic church.

In January 1851 the Vestry returned to the subject of the window tax which, 'interfering as it does with light, one of the greatest blessings of providence and ventilation, the greatest preservative of health, is peculiarly injurious to the wellbeing of Society'. But after repeating that the tax bore particularly heavily on the keepers of lodging houses who gained a precarious living in a season which was limited to only part of the year they rather gave the game away by adding that any window or inhabited house tax lessened the daily comforts of residents by 'preventing them from residing in more commodious dwellings'.

But when in the following month the Chancellor of the Exchequer prepared to introduce a house tax instead of a window tax the Vestry thought this equally unjust and 'unnecessary in a time of peace with the present enormous revenue of the Country'. A committee was appointed to collect signatures to a petition against such a tax.

A further petition followed in April in favour of adult male suffrage which had already been mentioned in previous years in the Peoples' Charter.

In November 1851 the Hungarian patriot, Louis Kossuth, arrived in London on his way to the United States. The Vestry drew up an address to be presented to him by the High Constable, Montagu Dana Scott.

This[1] addressed Kossuth as 'the National Representative of the ancient constitutional Kingdom of Hungary and elected Governor by the suffrages of its free and enlightened people as the man who could proudly assert amidst the assembled delegates of the working classes of the English Metropolis that 'he had lived his whole life by his own honest and industrious labour'. It went on to express sympathy, not only with Hungarian independence but also with Italian, German and even European liberty. The petitioners wished that Kossuth might be 'wafted by fair Winds and on smooth waters to the hospitable shores of that New World which has been peopled in a great measure by the descendants of those Pilgrim Fathers who, like yourself, became exiles and wanderers rather than submit to despotism'. It is interesting to note in passing that only three years before, during the revolutions of 1848, the great Austrian Chancellor, Prince Metternich, had arrived in Brighton. He had been welcomed at the station by the Master of Ceremonies, who represented a different section of Brighton life, but did not form the subject of any comment in the Vestry minutes.

In November 1852 it was again the turn of vote by ballot to form the subject of a petition following the corrupt practices which had arisen from a recent general election. In the following month the Chancellor of the Exchequer proposed to double the house tax, which the Vestry again considered to be most unjust. The rate of taxation then stood at 9d. in the pound on dwelling-houses, 6d. in the pound on shops, and 7d. in the pound on income. The Vestry suggested instead a probate and legacy duty on real estate similar to that imposed on personal property and that the income and property taxes should be extended to Ireland.

In March 1854 when Lord John Russell's new Reform Bill was before Parliament the Vestry recommended its acceptance as it would add about one million voters to the electorate, though it thought that certain clauses needed

1. Owing to the High Constable's illness it was actually presented by a Mr. Cunningham and a German named Dr. Arnold Ruge.

amendment in committee. This is the last political comment that the Vestry book contains.

National Affairs: (c) Non-political Matters

Non-political matters of more than local significance do not often make their appearance in the Vestry minutes other than in grievances forming the substance of petitions to the King or Parliament. But on 31 October 1831 it was resolved that, in deference to a recommendation of the Privy Council, a local Board of Health should be established to consider precautions against cholera morbus. But with the complacency so often displayed by the authorities of a holiday resort when confronted with an epidemic, it was added that the Vestry had no reasonable grounds for thinking that the disease would be introduced into the area, and, if it were, 'there is every reason to believe that, from the situation of the place, the habits of the people and the Acknowledged salubriety of the Air, it will not be attended with the deplorably fatal consequences which have hitherto marked its progress on the Continent of Europe'.

Six months later (6 April 1832) a committee was appointed to 'take the Subject of emigration into serious consideration'. A month later this committee reported with unconscious humour that 'they cannot recommend Emigration generally to the Parish'.

A year later (23 January 1833) the Vestry turned to the subject of the observance of the Lord's Day. A Select Committee of the House of Commons had recently considered the subject. The Vestry petitioned both Houses to enforce the law on the subject strictly in view of 'the increasing evils which flow from Sunday Trading as it respects the Temporal Condition and moral and Religious habits of a large portion of the Community'.

The Great Exhibition of 1851 twice made an appearance in the Vestry minutes. In March 1850 a committee of 17, including the Vicar of Brighton and the Vestry Clerk, was appointed to obtain subscriptions for the promotion of the Exhibition 'as an object at once noble

in its original concention and calculated to be beneficial
to the Community of the World'. The Vestry viewed
'with feelings of the highest gratification the exertions
which are being made throughout the Kingdom by all
classes' to render the Exhibition effective. When the
Exhibition took place a special meeting of inhabitants
was held on 26 July 1851 to consider 'what steps should
be taken to enable certain classes of their Fellow Towns-
men and Townswomen and the children of the Charity
Schools to visit the Great Exhibition who, without some
aid, will be debarred from the opportunity of enjoying
a privilege which has afforded so much gratification and
improvement to the Community at large'. A committee
was appointed to collect subscriptions for sending the
children of the charity schools. According to Bishop's
Brighton in the Olden Times a party of more than 120
bathing men and women, with their relations, and led
by Lewis Slight, the Clerk to the Brighton Commissioners,
and Samuel Thorncroft, the Assistant Overseer of the
Poor, visited the Exhibition in August 1851.

Part II
The Brighton Commissioners

1.—1789–1810

The first Brighton Act of 1773 set up a body of 64 Commissioners who were nominated in the Act. When subsequent vacancies in their number occurred they were authorised to fill these themselves. The qualifications for membership were the ownership of land in Brighton valued at not less than £10 a year, the occupation of premises valued at not less than £20 a year, or the ownership of personal estate worth £400.

The Act had two principal objectives. The first was to arrange for the paving, lighting and cleansing of the streets. The streets, pavements, footways and lamps in public places vested henceforward in the Commissioners, who were empowered to pave, maintain, water and drain the streets and pavements and to erect lamps to light these. No unauthorised person was permitted to remove dirt or ashes from the streets, but house-holders were allowed to dispose of their own dirt and ashes unless this disposal caused annoyance to their neighbours. They were moreover compelled to sweep the pavements before their houses or shops every morning except Sundays between the hours of eight and ten. To carry out these obligations the Commissioners were authorised to levy a general rate of up to 3s. in the pound which was to be assessed on the same basis as the poor-rate of the parish. Relief of rates could be granted in appropriate circumstances, with appeal on refusal to Quarter Sessions.

With these obligations went very elementary planning powers, as they would be called today. New buildings could not be brought forward beyond the foundations of the old ones in such a way that they obstructed the

street. The Commissioners had power to regulate signs,
gutters, stalls, wells, pumps, pits and posts. They had
power to remove obstructions on the complaint of inhabitants. Fines of up to 5s. could be imposed for cleaning
or loosing horses in the street or for shying at cocks,
and of up to 10s. for allowing cattle to stray or be
slaughtered in the streets.

A specific power was granted to hold a market, and
the sale of provisions elsewhere, except of fish by the
fishermen on the beach, was prohibited. The Commissioners were authorised to borrow up to £3,000 for the
purpose of building such a market. They could also raise
up to £1,500 for the purpose by issuing annuities.

The second main objective of the Act was to provide
groynes in front of the town and to repair those that
already existed with a view to preventing the coast erosion
that had engulfed the original town below the cliff. For
this purpose the Commissioners were given a specific
source of income. They were empowered to levy a duty
of 6d. a chaldron of 36 bushels on all coals brought into
the parish of Brighton either by sea or by land. They
could also borrow up to £1,500 on the security of this
coal duty for the purpose of erecting groynes.

The Commissioners

The first meeting of the Commissioners that is recorded
took place at the *New Ship* tavern on 16 November 1789.
The meetings were all held at hotels: the *Castle*, the *Old
Ship* or the *New Ship*. They occurred at approximately
monthly intervals but were often adjourned without
any business being transacted, sometimes on several
consecutive occasions: for instance on 8 August, 12 September, 17 October, 14 November and 12 December
1791; and again on 4 July, 10 August, 7 September,
5 October, 2 November, 30 November and 14 December
1796. The time of the meetings was 7 p.m. But in
September 1807 it was provided that between Michaelmas
and Lady Day the meetings could be adjourned until
8 p.m. or 9 p.m. if a sufficient number of Commissioners

was not present at the earlier time. The minutes were signed on each occasion by all the Commissioners present.

The Commisissioners were not what would be called today a democratic body. They were empowered themselves to fill vacancies within their number. This was not done immediately a Commissioner died, resigned, left the district, or ceased to hold the necessary qualification to serve. The matter was left for a year, or occasionally longer, until there was a number of vacancies. The Commissioners then nominated a large number of candidates, usually about four times the number of places that there were to fill, and at the next meeting the requisite number of names were chosen from among them by those Commissioners who were present. Only nine such elections took place between 1789 and 1809. In June 1794 five Commissioners were chosen out of 22 nominations; in May 1797 eight out of 15 nominations. On this occasion two of the people chosen had previously acted as Commissioners without being regularly elected as such. In December 1801 three Commissioners were elected out of 16 nominations; in December 1803 three out of eight nominations; in December 1804 four out of 11 nominations; in July 1805 two out of 11 nominations. One of the four Commissioners chosen in 1804 was the new Vicar of Brighton, the Rev. Robert James Carr,[1] and one of the vacancies which he filled was caused by the death of Samuel Shergold, the proprietor of the *Castle Hotel.*

The two new Commissioners chosen in 1805 were or became well-known solicitors. One was Thomas Attree, the future clerk to both the Vestry and to the Commissioners, and the other Thomas Hill of Furner and Hill (now Fitzhugh, Eggar and Port,) of 3 Pavilion Parade. In November 1806 five Commissioners were chosen out of

1. R. J. Carr was Vicar of Brighton from 1804 until 1824. From 1820 onwards he was also Dean of Hereford. In 1824 he was promoted to the see of Chichester and in 1831 became Bishop of Worcester. He died in 1841.

18 nominations, and in September 1809 six out of 14 nominations. One of those elected in 1809 was Charles Elliott who built St. Mary's church.

On one occasion, 29 June 1792, three Commissioners named Beach Roberts, Thomas Paine, and Henry Cheeseman were warned that unless they attended the next meeting or sent their reasons for not doing so they would be struck off the list and replaced. None of them did attend the next meeting, but Beach Roberts must have sent satisfactory reasons for non-attendance, as he attended subsequent meetings. Thomas Paine and Henry Cheeseman were in due course replaced when the next election took place in June 1794.

One disturbance took place during a Commissioners' meeting, when, on 20 October 1802, Edward Thunder intruded. When asked to withdraw, he refused to do so and expressed his determination to attend during the public business of every other meeting. As it was not possible to transact any business, the meeting was adjourned until a week later. On that occasion he repeated the performance, this time accompanied by John Smith. The Commissioners therefore decided to prosecute both parties for obstructing them in the exercise of their duty. Counsel named Partington was consulted, but the offenders, through their solicitor, tendered their apology for their action and undertook not to repeat the offence. On counsel's advice the Commissioners therefore withdrew their prosecution. Thunder and Smith subsequently claimed that the apology attributed to them was false, but the Commissioners' counsel confirmed that, when he had attended before the magistrate, their solicitor, Langridge, had read out their apology, whereupon counsel had agreed to withdraw the prosecution.

The Rates

When the surviving minutes begin in 1789 the rate for that year was fixed at 2s. in the pound at a meeting held on 14 December. The rate remained at that amount until 1798, when it was increased to 2s. 6d. The year 1799 brought a further increase to 3s., but in 1800 it returned to 2s. 6d. From 1801 to 1809 the rate remained at 3s.

There were few references to prosecution for default in paying rates. In July 1794 a decision was taken to obtain a writ of mandamus to compel the magistrates to distrain for rates, which they had previously refused to do. The name of the defaulter was not mentioned. But in similar circumstances in the following November the defaulter was specified as Edward Thunder. He defaulted again in December 1796, when a distraint was issued against his goods. He seems to have been a real trouble-maker as he was one of two persons who created a disturbance at a Commissioners' meeting in October 1822.

For the financing of the town, in addition to rates, a number of debentures had been issued which bore interest at five per cent. In November 1801 these amounted to £4,420 on the town account and £1,500 on the groynes account. By November 1809 these sums had been reduced to £3,720 on the town, and £1,140 on the groynes account.

The Officers

The officers of the Town Commissioners were the Clerk and Treasurer, who were usually the same person, and the Surveyor and Collector, who likewise combined office. The Clerk and Treasurer at the time when the surviving minutes opened was William Attree of 8 Ship Street, who was also Clerk to the Vestry. His salary seems to have been £4 10s. a year. William Attree resigned his offices of Clerk and Treasurer in January 1810, no doubt in anticipation of the new Act of Parliament which was then under discussion. He was succeeded in both offices, as well as in that of Vestry Clerk, by his son, Thomas Attree, on his providing a security of £1,500. Thomas Attree became one of the most influential people in Brighton during the next 30 years or more.

The offices of Surveyor and Collector were also at first united in one person. William Lee held office until 1796, and Thomas Bridger from then until March 1800. Four Commissioners named Thomas Howell, William

Tuppon, John Baulcomb and Benjamin Pearce thereafter acted as Surveyors and Collectors in an honorary capacity for one year.

In the following March (1801), when they were thanked for their services, four other Commissioners were asked to volunteer to act on the same basis. But as no such offer was received by the following meeting it was decided to appoint a salaried official. The choice fell on Thomas Harman, who was appointed Surveyor and Collector for one year from 24 June at the salary of 26s. a week. His appointment was continued after the initial year, but in December 1802 it was decided to separate the two offices, and William Gates of 16 Ship Street was appointed collector at a salary of £21 a year.

The Market

The municipal buildings consisted of the Town Hall in Bartholomews, which also contained the gaol or black hole, and the market-house adjoining. There are frequent references in the Commissioners' minutes to the market. In 1797 it was decided to put up to auction the tolls of the market at the average produce of the last three years, namely £203. An advertisement to this effect was inserted in the *Sussex Weekly Advertiser*. Three bids were received, and the highest bidder, John Shoesmith, was declared the lessee of the tolls at £209 a year from 1 June.

The market tolls at the time were as follows: butchers were charged 1s. a day for a stall from 1 June to 1 December, and 6d. a day from 1 December to 1 June; fishmongers 10d. and 6d. respectively; all other stall-holders 6d. A fisherman selling his own fish had to pay 6d. a basket. On other merchandise the largest toll was 8d. on a cartload of oysters or mussels. On a dozen lobsters the toll was 3d. and on 100 prawns ½d. For a live pig only 1d. was taken, but for a dead pig 2d. On a turkey, goose or a dozen pigeons the toll was 1d.; on six chickens, ducks or rabbits 2d., with a lower scale for a larger number, up to 1s. for four dozen of each. Twelve pounds of butter brought a toll of 2d, and two dozen eggs 1d. The sale outside the market of commodities specified in the Brighton Act of 1773 gave rise to penalties. In June 1798 the expenditure of £46 was authorised for repairs and improvements to the market.

John Shoesmith continued to be the successful bidder for the tolls of the market for several years. In 1798, 1799 and 1800 he paid £213 a year, but in 1801 the tolls fetched £263. In March 1802 the market was enlarged on the east side, adjoining the poultry market, for a width of 12 feet to contain two rows of tables with pillars between them. Despite this measure, when the tolls were auctioned two months later there was no bidder. As a result the rent of fish stalls was raised from 10d. to 1s. a day per stall from 1 June to 1 December, and the market was enlarged on the west side, as it had previously been on the east. John Shoesmith thereupon made a renewed bid of £263, with the addition of one year's interest on the cost of enlargement, and was declared the lessee for three years.

When this period of three years elapsed it was again decided to enlarge the market to make a proper place for the fish-sellers. John Shoesmith again secured the lease of the tolls for a further period of three years for a bid of £267 a year, but he was required to pay the additional amount of £7 10s. on account of the improvements to be effected by the Commissioners. The churchwardens were asked to call a Vestry meeting to consider the Commissioners' application for a piece of ground at the back of the market for the necessary enlargement. This meeting was held, but the subsequent communication (whatever this was) by the Vestry which proceeded from it was not approved by the Commissioners. The enlargement and repairs were, however, carried out in June 1806. In January 1807 it was decided that the additional rent for the enlarged market would be £5 from the time when John Shoesmith took possession of it until 1st December 1806, and thereafter £30 a year for the remainder of his contract. This was John Shoesmith's last appearance in the Commissioners' minutes. The enlargement effected to the market in 1806 must have been considerable because, when the tolls were next put up to auction in 1808, they fetched £900—a large sum for those days. The successful bidder was Allen Anscomb.

Scavenging

One of the principal duties of the Town Commissioners was the collection of refuse. In a world where all transport was by horse, and water closets hardly existed, this consisted largely of ordure. In a largely agricultural country ordure had a value. Therefore the Commissioners' method of disposing of it was to let out to contract the right and obligation to clean the streets. On 5 May 1790 Stephen Paine and John Piper 'contracted for the Dung and Soil of the Town' for one year for £14. Any other person was forbidden to take away dung or rubbish thrown into the streets, and it was specifically provided that, if the Commissioners did not take proceedings against such offenders, the contract with Messrs. Paine and Piper would be void. In the following year Robert Allen paid £10 10s. for the right of collecting dung.

But in June 1792 Nathaniel Bradford's proposal for the collection of refuse were not accepted, and it was resolved that the streets and other public places in the town should be cleaned under the inspection of the Town Surveyor. Horses and carts were to be provided by contract for this purpose. In November Robert Allen and Thomas Coppard were prosecuted for 'taking away the Town Dung'. In September 1793 it was resolved that 'the farmors [sic] adjoining this Town shall have the Dung of the Town laid down upon their Grounds at a near distance from the Town at 1s. per Cart Load and that the Dung now in a heap be sold at 1 and 4d per Cart Load and 4d. per Waggon Load'.

Nothing further was heard of refuse collection until November 1797, when it was decided to revert to collection by contract, and advertisements were inserted in the *Sussex Weekly Advertiser*. The contract was given to Daniel Izard. In 1798 John Piper reappeared as the contractor. He was followed by Joseph Davison in 1799. By January 1801 the amount to be paid was £30, when John Izard was the contractor. But in September he and his surety, William Izard, were informed that the cleaning of the streets was unsatisfactory and unless it was improved they would be sued. They were instructed to remove the dung-hill at the north of the town. In November an action was in fact brought against the contractor, and a month later a new tender by Daniel Izard was accepted. The latter, however, did not prove any more satisfactory, and after repeated complaints his contract was also declared void, and new advertisements were inserted in the paper. Joseph Davison then reappeared, but this time without payment, 'on having the Soil for his Trouble'.

In November 1802 handbills were printed offering a reward of £5 5s. for information of any person 'employing Night Soil or other noisome Matter in any of the streets'. By May 1803 a contractor named Edward Linn was prepared to pay £31 10s for the yearly contract, but this was subsequently declared void because his sureties were not approved. The contract went instead to William Stanford for £15. In 1804 Joseph Davison again reappeared and obtained the contract yearly until 1807 for £15 or £16, though he was threatened with proceedings in December 1806 if he did not carry out his contract satisfactorily. But in June 1808 it was decided, instead of inviting tenders for cleaning the town, to put this up to auction for three years and to advertise the fact in the local papers. William Scrase was declared the winning bidder at the sum of £64, and a sub-committee was appointed to fix the days and times when the different streets should be cleaned and to provide badges for the scavengers in order to facilitate their operations. Joseph Davison, who had acted as scavenger for so long, evidently continued to operate in the neighbourhood, because in December 1808 it was resolved that a person should be employed by the Commissioners for one month to follow Davison's cart and inform people from whose houses ashes might be taken by his men that he was not the town scavenger. In January 1810 William Scrase was informed that, if he did not sign the contract for scavenging, advertisements for a new contract would be inserted in the papers.

Lighting

The second principal duty of the Commissioners in the early days was the lighting of the streets. Like the scavenging, this was put out to contract, but naturally on a basis of paying instead of being paid. The contractor was supposed to supply the oil for 150 lamps with glass burners containing two wicks each and to light them on 120 nights in the year from sunset to 3 a.m. But the period during which they were to be lighted was most curious as this was generally specified as between the end of July and the beginning of February, which coincided neither with the winter nor with the darkest half of the year. Sometimes the opening date was given as the Monday before Brighton or Lewes races.

Richard Knighton was the contractor who undertook the work for many years. In 1792 and 1793 he was paid 14s. 9d. a lamp, but in the second year he was threatened with forfeiture of the contract if the lamps were not better lighted. In 1794 the basis of payment was changed to £30 a year. In September 1797 a committee was appointed to survey the town and decide where additional lamps were needed. They reported that 17 more lamps were required and these were duly erected.

In September 1798 Joseph Hughes's offer of £1 8s. per lamp for the forthcoming season was accepted, but he was discharged in December on payment of £5 5s. Richard Knighton then returned at a contract of £62 10s., renewed in 1800 for £60. Handbills were distributed in the town to say that a reward of five guineas would be paid to anyone giving information about the breaking of lamps. Richard Knighton does not seem to have been paid yearly at this time because in February 1801 the treasurer was instructed to pay him the balance of the account due to him which amounted to £161 10s. 9d., on his making up the number of the lamps. By June 1801 the number of lamps to be lit had gone up to 200, and Richard Knighton again took on the job of lighting them at 20s. per lamp on the condition that he made good all damage to the lamps. However, his work did not give full satisfaction, and in November he was warned that he would be sued if the lamps were not better lighted in future.

The advertisement for the contract in 1802 stated the period to be covered as 23 July to 28 February, except seven nights each month which were the days of the full moon. Richard Knighton's offer was again accepted. Twelve new lamps were erected in July in the streets east of Old Steine which had been newly erected, such as Manchester Street, Charles Street, George Street, German Place (now Madeira Place), New Steine, and Royal Crescent. Richard Knighton continued to be the contractor until 1806. In 1803 he was paid £1 2s. and in 1804 £1 1s. 6d. per lamp. On this occasion a lamp was erected at the corner of Donaldson's Library to cast a light up St. James's street and along the path across the Steine to the *Castle* hotel. In May 1805 the price paid to Knighton was £1 2s. per lamp for 230 lamps. When the end of the contracted period came it was decided for the first time to extend the lighting of the lamps from 1 March to 30 April 1806 for 4s. 6d. per lamp. On the next occasion the contract was given to James Smethurst from 26 July 1806 to 30 April 1807 for a guinea per lamp. But in November he was warned that proceedings would be taken against him if the contract was not better carried out.

Such defects as this evidently influenced the Commissioners to make different arrangements. In June 1807 they resolved to have the lamps lit under their own supervision, and a committee was appointed for the purpose. A warehouse near the market was fitted up to house the lamps and the oil. This arrangement seems to have proved satisfactory because it was repeated in 1808 and 1809. A fairly large number of extra lamps was bought in 1809, and it was agreed to pay the lamplighter £3 15s. a week in consequence of his being obliged to employ an additional hand.

Roads

The third principal duty of the Town Commissioners was to provide and maintain roads and pavements in the town. One of the earliest surviving references to this occurs in May 1790. The Commissioners then decided to make a brick road 12 feet wide across the Steine from the *Castle* hotel eastwards and to take up and turf over the brick paths which had previously run from opposite Marlborough House to Crawford's (later Donaldson's) Library, which stood at the south-west corner of what came to be St. James's Street, and to the north-east corner of the Steine. Permission for this was obtained from the lords of the manor of Atlingworth. But at a subsequent meeting on 21 July certain Commissioners protested that such a step involved the sacrifice of part of their rights to herbage on the Steine and that their permission had not been asked. The surveyor was directed to obtain the consent of all the necessary persons. No further reference was made to the matter; so presumably this remained an insuperable difficulty, and no road across the Steine was in fact made until 1834.

The dispersal of rain water was also a serious problem. In May 1790 a cesspool 12 feet deep was made at the cost of £7 10s. in a hollow in Union Street to take the surplus water. In July 1791 similar arrangements, this time described as a reservoir, were made in the north-east corner of Bartholomews. But in April 1792 the well in West Street was stopped up as it was dangerous. In January 1803 a new well was dig in Brighton Place. The latter had been the site of the communal town water supply since time immemorial.

In January 1793 there was a fall of loose earth on the cliff opposite the gun or battery east of the Steine, which had been erected in 1763, but the Commissioners thought that this ought to be made good by the Surveyor of the Highways to the parish. In May of that year it was resolved to make special bathing places for people who did not use the bathing-machines and to provide a gravel walk 'east of Miss Russell's house' for the accommodation of ladies bathing. Previously, in June 1791, boards had been fixed against the groynes to prevent people bathing 'before the town'.

The minutes do not refer to the enclosure in an underground channel of the Wellsbourne stream which took place in 1793. This was because the expense was borne by the Prince of Wales and the Duke of Marlborough for the protection of their own houses against floods. Two years later trouble arose which presumably related to this work. Floods had occurred. The arch 'at the north part of the town' had to be repaired and the head kept open. The water running down Church Street had to be diverted from Great East Street and the road in front of Marlborough House lowered to conduct the water into its original channel. A conduit also led from opposite Crawford's Library into the Wellsbourne channel. This was lengthened so that its full length was 96 feet. The same trouble occurred at the end of 1798 and at the beginning of 1799, when it was found impractical to divert water from Church Hill (Dyke Road) down West Street, but the level of Church Street was lowered so that the water could flow more easily into the Wellsbourne channel, and a new entrance to it was made opposite the *Castle* hotel.

In February 1797 the Surveyor was ordered to see that the town cart should be employed daily from 7 a.m. to 4 p.m. and that if either of the men employed should refuse to obey his orders, they should be discharged and replaced.

In October 1802 directions were given to the Surveyor to remove the timber and chain at the bottom of Great East Street to which the fishermen attached their capstan for drawing up their boats.

In August 1805 a committee was appointed to ascertain the cost of acquiring the necessary properties to widen Ship Street Lane and of making a new road from North Street to Ship Street. But this was not actually carried out until soon after the Act of 1810 came into force.

In July 1805 it was decided that the posts and rails opposite Marine Parade should be continued to the corner of the wall of Russell House, Old Steine, with openings for sedan chairs at each end. In the centre was to be an entrance for carriages and horses, but this would normally be barred and a key left with the Surveyor, Thomas Harman; also at St. James's Court, St. James's Street, and with the principal fishermen for the accommodation of gentlemen's carriages and of boats carrying sand. A year later directions were given for the Steine to be paved with bricks, but this presumably related to the paths round it which had been turfed over in 1790, rather than to the open space itself.

In November 1806 a petition was presented to the Board of Customs concerning ships unloading to the east of the town, which had damaged the groynes. The Board was asked to see that ships unloaded only between the two stone pillars which had been specially erected some years previously to prescribe limits for unloading. In November 1807 the Commissioners had to address themselves to another public body, the Board of Ordnance, requesting them to rectify the dangerous condition in which the spot lately occupied by the battery opposite German Place (now Madeira Place) had been left.

In November 1808 Sir Robert Burnett and others drew the notice of the Commissioners to the bad state of Marine Parade owing to falls of the cliff. But the Commissioners replied that this was the responsibility of the Surveyor of the Highways to the parish. At the same meeting they decided that the railing at the bottom of the Steine should be so arranged as to prevent donkeys being stationed to the south of it.

Nuisances

The obligation to provide and maintain roads and pavements led to the prevention of nuisances thereon. There seem to have been three main kinds of nuisance. The first comprised the actual obstruction of the roads by solid materials. For instance, on 19 April 1790 it was ordered that the 'Dung, Stones, Hogstyes and Rubbish at the East and West side of the Turnpike Road near the North Row at the North Entrance of the Town be removed and taken away'. A similar provision was made in March 1792 'in a certain Street formerly called ye North Back Side now Spring Walks (by the desire of the Commissioners is intended to be henceforward called the Church Street)'. This was the east end of Church Street opposite the present Library. Only three months later the Surveyor was ordered to inspect all buildings in the town and to give directions for the enclosure of all building materials or rubbish that were unfenced, on pain of prosecution. Again in September rubbish placed in the streets was declared to be a nuisance to be impounded and giving rise to proceedings.

Six months later (March 1793) it was resolved that 'sufficient Notices to persons that do not sweep the Foot Pavements before their Doors, etc., for running barrows, etc., upon Pavements and dressing horses, etc., will be prosecuted be immedy Printed and stuck up distributed and that all persons so offending after such Notices be prosecuted'. In June of the same year the Commissioners directed that the goods of Matthew Leame which were placed before his house in Castle Square should be taken into the 'Town House' and sold if the fine for which he was liable was not paid. In June 1798 a complaint was made against a shipwright named James May that boats and timber on which he was working were obstructing the passage of Margaret Street. He was also accused of having dug out the foundations of a house adjoining his premises without having railed these off. He was ordered to remove the timber and to fence the hole. A note was made in the margin of the minutes to the effect that both nuisances were removed.

The second kind of nuisance related to horses and other animals. In September 1792 it was directed that persons dressing horses in the street should be indicted. In January 1796 the Clerk was ordered to wait upon the Commanding Officer of the Somerset Forcibles to request that the soldiers should not exercise their horses in the streets. In September 1797 the surveyor was directed to remove to Bartholomews any carriage belonging to Mr. Maibon which should be found standing in or near Princes Street, and any chaise belonging to Mr. Hicks which was found in Duke Street, and that these should be detained until the fines incurred thereby were paid. A similar provision was made a month later for any carriages without horses which were found in New Street (now Bond Street).

A rather different situation arose in November 1797 when Mr. Piper was warned to discontinue keeping hogs in the coach-house 'opposite to the back part of Mr. Crawford's House'. In December 1803 handbills were printed prohibiting the wheeling of wheelbarrows on the pavements. On one occasion in 1805 a gig had been impounded in Bartholomews, as in the instance already mentioned. Someone, however, broke the chain binding it and removed the gig. A reward of £3 3s. was offered for information leading to the conviction of the offender.

In September 1809 it was decided to proffer a bill of indictment against the two or three people who kept horses and asses for hire opposite the south end of the Steine.

The third form of nuisance verged almost upon town planning powers. Nothing equivalent to planning permission was required for building a house, but if, in doing so, a person erected a bay window which created an obstruction in the road or pavement, he could be ordered to remove it. It is not clear exactly what constituted an obstruction. Each case was treated on its merits, and an *ad hoc* sub-committee of Commissioners made an inspection. But many complaints of such steps occurred. Probably some were more cases of rows between neighbours than anything else.

The first reference to a projection forming a nuisance was on 6 June 1791, when it was ordered that all signs which projected in a triangular or any other form should be taken down and fixed flat against the buildings in question. In March 1792 a butcher named Richard Russell was ordered to remove from the front of his house the range on which he occasionally hung meat and not to suspend offal under the penthouse. As he did not comply with this order a prosecution was instituted. The Commissioners present at the meeting of 12 June 1793 were asked to inspect the bow window of Edward Hales's house in Middle Street. Presumably it was not thought to cause any offence as no further reference to it was made at subsequent meetings. In September 1797 similar action was taken to see whether Mr. Crawford, who was erecting a building on the side of the Old Bank in North Street, had advanced the foundations on the north side farther than those of the old building. In April 1798 directions were given to George Walker to remove from his house in North Street bow windows which were held to be a nuisance. A note was made in the margin of the minutes to the effect that the order had been complied with, but in the minutes of 16 May it was recorded that these bow windows could not be held to be a nuisance. In July 1803 enforcement action was recommended against bow windows on the west side and steps on the south side of a house on the Cliff, but the name of the offender is left blank in the minutes.

The buildings mentioned in the preceding instances cannot now be identified, but in 1807 occurred a more interesting example as it related to a well-known building. An entry in the minutes of 15 April 1807 read: 'Resolved that in answer to a request made by Mr. Cobb, proprietor of the New Theatre, for Liberty to erect the portico in front of the same a short distance beyond the

limits of the present foot path, so as to obtain eight feet
in the clear from the building; that he be informed that
the Commissioners have no right to grant his request;
but on the contrary, should such a portico be erected
and the same be complained of and adjudged by the
Commissioners as a Nuisance, they would be under the
necessity of instituting proceedings to remove the same'.
This was followed by an entry of 15 July to the effect
that no further discussion should take place concerning
this portico without the proprietor having given the
Commissioners three months' notice, but of what he
was to give notice was not stated. These entries related
to the building of the earliest theatre on the site of the
present Theatre Royal in New Road, of which the
foundation stone had been laid by the manager, Mr.
Brunton, senior, on 10 September 1806. The first
performance took place on 27 June 1807. The previous
theatre had been in Duke Street, and its street elevation,
illustrated in Bishop's *Brighton in the Olden Time,* faced
in weather-boarding grooved to imitate masonry, shows
just such a portico as was evidently envisaged for the new
Theatre in New Road. If a similar portico was first built
in New Road it must have been replaced by the existing
colonnade 13 years later.

In October 1807 it was decided to prosecute John Slee,
junior, for encroaching on the street by bringing forward
the front of his house in Manchester Street. However,
at the following meeting the prosecution was suspended
until the premises had been inspected by a committee
of the Commissioners, presumably with satisfaction, as
the matter was adjourned and no reference thereafter
made to it. In January 1808 Thomas Hill was warned
that if he should erect a bow window or 'bulk' in front
of his house in Ship Street this would be removed by
order of the Commissioners. In March 1808 a somewhat
different entry was made. A committee was appointed
to examine the position concerning the public house in
Middle Street belonging to Wigney's Brewery which
had lately been called the *Spotted Dog* and to see

whether 'the giving up not less than three feet at the North end will be of advantage to the Town and what will be the probable expense of taking down the front of the House and rebuilding the same'.

Groynes

One of the principal causes of expenditure to the Commissioners comprised the groynes in front of the town, and a separate financial account was kept concerning them. Special debentures had been issued for their construction in the past. On 13 February 1792 a petition was presented to the Commissioners asking for groynes to be erected to the east of the town. The Commissioners decided to obtain, at the expense of the petitioners, an estimate of the cost involved. They also decided to examine the existing groynes and to obtain an estimate for supporting them. The necessary repairs were estimated at £200, but on 30 April it was decided to spend £670. This was to be borrowed on the security of the coal duty. The repair of the groyne east of Pool Valley was ordered on 28 May, but no new groynes were built.

In February 1800 the groyne opposite Pool Valley was found to be out of repair, but none of the carpenters present at the meeting was prepared to give the town credit for the work needed. It was not until 16 April that repairs up to the sum of £20 were authorised to be carried out under the supervision of the town surveyors.

In October 1802 a report was made on the east groyne which recommended the erection of a new groyne 'near the east end of Mr. Siddon's wall', and an estimate for building this was requested. But there is no record that it was erected.

In February 1803 the proprietors of houses in Marine Parade and of the land adjoining offered to erect three more groynes to the east of those which already existed at the cost of £600, if the Commissioners agreed to pay £300 towards this. The Commissioners resolved to do so provided that the easternmost groyne to be erected was 75 feet east of the east wall of the garden to Rock

Building and that the proprietors, at their expense, built a sea wall along the cliff as far as this groyne. Despite this expenditure the Commissioners were able, in November 1803, to pay off five debentures of £20 each on the groyne account and two debentures of £100 each on the town account, and, in November 1804, £200 on the groyne account and £300 on the town account. As no further expenditure on groynes took place during the next four years nine more debentures of £20 each on the groyne account were paid off in November 1807.

In March 1808 the proprietors of east Brighton again approached the Commissioners about erecting more groynes opposite their property as the town had begun to expand considerably in this direction. Two surveyors were appointed to confer with two other surveyors appointed by the proprietors of the houses to be affected. Their report was to the effect that eight groynes 120 feet long would be required and would cost £2,400. The proprietors of east Brighton decided to erect these eight groynes, and in May the Commissioners agreed to pay £100 per groyne towards the expense within a month of the completion of each groyne on the condition that the proprietors subsequently kept the groynes in repair. The makers of the groynes were lent the town's 'humboy', and £400 was paid for completed groynes in November.

Miscellaneous Matters

There was a number of miscellaneous items of interest that really come under no general heading. For instance, on 4 July 1791 a reward of £10 10s. was offered for the discovery of persons destroying the nets placed round the Duke of Marlborough's house.

In May 1794 Bond Street was renamed New Street, and the street joining West Street and Russell Street was given the name of Little Russell Street. In April 1797 there occurred a curious entry concerning the lodging houses on the east side of the Steine. It having been understood that, though these houses were liable for town rates, they were not entitled to the privileges arising from the local Act of 1773, the Commissioners held that they were so entitled.

At 5 a.m. on 5 May 1798 a fire occurred in the Royal Pavilion which was thought not to be accidental. The Commissioners therefore offered a reward of 200 guineas— a very large sum for those days—for information leading to a successful prosecution of an offender. The only other occasion on which the subject of fires is mentioned in the minutes of the Commissioners at this period was on 23 September 1801, when the question arose of repairing the hose of the fire engine or providing a new one. The Commissioners held that the fire engine did not come under their jurisdiction.

The Royal Pavilion was however mentioned on two other occasions. On 10 March 1802 a proposal was received from the Prince of Wales's architect, Henry Holland, to bring the gates and fence on the south side of the Royal Pavilion four and a half feet further forward and to widen Great East Street on the west side 'in a Line from the Great Gates to the House now in the occupation of Mrs. Sayers'. The Commissioners agreed to this proposal and in July sent a reminder to Henry Holland, asking him to carry it out.

In the following year the north end of Great East Street, which had hitherto run virtually under the west windows of the Royal Pavilion, was stopped up and the Prince of Wales gave the town in exchange land further west for the creation of what is now New Road. Henry Roberts in his *History of the Royal Pavilion* quotes a minute of the Commissioners for 25 August 1803 approving the diversion of this road. But curiously enough in the surviving Commissioners' minute books there is not only no record of such a resolution but not even of a Commissioners' meeting on that date.

Brighton races were mentioned in September 1800, when £3 3s. and £8 16s. 8d. were paid to Mr. Gourd and Richard Lashmar respectively for watching the town during the races of 1798 and 1799.

A New Act of Parliament

In January 1799 the Commissioners appointed a committee to consider the defects of their existing Act of
Parliament of 1773, and what additional powers were
required. Charles Scrase Dickens, Samuel Shergold, William
Wigney, Thomas Kemp, and Nathaniel Kemp were among
the members of this committee. It reported in March, and
it was decided to summon a town meeting on 2 April to
consider the desirability of applying to Parliament for a
new Act. The Vestry minutes, however, do not record
that any such meeting was held.

The matter did not come up again until 1806. In that
year the Vestry discussed the possibility of obtaining a
charter of incorporation and recorded on 13 March that
'a Charter, if the same can be obtained with an adequate
Revenue, would be greatly to the benefit of this parish'.
This was signed by the Vicar, the Rev. R. J. Carr (afterwards Bishop of Chichester) and by the High Constable,
Thomas Saunders, as well as by the churchwardens and
overseers. But the Vestry was afraid that a corporation
could not be supported and would not meet with the
approval of the inhabitants unless the town was endowed
with permanent property—which did not in fact exist.
This in fact proved to be the case. A public meeting
was held at the *Old Ship* hotel at the suggestion of the
Prince of Wales to consider whether the town should be
incorporated, but the proposal to that effect was negatived.

The Town Commissioners returned to the consideration
of improved powers on 13 September 1807. They decided
to give formal notice of their intention to apply to Parliament for a new Act, and the 10 Commissioners present
at that meeting were constituted a committee to prepare
a new private Bill.

Once more this did not get off the ground and it was
not until March 1809 that steps towards a new Act were
in fact taken. Another formal resolution was passed
expressing the intention of applying to Parliament for
a new Act, and a committee of nine Commissioners,
including William Wigney, Dr. Scutt and the Vicar of

Brighton, Dr. R. J. Carr, appointed to frame this. The draft Bill was laid before Sergeant Runnington, who was a local resident and magistrate, in September. As the result of his advice it was resolved to increase the number of new Commissioners, to be appointed by the existing Commissioners, to 80, and that the clause relating to the qualification of Commissioners should only apply to new Commissioners. It was resolved to have the Bill printed in the local papers, to invite comments thereon and to obtain signatures of the inhabitants to a petition to Parliament in favour of the Bill.

The promotion of this Bill led to a sharp dispute with the Vestry. According to the Vestry minutes the Commissioners held a meeting on 23 October 1809 at which the conduct of certain members of the Vestry was criticised. But no meeting of that date occurs in the minutes of the Commissioners. However, the real cause of dissention was the provision in the Bill whereby the appointment of the Directors and Guardians of the workhouse should be appointed by the Town Commissioners instead of by the Vestry. On 13 December the Vestry passed a resolution that was confirmed by a public meeting on the 20th to the effect that the Town Commissioners had no right to frame a new Act of Parliament or to make any alteration in the method of raising rates without first calling a town meeting; that the proposed Act of Parliament should not be proceeded with; and that no expense of preparing the same should fall upon the inhabitants, but should be paid purely by the Town Commissioners who had suggested this Act. A committee of 21 people was appointed to prepare a petition to be signed by all inhabitants who paid scot and lot, praying the House of Commons not to pass the proposed Bill, should this be presented to them. The committee was also authorised to frame an alternative Bill after consulting the accounts of the Vestry and of the Commissioners.

As the result of this opposition the Commissioners appointed 10 of their members in January 1810 to confer with 10 representatives appointed by the Vestry. This step in due course led to agreement. The Vestry was anxious that the qualification for Town Commissioners should be the payment of scot and lot and the occupation of premises of the annual value of £50 or the ownership of property to the value of £1,000. The Commissioners at first thought that the number of Commissioners under the new Act should be increased from 64 to 164; the additional number being appointed by the existing Commissioners out of 200 names put forward by the Vestry. But they subsequently agreed to an increase of only 36 new members, to be chosen in the same fashion, and that the Bill as a whole should be presented to a town meeting before being submitted to Parliament.

On 31 January a last minute attempt was made to challenge this agreement concerning the reduction of the number of the new Commissioners from 164 to 100 on the grounds that, at the meeting at which it was approved, the chairman had not voted because exception had been taken to his doing so, whereas, had he done so, the voting would have been equal. The number of 164 was therefore re-substituted. But agreement was subsequently reached with the Vestry on the figure of one hundred.

A petition was then presented to all the inhabitants for signature in favour of the Bill. But this was first submitted to the Prince of Wales. The covering note stated: 'That Brighton has risen to its present state of Prosperity that it has become the first Watering Place in the British Dominions is to be ascribed to the fostering kindness of Your Royal Highness, and it is the united wish of the Inhabitants, as it will be their constant endeavour, to render it increasingly worthy of your high regard'.

2.—1810–1825

The Act of 1810 was duly passed. The preamble specified as the reason for its enactment that the powers given to the Commissioners of 1773 were then inadequate. The population of the town had since grown greatly, as had the number of the poor. The workhouse needed enlarging and there was a need to appoint Directors and Guardians of the Poor with a paid overseer. The Act repealed all the provisions of the earlier Act except those relating to the market.

The number of the Commissioners was increased from 64 to 100, but 43 existing Commissioners were again nominated in the Act. Thereafter vacancies were to be filled more democratically. Except for the High Constable, the churchwardens, the Overseer of the Poor and the Vicar of Brighton, who served *ex officio,* vacancies were to be filled more democratically. Elections were to be held for the purpose. All inhabitants paying scot and lot and assessed to taxes on a rent of more than £20 a year were eligible to vote. The qualifications for acting as a Commissioner were extended to the ownership or occupation of premises to the value of £50 a year.

The Act of 1810 very greatly extended the general powers of the Commissioners. They were empowered to appoint a clerk, treasurer, surveyor and collector of rates, who were precluded from themselves acting as a Commissioner, though in at least one case at a later date such a duplication of functions seems actually to have happened. The power was also given to appoint watchmen to patrol the streets.

Somewhat similar provisions were made for the paving, cleaning and lighting of the streets as in the old Act. But it was specifically provided that, when new houses were built, the owners were themselves responsible for the cost of providing a pavement in front of their houses which would thereafter vest in and be maintainable by the Commissioners. From then onwards the house-owners would not be able to alter the pavements without permission, though the Commissioners themselves could alter their level. It was laid down that authorised scavengers were to collect dirt from the street and houses (except the night-soil from privies) on Wednesdays and Saturdays between the hours of seven and twelve. Night-soil was to be collected separately, and no unauthorised person was to remove it or dump it in the street.

The prohibition of nuisances was extended. It was made a specific offence to run carriages on the pavement, to shoe or expose horses for sale, to drive or ride furiously, to play ball games, let off squibs, kill animals, or expose meat for sale in the streets. Wandering animals or carriages left in the street would be impounded.

The rudimentary planning powers were also strengthened a little. If the roof of houses would discharge rain-water on the pavements rain-water pipes were to be affixed thereto. The old provision concerning the projection of new houses beyond the foundations of old ones or the line of adjoining buildings was repeated. But there was a reservation in favour of verandas not projecting beyond the areas of the houses and for verandas and balconies not projecting beyond those of the adjoining house. The Commissioners could require the removal on notice of such projections or signs if they considered that these obstructed the street. New houses should rise perpendicularly from their foundations except for shop windows which were allowed a projection of 10 inches on brackets. Party walls were to be nine inches thick and to be made of brick or stone without timber. No buildings, other than existing farm buildings, were to be thatched. Owners might built vaults in front of their houses but must insert gratings as directed.

The Commissioners were directed to have the name of each street displayed, and moreover to require the householders to exhibit the number of their houses. They were empowered to widen certain streets which were mentioned in the schedule to the Act and to acquire buildings by agreement for the purpose. Failing agreement, they could appeal to a jury at Quarter Sessions, and, unless the jury awarded a larger sum than the Commissioners had offered, the expense of the appeal would be paid by the owner.

To carry out these liabilities the rate which the Commissioners were entitled to levy was increased from 3s. to 4s. in the pound on the basis of the poor-rate. Relief could be granted, and an appeal against assessment could be made to the Commissioners themselves, to the Justices of the Peace, and, if necessary, to Quarter Sessions. In new streets, if the road had been made up, owners were liable for two-thirds of the cost of providing a pavement in front of their houses, even if the houses were unoccupied, and for a third of the cost if the house was still unroofed.

The amount borrowed by the previous Commissioners had reached a total of £3,720. The Act of 1810 authorised the new Commissioners to borrow a further sum. But, except for the purpose of building a new Town Hall, the additional amount was not to exceed £3,000 until the old debt had been reduced to £2,000. Loans could take the form of annuities issued to a person of over 40 years of age at a rate of not more than £10 per £100 loaned, and not more than £100 could be borrowed from any one person.

Further powers were granted in matters relating to trade. The market established by the Act of 1773 was to be continued, but the existing building could be extended on land which had already been purchased for the purpose. Five thousand pounds could be borrowed for this extension on the security of the market tolls. These could be leased for three years at a time. A similar amount of £5,000 could be borrowed in order to build a new Town Hall.

For the purpose of securing fair dealings in shops the Commissioners were directed to nominate annually nine householders to act as inspectors of balances, weights and measures in an honorary capacity. Anyone who refused to serve as such once in three years was to be fined five pounds. Many instances occurred in future years of such refusals being made and a fine being consequently imposed. Of the inspectors appointed three acting together, were to enter once a month all shops, inns, warehouses, breweries and other buildings where articles were sold by weight or measure. If the traders were discovered to be giving short weight the inspectors could fine them up to 20s., break their weights and publish their names in the local papers. They were similarly authorised to test the quality of bread in bakeries. Under the inspectors a paid officer was to be appointed to seal or mark all the weights that were brought to him. The use of all other weights was to be illegal. The fees were 3d. for a bushel weight, ½d. a peck, 2d. a sack or hundredweight, and 1d. for a measure of ale, beer or milk. Half the fees were to be handed over to the Commissioners and half retained by the officer as his fee.

The Commissions were authorised to licence hackney carriages, sedan-chairs and bathing-machines, and also to regulate bathing. The annual fees for licences were 10s. for a carriage, 5s. for a sedan-chair, and 2s. for a bathing-machine.

In order to finance the building of groynes in front of Brighton the Commissioners of 1773 had been authorised to levy a duty of 6d. a chaldron on all coal brought into the town and to borrow £1,500 on the strength of this duty. Though this maximum amount had been borrowed, the total sum available had not been sufficient for the purpose. The Act of 1810 therefore increased the maximum duty to 3s. a chaldron, and the borrowing powers to £5,000. A relief of duty, known as a 'draw-back', on up to two chaldrons a year could be given to poor people by the overseer of the poor-rate.

Six Land Coal Meters could be appointed to collect this duty. Customs officers at Shoreham were not to discharge ships from that port without a certificate to the effect that the coal duty on their cargo had been paid.

The most important new powers included in the Act of 1810 related to the poor and to the workhouse. This building had hitherto been administered by the Vestry itself. Henceforth the Commissioners were authorised to appoint 30 'substantial and discrete' inhabitants and householders as Directors and Guardians of the Poor, in addition to the High Constable, the Vicar, the churchwardens and the Overseer of the poor-rate, who would serve *ex officio*. These Directors and Guardians would appoint six committees which would each hold a meeting on one day a week. They would make bye-laws concerning the poor. But henceforth the whole administration was not to be on the amateur basis which had characterised it hitherto. The existing workhouse could be sold and a new one built on another site. Ten thousand pounds could be borrowed on the strength of the poor-rate for the purpose. The Directors and Guardians were authorised to appoint their own officers. These were a governor, matron and surgeon of the workhouse and also a clerk, treasurer and assistant overseer. The latter was the key official and could be paid up to £200 a year. In future the assistant overseer was to assume all the duties of the hitherto honorary overseer of the poor-rate, and the churchwardens and overseers were not to meddle in the matter. Their function would be only to collect the poor-rate and pay this over to the treasurer of the Directors and Guardians.

The latter were to set the poor to work; to compel 'idle and disorderly persons' who refused to maintain their families to come into the workhouse and there put them to work until they had earned sufficient to pay the expenses previously incurred on their behalf or that of their families, or, failing that, to have them detained for up to 30 days hard labour. Vagrants and beggars were to be confined in the workhouse and kept for 14 days hard labour before being passed to the parish of their origin. The Guardians could employ the poor in any trade, and could stock flax, hemp, wool, cotton, thread, iron, stone, wood, or leather to give them material on which to work. To encourage the poor to 'apply themselves to labour . . . such small Rewards shall be distributed to the Industrious and Skilful . . . as shall seem reasonable to the Assistant Overseer'. Children born or taken into the workhouse when very young should be kept there till the age of 14 and then apprenticed for seven years to 'any reputable Person in England and Wales' or 'employed in the Sea Service'. Either above or below the age of 14 children could be hired out as domestic servants or for work on the harvest.

Half the expenses of the Act of 1810 were to be paid by the Commissioners out of the general rate, and half by the Directors and Guardians of the Poor out of the poor-rate.

These expenses amounted to £943 8s. 9d. Of this sum £643 8s. 9d. was paid to William Radley Mott, who was presumably a parliamentary counsel or agent and was later a Commissioner, and £300 to Thomas Attree as Clerk.

The Commissioners

As provided by the Act, the new Commissioners met for the first time at the *Old Ship* hotel on 2 May 1810 between the hours of 10 and 12 in the morning. Their first obligation was to sign the oath, or, in the case of Quakers, the affirmation, both of which are inscribed on the first pages of the minute book. Those subsequently elected testified on their first appearance that they were householders paying scot and lot, that they occupied a house to the annual value of £50 and owned property in the town to the annual value of £50. The chairman was elected at each meeting. Among the original Commissioners were the Vicar of Brighton, the Rev. R. J. Carr, William Wigney, Samuel Brown, Thomas Pocock,

Thomas Kemp, his brother Nathaniel, his son Thomas Read Kemp, Thomas Hill, Henry Brooker, Benjamin Scutt, Harry Attree, and John Perkins. Four Quakers signed the affirmation in the first instance and one subsequently. Among those who subsequently became Commissioners were Thomas R. Attree in December 1819 and George Wigney in March 1822.

On 9 May 1810 the Commissioners appointed a committee to ascertain why some of the persons recommended to be Commissioners had not in fact been appointed and others had taken their place. This committee exonerated from blame for this occurrence the committee who had supervised the passing of the Act but did not give the explanation.

By April 1811 it had become necessary to ascertain what vacancies existed amongst the number of Commissioners. William Attree, Thomas Kemp and two others had died, and five other Commissioners had resigned. Nine new Commissioners were therefore elected to take their place in May. These included Edward Thunder and William Izard who were to be a source of future trouble.

Thereafter vacancies were filled, not as each individual one occurred, but at yearly or longer intervals when there were a number of empty seats.

For instance, nine new Commissioners were elected in November 1813. These included Sergeant Runnington, the chairman of the local magistrates, and Hyam Lewis. The latter duly attended a meeting but declined to take the oath as he stated that he was not qualified to act. However, he must have acquired the necessary qualifications by 1822 as he was re-elected on 15 February of that year and duly signed the oath.

David Spector in his article on 'The Jews of Brighton, 1770-1900' says that this is probably the first instance in England of the entrance of a Jew into local government. Hyam Lewis had been born in Prague in 1769 and became a naturalised British subject in 1816. He was a silversmith and pawnbroker by profession—perhaps the first pawnbroker in Brighton. His shop was at first in

Ship Street Lane and, after this was widened, at 31 Ship Street. He died in 1851.

Seven new Commissioners were elected in April 1814; five in October 1816; six in December 1819; 23 in March 1822; five in March 1823; four in March 1824; and three in March 1825. One of these last was the solicitor, George Faithful, who was Member of Parliament for Brighton from 1833 to 1835. Thomas Read Kemp took his seat for the first time in April 1823. Following the election of 1816 it was claimed that the election was invalid because some people who were qualified to vote had been denied admission during the ballot and that some candidates had voted for themselves. Counsel's opinion was taken and laid before a public meeting, which directed that a new election should be held. This took place on 2 December.

The Rates

The last town rate fixed under the old Act of 1773 had been 3s. in the pound. The first rate under the new Act was fixed at the same rate in December 1810. A year later this was reduced to 2s. 6d. and continued at that sum until December 1813. In December 1814 this was increased to four shillings. An amendment was made to the effect that the amount should be 3s. but this was defeated. The rates remained at 4s. until 1824. In May 1820 the Audit Committee found that the rates were always in arrears because the amount of the rate was not fixed until the end of each year and the sums due were not collected until the following year. The committee therefore recommended that in future the rate should be collected during the year for which it was made. But in February 1824 the position appeared to be unchanged, and people were still evading payment by leaving the town before the rates could be collected.

The Officers

After signing the oath the first task of the original Commissioners was to appoint their officers. The choice for

Clerk and Treasurer naturally fell on Thomas Attree who had been acting in both capacities since the resignation of his father William earlier that year. His salary was increased by £30 in October 1811. In August 1821 it was decided that it was mutually incompatible to combine the functions of Clerk and Treasurer in one person. Attree resigned the treasurership and it was decided to appoint the local banks to act as Treasurer for one year each in rotation, beginning with the Brighton Old Bank or Michell, Mills and Co. of 103 North Street. But when their year of office expired in 1823 John Mills was appointed sole Treasurer.

Thomas Attree's main responsibility was to the Brighton Vestry and as the complexity of life increased it was presumably found awkward that he was Clerk both to the Vestry and to the Commissioners. In September 1822 his partner, Frederick Cooper, was appointed joint Clerk to the Commissioners with him, and in May 1823, Thomas Attree resigned wholly in his favour as the result of a decision of the magistrates.

Under the new Act of 1810 the existing Collector of the town rates, William Gates, was also confirmed in office on giving security of £1,000. He served until March 1821, when he was thanked by the Commissioners for his 'disinterested faithful conduct as collector and servant of the Commissioners during the long course of 20 years'. Nevertheless, he left something of a crisis behind him. He was found to owe the Commissioners £1,377 7s. 1d. After treating with his creditors the liability seems to have been reduced to £898 4s. 10d. From the tone of the minutes it is clear that this was far more a case of a muddled system than of dishonesty on the part of the employee concerned. The Commissioners magnanimously recorded that 'as Mr. Gates has collected a large Revenue for the Comrs. for the last 20 years at the small annual stipend of 25 guineas he is entitled to the consideration of the Comrs. and that had he been paid the same as the present Collector the pr. Centage would have amounted to nearly the debt due from

Mr. Gates'. He was therefore discharged from this debt. His immediate successor, S. F. Saunders was given a commission of 4d. in the pound instead of a salary. But within a year a committee came to the conclusion that this remuneration was quite inadequate and that Saunders was incapable of collecting the rates within a reasonable time. He was therefore replaced by Trist and Grenville, the Collectors of Assessed Taxes, who were paid a commission of 6d. in the pound.

Thomas Harman, the existing Surveyor in 1810, was removed from that office and reappointed Street-keeper at the wage of £1 6s. a week, which was increased by £10 a year in 1811. After an advertisement in the *Brighton Gazette* Thomas Vine was appointed Surveyor at the salary of £50 a year. The office lasted until 1816, when Thomas Vine was dismissed, not because of any dissatisfaction with his conduct but because it was thought that the office might be dispensed with. The office was revived in June 1823, when Thomas Furner was appointed at a salary of £100 a year to superintend all public works and particularly to prevent new houses from encroaching on the streets and to see that proper party-walls were inserted therein. At the same time Thomas Harman was appointed Master Pavior and Inspector of Lamps at £60 a year.[1]

James Penfold was appointed Marker and Stamper of Balances, Weights and Measures in 1810. He was replaced in October 1811 by George Jenkins at a salary of £10 a year. Jenkins, however, was dismissed in February 1813 for neglect of his duties and for having attended a meeting of the Commissioners in an intoxicated condition. Thomas Palmer succeeded him until 1820, and then Martin Lashmar.

Then there were the offices of Coal Meters and Inspectors of Balances, Weights and Measures. The first Coal Meters were John Lucas, Thomas Kent, Thomas Parker and E. Cobby. From 1822 the collection of the

---

1. In June 1825 a William Harman was dismissed, but it was not stated from what office.

land carriage coal duty was given to Carter Thunder for a commission of 6d. a chaldron, John Lucas was paid 10s. 6d. a week as Coal Meter. The office of Inspector of Balances, Weights and Measures, however, was an honorary obligation that citizens were expected to accept if they were nominated for it. An allowance of £12 was made to them provided that the fines imposed by them did not exceed this amount. But it was not stated whether this sum was allowed to each inspector or to all of them collectively. As many as 23 people were nominated to hold this onerous office in the first two months' operation of the new Act. Three of these refused to serve and were fined £5 each. On several subsequent occasions people who were nominated refused and were fined.

In May 1810 the Commissioners for the first time appointed the Directors and Guardians of the Poor, amounting to 30 in number. These had previously been appointed by the Vestry in public meeting.

The last officer appointed was the Beadle, whose function was to apprehend vagabonds, to prevent people bathing without a machine between the *Norfolk Arms* and Royal Crescent and to impound animals straying in the streets. The post was advertised in the local paper at the wage of a guinea a week. But when Henry Hobden was appointed in June he was only given 19s. a week and was not sworn as a special constable. Henry Hobden left the town in September 1812. His place was taken by Thomas Measor, who was paid the guinea a week that had been advertised in the first place. He was supplied with a blue coat with yellow buttons and a cocked hat similar to those worn by the town crier; also with a brown greatcoat and a gilt staff bearing a silver plate with the insignia of the town. Thomas Measor, however, did not last long. In June 1813 he was dismissed for neglect of his duties. His successor was William Catling. Catling got into trouble in 1822, when he was accused of using Sir David Scott's name improperly, and was dismissed. But on the intercession of Sir David he was reinstated.

Four more Beadles were appointed in 1821, namely Henry Martin, William Sheppard, John Mills, and John Knight. Each was given a district of the town. Beadles named Thorburn and O'Connor, who were referred to as extra beadles, were discharged in April 1823.

The Market

The tolls of the market were let by auction in May 1810 for two years. Henry Cuddington paid £865 for them. In 1812 Allen Anscomb, who had been the successful bidder in 1808, made his reappearance. In August he was warned that, if the arrears of rent were not paid, he would be prosecuted. He had surrendered possession of the market by May 1814 when the stalls were re-advertised, but owing to collusion on the part of the renters no bids were received. The stalls were therefore re-let individually direct at sums varying between 1s. and 2s. 6d. per day, which constituted an increase on the old rates. John Baldry was appointed collector of the rents at a commission of seven per cent. The stallholders objected to the increases and a committee consisting of the Vicar, the Rev. R. J. Carr, Sergeant Runnington and S. F. Milford was appointed to settle the dispute. Their report recommended some reductions, but not enough to please Sergeant Runnington who dissented from their conclusions. The Commissioners accepted the compromise and thanked the committee for having restored tranquility to the town.

In June 1820 the Commissioners reverted to the practice of letting the market tolls as a whole. John Martin paid £915 for the year. The following year George Shelley paid £1,010, and in 1822 William Head £1,200. By this time the market was not proving large enough for the requirements of the town. So the Commissioners agreed to buy the adjoining poor-house from the Directors and Guardians of the Poor for the amount of the mortgate outstanding on the building, £4,333 6s. 8d. The first instalment of £125 on the purchase price was paid in January 1823. Five months later William Head again rented the market for £1,285. During the year he fell into arrears with his rent and applied for a reduction on account of extensive hawking in the town. This was refused as having been specifically precluded by the agreement between him and the Commissioners. The next rent comprised a slight reduction, namely £1,190, but the renter was Robert Snelling. In 1825 the tolls did not fetch £1,400 at auction and were bought in by the Commissioners.

Lighting

As one of their first tasks the new Commissioners proceeded to elect a committee to superintend the lighting of the town, to examine what lights should be moved, and where new ones should be placed, to contract for oil and to provide vats for its storage. In November 1811 this committee reported that many lamps had been stolen, and they were empowered to engage men to apprehend the offenders. In November 1812 the lamp-lighter asked for an additional payment on account of the great increase in the number of lamps to be lighted. He was granted £22.

In July 1814 the Commissioners decided to try a new system instead of employing their own lamp-lighter. The lighting of lamps was put out to contract at a fixed price per lamp including breakages. William Smith of South Audley Street, Grosvenor Square, London, undertook to light the lamps for the sum of one guinea each from 28 July to 30 April following save for the day of the full moon each month, the four days preceding it and the two days following it. He undertook to use his newly-invented reflector. When this period of this contract elapsed Thomas Harman, the Street-keeper, was appointed inspector of lamps under a committee of three Commissioners whose job it was to dole out the quantity of oil required each night according to the length of the night, to keep an account of breakages, and to proceed against offencers.

The possibility of using gas-lighting was first mentioned in May 1816, when Sir Benjamin Bloomfield informed the Commissioners that, if they decided to light the town with gas, the Prince Regent, as an inhabitant of the town, would largely contribute to the lighting of the exterior of the Royal Pavilion and its outbuildings. The communication was received 'with every sentiment of respect'. The Commissioners then proceeded to consider whether they should light the town themselves or whether they should entrust this to a private company. On 2 April 1817 they decided to grant a private company the right to put down a main pipe to light St. James's Street, the Steine, Castle Square, Great East Street, and North Street. The Prince Regent having authorised Jonathan Taylor to supply the Pavilion with gas, the Commissioners in January 1818 granted him permission to lay the necessary pipes for the purpose. They also decided to treat with him concerning the laying of pipes in such streets as he might think necessary to light the town with gas and to build a gasometer. In April Taylor applied for further time, which was refused. But by this time a Bill was being promoted in Parliament, which was presented to and approved by the Vestry. In June the Surveyor, acting under the directions of a committee, was instructed to proceed with taking up the streets within two months so that the Brighton Gas Company could lay gas pipes. A Commissioner named Edward Thunder protested in the minutes against this action. But the Bill did not run its course.

In July 1818 Jonathan Taylor informed the Commissioners that he had not been able to obtain the land necessary to erect a gasometer. He therefore wished to place this near the cricket ground, now the Level. The Commissioners did not like this idea, and the application was therefore abandoned for the time being.

No further action appears to have been taken until March 1820, when a committee was appointed to consider the whole question of the cost of lighting the town with gas in comparison with that of the existing system of oil lighting and exactly how many lamps would be required.

1. The Old Town Hall of 1727 in Bartholomews.

2. The Town Hall of 1830.

3. St. Nicholas's church in 1853 before the restoration.
   Water-colour by W. A. Delamotte.

4. St. Nicholas's church in 1853 before the restoration, interior looking west.
   Water-colour by W. A. Delamotte.

5. St. Peter's church with spire, as originally designed by Sir Charles Barry.

. Design by Amon Henry Wilds for St. Nicholas's church-yard extension in)yke Road. (c. 1841).

8. The Rev. H. M. Wagner, Vicar of Brighton 1824-1870.

7. The Rev. R. J. Carr, Vicar of Brighton 1804-1824.

9. The North Street Colonnade. Drawing by W. A. Delamotte, 1853.

10. The Workhouse of 1822 on Church Hill. Drawing in Erredge's illustrated History of Brighton.

11. The projected harbour of 1841-6, designed by William Henry Smith

12. Captain I. N. Taylor's proposed breakwater of 1841.

13. (*left*) Archway erected for William IV's first visit to Brighton in 1830.

14. (*below*) Archway erected for Queen Victoria's first visit to Brighton in 1837.

15. Amphitheatre erected for Queen Victoria's first visit to Brighton in 1837.

16. Queen Victoria landing at Chain Pier in 1843, by Richard Henry Nibbs.

17. The Market of 1830, exterior.

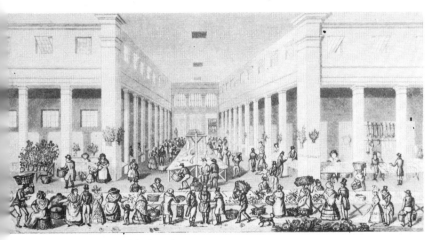

8. The Market of 1830, interior.

20. Somers Clarke, Clerk to the Vestry 1830-1892.

19. Lewis Slight, Clerk to the Commissioners 1826-1854.

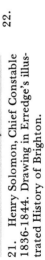

21. Henry Solomon, Chief Constable 1836-1844. Drawing in Erredge's illustrated History of Brighton.

22. Phoebe Hessell. (1713-1821).

24. Admiral Sir George Pechell, Member of Parliament for Brighton 1835-1860, by L. W.

23. John Pocock. Parish Clerk 1808-1846.

The approval of the Vestry was obtained for the idea of lighting the town by gas. Nothing seems to have been done for two years. In April 1822 the Commissioners agreed that if the inhabitants of the town would erect lamp-posts at their own expense the Commissioners would light them on the terms agreed with the Gas Company. The inhabitants of Regency Square decided to take advantage of this and approached the Commissioners on the subject. The Commissioners agreed to allow them towards the expense of gas lighting the amount that it cost at present to light the Square with oil.

In February 1823 Josias Goodman offered to light the town with 300 gas lamps at the price of £3 10s. per light, which he claimed was £1 15s. per lamp less than 'is usually charged in Brighton'. The Commissioners negotiated with him, but concluded nothing, and he was subsequently paid £10 10s. for his services relative to the arrangement which was about to be made with the Gas Company. In July the Gas Company reported that their Act of Parliament had been passed and that they were prepared to light the town on the terms set out in the clauses which had been rejected by Parliament. These odd terms not unnaturally did not appeal to the Commissioners and the matter was deferred.

It was not until February 1824 that an actual decision was made to light Old Steine for the period of one year during the months of January to May, and August to December, omitting the four days of full moon each month. The rate was fixed by an award of Messrs. Clegg and Lidbetter. Mr. Trevatt was paid £99 18s. 7d. for adapting the lamps in the Steine for gas. Towards the end of this experimental year a committee reported on the advisability of extending gas lighting to the whole town. Oil lamps cost only £500 a year and the estimate for gas lamps was £1,600 a year. But the committee thought that it was 'a subject of general surprise and regret to the inhabitants and Visitors of Brighton, and in short to everyone feeling any Interest in the Town that Brighton should be so inefficiently lighted'. As many other towns, some of

which were 'by no means in so flourishing a situation' as
Brighton had already turned over to gas, the Commissioners decided to take the plunge and to advertise for
tenders. Messrs. Grafton, Lashmar and Co.'s tender was
slightly more than half that of the Brighton Gas Company.
In March 1825 they were therefore given the contract to
light the town by gas from 29 September for 14 years
with two kinds of fitment burning four and a half or five
cubic feet per hour at the cost of £2 16s. or £2 19s. 6d.
per hour.

Scavenging

The letting by auction of the right to scavenge the
streets of the town continued after the Act of 1810, as
before. In July 1811 Benjamin Tillstone paid £110 and
£145 a year respectively for two years for the two
districts of the town separated by the common sewer
under the Steine. He did not, however, give satisfaction,
and in November the Beadle was ordered to attend him
in order to see that the streets were scraped and the
dirt removed in wet weather: North Street every Monday,
Great East Street, Castle Square and Market Street every
Tuesday, and St. James's Street and its area every Wednes-
day and Thursday. In dry weather the streets were to
be swept under the direction of the Beadle when required.
The scavenger was supposed to give notice of his approach
by ringing a bell.

For the period of two years from 26 July 1813 the
contractors were John Smith for the east district at £110
a year, and John Smith with William Mott for the west
district at £145 a year. The latter contractors asked for
the contract to be extended to five years, but this does
not seem to have been agreed to. A fortnight later they
asked that the contracts should be interchanged, John
Smith taking the west district, and William Mott alone
the east district. The Commissioners rejected this. As
both parties refused to carry out their original contract
it was decided to proceed against them. Both Smith and
Mott were themselves Town Commissioners and they were

suspended from membership during the continuance of their contract. Mott was also reprimanded for having, as a member of the lamp committee, ordered oil and erected lamps without the agreement of the rest of the committee.

Two years later difficulties again rose over the scavenging. William Phillips submitted a tender, but this was not accepted. The right of scavenging was put up to auction at £170, but no bids were received. The Clerk was therefore instructed to ascertain the cost of carrying out the work by direct labour and what would be the value of the night soil. William Scrase then tendered £5 for two years. This was not accepted. Direct labour was introduced, and continued for three years, at first at a loss, but in 1817 at a small profit.

In December 1818 the scavenging contract was again auctioned, this time in three districts, in order to increase the revenue of the town. The east and west districts, as formerly, were separated by the common sewer under the Steine, but their northern boundary was defined as Edward Street and Church Street respectively. The land north of these two streets formed the new third or north district. A Mr. Cunningham paid £135 a year for the east district for two years, and John Cheeseman junior £155 and £60 respectively for the west and north districts. In March 1820 complaints were made as to the filthy condition of the streets, and the Commissioners resolved that this should be investigated. Individual Commissioners were asked to attend before the magistrates whenever the situation justified it to see that the contract was enforced.

Further complaints were made in May, and the audit committee recommended the Commissioners to treat with the Directors and Guardians of the Poor for 'the Employment of the Poor when most in need'. In December the Commissioners agreed to pay the Directors and Guardians £200 a year to clean the streets and take away the market soil, but the collection of ashes would be let by contract separately as hitherto. However, when this right of collection was put up to auction it was bought in by the Commissioners for £490. They then let it to Mr. Cunningham for £500. In the following year the right of collection was bought in for £430. In February 1822 Carter Thunder was appointed superintendent of the collection of ashes and given a commission of five per cent. on the first £400 and seven and a half per cent. above that amount.

In May 1822 complaints were made about the dustiness of the streets in dry weather. The Commissioners determined to provide six water carts to water the main streets with sea water during the summer, and instal pumps at the West Street gap and the Old Steine groyne, but no action was taken for a year. Later the complaints were renewed and a similar resolution was passed. The scavenging of the streets by the poor was not considered satisfactory either, and in August 1823 the Directors and Guardians were asked to see that this was better done.

In February 1824 the audit committee expressed the opinion that the whole system of scavenging was unsatisfactory and that it would be more economical for the Commissioners to acquire horses and carts for the purpose themselves, which could then be used for watering the streets in dry weather. But when they went into it the Commissioners found that the capital outlay involved in direct action would be £1,260 (the erection of stables £500, the purchase of 12 horses £360 and of the carts and harness £400) and the annual expenses would be £1,376, whereas, under the present system in 1823 they spent £1,583 under all headings. They therefore preferred to let both the scavenging and the collection of ashes by contract. In June W. Hall agreed to pay £560 a year for two years for both rights for one district and James Phippen and John Lower £430 for the other district.

This system did not solve the problem of the dustiness of the streets, which was not surprising as only two wells and pumps were in existence. It was therefore decided to employ Mr. North to water the streets. Additional wells were sunk and four pumps purchased. Three months later the scavenging of the streets was found unsatisfactory and proceedings were authorised against the contractors.

Roads

The construction of roads and pavements continued to be one of the principal responsibilities of the Commissioners. One of the first instances comprised improvements to St. James's Street, as provided by the schedule of the Act of 1810. A committee considered in what ways proprietors could give or sell their land for the purpose, and £100 was offered to them to enable the road to be widened. Some seem not to have been willing to sell, but the Commissioners proceeded with the road-widening. Mrs. Lamon agreed to accept £70 in January 1811 on the condition that her fence was moved and repaired. Other owners were thanked for their co-operation in giving up land free of charge.

Another contemporary project was the enlargement of Ship Street Lane or what is now the part of Ship Street containing the General Post Office. The committee appointed to consider the matter expressed themselves strongly in favour of making an entrance into North Street which would join this to Ship Street, and the Commissioners sought private subscriptions to enable them to carry out this work. The slightly oblique line taken was due to the fact that the property on the direct line was more expensive to purchase. Most of the land involved seems to have belonged to Mrs. Styles, who claimed £2,000 for it. She was subsequently paid £1,700 in the form of debentures specially issued for the purpose. Five debentures of £100 each were issued to Thomas Best. Further debentures of £2,000 were issued in December 1813 on the security of the rate and coal-tax funds, to be repayable in four instalments at six month intervals; of £1,500 in January 1814 on the groynes' account; and of £500 to T. West in April 1814 on the coal-tax fund.

Another early project (May 1810) was a plan made by two Commissioners, Cornelius Paine and Thomas Pocock, for uniting the two halves of the West Cliff into a carriage-way supported on arches. But this seems not to have been carried out until 1820. In September the Surveyor and the Street-keeper were instructed to put up the names of the streets and the numbers of the houses. The latter represented a measure which is not always to be found today and is much needed. The instruction was repeated in 1813, when householders were told to replace the numbers on their doors after re-painting. On 31 October 1810 the Duke of Marlborough applied for leave to enclose part of the road to the north and west of Marl-borough House, but the Commissioners replied that it was beyond their power to grant His Grace's request.

In December 1810 trouble was caused by a fall of land along Marine Parade and the consequent narrowing of the road to Black Rock. Four Surveyors of the Highways attended a special meeting and reported that they would be able to move the fence along the cliff and make a new road. Investigations were authorised to try and preserve the road from further encroachments. A year later the fence from Russell House to Royal Crescent was moved back and steps down the cliff were made at the south-east corner of the Steine. At the same time a wall of flints and Steyning lime was built under the cliff between Black Lion Street and Ship Street. In December 1811 a resolution was made to build a similar wall between Rock Gardens and Royal Crescent. Jesse Lower's tenders for these walls were £990 10s. and £98 10s. respectively. The backing of the walls was carried out by the Com-missioners with direct labour. In March 1813 Sir Thomas Barnard, Thomas Read Kemp, Nathaniel Kemp, and John Mortlock approached the Commissioners concerning the possibility of making a terrace on Marine Parade which they called 'the finest Terrace in the Island'. The Commissioners expressed themselves in favour of the proposal provided that it could be done principally by private subscriptions in which case they would probably contribute towards it. A committee was appointed to explore the possibilities, and there the matter seems to have rested. But a new groyne 120 feet long was erected behind Russell House by John Pocock at a cost of £240.

One minor matter was a decision in December 1811 to make crossings covered with pitch connecting the Steine lawn with South Parade, North Parade, and the Blues and Buffs. It is interesting to note the official use of the latter expression. In January 1814 it was resolved that the pools on the west side of the Steine should be moved so that sedan-chairs could pass right round the Steine. In January 1817 the north Steine lawn was enclosed at a cost of £500.

Falls of the cliff continued to be troublesome. In December 1816, 10 of the house-owners in Royal Crescent petitioned that the fence opposite their houses should be set back on this account. The remainder of the proprietors having subsequently concurred, it was resolved that the fence should be set back and that the paving committee and the clerk should wait on Lord Hertford to ascertain what part of the railing he considered dangerous. Lord Hertford's appearance on the scene is not explained as he had not signed the petition. Neither was he the proprietor of a house in Royal Crescent.

Upper Rock Gardens was paved in April 1812, Marine Parade in September 1818. In January 1819 there occurred a rare instance in which the naming of a new street was mentioned. It was resolved that the buildings from Knaptor's Corner to the end of North Row should be called Marlborough Place and numbered as such. In March 1819 John Cheeseman junior was authorised to replace the fence along the West Cliff from the Battery to the parish boundary for the sum of 1s. 11d. per foot, and the old fence was given to the racecourse committee to enclose the racecourse. A groyne was built below the East Cliff (now the east end of King's Road) in February 1819. Later in the year the sea wall was again giving trouble, but the Commissioners decided that their funds were 'in such a dilapidated state' that it would be imprudent to agree to the proposal to build a wall 1,000

feet long under the East Cliff. It would be preferable to
join Middle Street to West Street by a road along West
Cliff. But even this had to be carried out by subscriptions
from inhabitants, though the Commissioners did
subscribe £500 and a special debenture was issued for
the purpose. Bishop's *Brighton in the Olden Time* says
that George IV gave 200 guineas, though the Commissioners' minutes do not record this. Thomas Read Kemp,
William Wigney and William Izard gave £100 each. The
new road was opened by the King in person on 29 January
1822. It was thereafter called King's Road and the name
was subsequently extended to cover the former East Cliff,
which lay between Middle Street and Great East Street,
and the continuation of the road along the front beyond
West Street. When the original portion of King's Road
was formed the Commissioners gave directions that all
streets should be named and the name of each street and
the number of each house displayed. This was necessitated
by roads like East Cliff and Old Steine having been divided
into several different sections.

In May 1821 it was resolved to spend £500 on improvements to the Steine which was said to be 'in a ruinous
state', and a debenture for that amount was issued for
the purpose. The work on the Steine was superintended
by John Furner. It involved raising the level of the ground
and surrounding it in two enclosures with an iron railing.
Paved paths crossed these enclosures from east to west.
Painting the railings and rolling the two enclosures cost
the additional sum of £35 in 1823. The enclosure of the
land involved a short dispute with the fishermen who
claimed right to draw up their boats under documents of
1579 and 1618. But after consultation with the lords of
the manor the Commissioners did not admit the fishermen's rights. The fishermen appear to have withdrawn
their claim on the advice of the Rev. Edward Everard,
and their boats were removed from the land. About the
same time the construction of the Grand Junction Road
south of Russell House cost £1,000 for which debentures
were issued.

In 1822 another committee was appointed to name and number the streets and the members were voted £2 a head for their labours. But no report from them found its way into the minutes.

Nuisances and Town Planning

The Commissioners continued, as before the Act of 1810, to proceed against inhabitants for recognised public nuisances and to exercise rudimentary town planning powers. A typical instance of the former occurred in May 1810, when dung-heaps in Charles Street were held to be a nuisance. A few days later it was the turn of old boats and other obstructions in Pool Valley. On 31 October 1810 it was resolved that all persons building new houses without nine-inch party walls should be prosecuted and in June 1811 William Izard and Thomas Webb were in fact prosecuted for this offence. In August 1810 a Mr. Tooke was ordered to remove a projecting bow window, and in December the surveyor was instructed to examine Mr. Bartholomew's veranda to see if it constituted an offence under the Act.

At the same time the Commissioners gave notice that if house-owners allowed the rain-water from their houses to fall onto the pavement they would take the necessary measures to have this remedied. The smells from slaughter-houses and lime-kilns were other causes of complaint. In August 1811 the Beadle was directed to cause the owner of a house in North Street to sweep the pavement in front of his house. In March 1811 W. Allen was warned that his new building in Great East Street must 'range in a line' with its neighbours. The same month William Gilburd was permitted an extension of an inch and a half beyond what was permitted by the Act for a bow window in Steine Lane because it did not project beyond its neighbours. At the same meeting complaints were made against the large numbers of dogs which were at liberty in the town and had bitten both people and other dogs. From 1 April onwards the High Constable was authorised to destroy all such roving animals.

In April 1811 Mr. Francis was permitted to take down a house in Great East Street in the occupation of Mr. Cook and rebuilt this as two houses according to the plan produced, on condition that it was aligned with a neighbouring building and on paying a fine of £5. Rather similar action was allowed to Richard Lasmar in May concerning buildings in Middle Street. Soon afterwards a meeting was summoned to consider the propriety of revoking the permission given to Mr. Francis but no quorum attended. A few weeks later brought a complaint of soil from a privy in North Street running into a well. In September Messrs. White and Proctor were warned to remove the verandas from the bow windows of their premises on West Cliff. In March 1812 it was the turn of someone named Sowerby for throwing soap suds and filthy water into the street from his house in St. James's Street. At the same same no less a person than Mrs. Fitzherbert made a complaint against William Bradford that water from a dunghole in his premises in Great East Street were running into her kitchen. On investigation the complaint was substantiated, and Bradford was taken before the magistrates. In May Messrs. Hall and Newnum were granted permission to erect a balcony on the *New Ship* inn.

Dogs again were the subject of a ruling in October 1812. A mad dog having been shot after being at large for some time, the Beadle was ordered to despatch any dogs found wandering in the streets. One of the beadles, named William Catling, acted under this order, incurred lasting derision by shooting a goat in North Street. This was apparently a well-known animal that lived in the stables of the *Castle* hotel which then stood opposite the *Coach and Horses* inn on the site of what became the Royal Colonnade at the corner of New Road. The goat had a free run of the yard and one day ventured into the street as far as the corner of New Street (now Bond Street). Catling mistook the animal for a dog at a distance and shot it. He was never allowed to forget this and for years afterwards was pursued by small boys calling out: 'Baa-aa! Who shot the billy-goat?'

In April 1813 the surveyor was directed to report on all bow windows or other projections which encroached over the road contrary to the Act, and in the next month this was followed by a provision that all signs projecting beyond the distance allowed should be removed.

In November 1814 the Street-keeper impounded a wagon that had been an encumbrance in the street, but was reprimanded by the magistrate, Sergeant Runnington. The Commissioners, however, supported their Street-keeper and declared that his action was fully justified. In September 1815 Mr. Ellis was granted permission to erect bow windows on a hotel in Great East Street in line with the bow windows on either side, though prosecution against him was subsequently considered and rejected. Three months later the clerk reported the agreement of a Mr. Fernehough to take off three and a half feet from the south front of his new house in Great East Street in return for the sum of £50.

The Prince Regent makes several appearances in the minutes in connection with matters of town planning. In December 1813 he was granted permission to lay two drains under Church Street which would connect with the common sewer. In October 1815 he was given leave to put down gratings over the drains near the improvements then under construction at the north end of the Royal Pavilion. In May 1817 Nixon, the Clerk of the Works at the Royal Pavilion, with the agreement of Sir Benjamin Bloomfield, applied to make an alteration in line of the frontage along Castle Square and a year later was granted permission to lay pipes under Great East Street in order to bring sea-water to the Royal Pavilion.

Several complaints related to the mixing of sea-water with fresh water. In February 1818 Edward Thunder and other inhabitants of the east side of New Steine complained about the seepage of foul water into their wells from the baths belonging to W. R. Mott in Devonshire Street. In August Mr. Fernehough of Artillery Lodge was granted permission to lay pipes to bring sea-water to his baths provided that the water was brought and returned without mixing with land springs. In January 1821 the inhabitants of New Steine complained of nuisances from sea water from the baths at the *New Steine* hotel.

A new form of nuisance appeared in September and the following May when complaints were made that the footpaths in West Street and elsewhere were being obstructed by women selling oysters. The Beadle and the Street-keeper were instructed to remove the offenders' barrows and trucks, subject to the payment of a fine of 5s. On 3 March 1820 a resolution was recorded against a bow window then in course of erection on Edward Thunder's house in South Parade, Old Steine, after a committee had inspected it. But at the following meeting Edward Thunder, who was himself a Commissioner, and a man of some nuisance value, entered a protest against this in the minutes on the grounds that the Commissioners had not said that the bow window either obstructed the street or was a nuisance. Ten names were added to his, though there is a note beside the entry to the effect that none of these persons besides Edward Thunder had in fact signed the protest.

In May 1820 it was found that Lord John Townshend's house, 1 West Cliff, and the railings in front of it in Artillery Place were an encroachment on the highway. The Clerk was requested to wait upon Lord John to ask him to remove the encroachment but, failing such action, the Street-keeper was instructed to pull it down. What transpired at the interview between the Clerk and Lord John is not recorded, but at a later meeting the resolution in favour of demolition was rescinded.

An interesting entry occurs on 1 September 1820. Messrs. Gotobed and Newnham were granted permission to erect a colonnade 'from the Theatre to the corner of Bond Street' provided that this was 12 feet high and did not exceed the width of the pavement. This came to be called the Royal Colonnade and it still exists in front of 6 and 7 New Road, though the portion in front of the Theatre Royal and the Colonnade Hotel (8 and 10) has been renewed later in the century. The very handsome bow windows on the first floor of these houses in New Road were also in course of construction at this time.

In March 1821 the Commissioners made an attempt to remove the Battery erected on the West Cliff in 1793, in order to widen the road. They heard informally that if a petition was presented to the King through Sir Benjamin Bloomfield, this might be granted. They took this action, but official procedures were as slow then as now. There is no record of a reply, and two years later the Commissioners approached the Board of Ordnance direct to know if they would agree to give up the Battery House and allow the Battery to be moved to a site 230 feet east of Russell House in Old Steine. The Board refused on the grounds that this site would not command such a good field of view and would be exposed to the sea. It was not until 1859 that the Battery on the West Cliff was given up. The Battery House behind it was demolished in 1861 and the *Grand* hotel built on the site.

When it was proposed to erect the Chain Pier a Bill was promoted in Parliament for the purpose. A committee was appointed to watch the Bill. The original site proposed was south of Old Steine, where the Palace Pier now stands. This would have been objectionable to the fishermen and to the proprietors of bathing-machines. The Commissioners therefore suggested an alternative site opposite New Steine 'near the Comb rocks'. This would also enable a handsome carriage drive to the pier to be made beneath the cliff. Samuel Brown accepted the proposal and the Commissions therefore granted permission in May 1822 for the pier to be built on that site.

The Commissioners subsequently recorded that the pier was, in their view, 'an object both useful and ornamental to the Town of Brighton' and Captain Brown was entitled to the warmest thanks of the Commissioners and inhabitants. At a dinner at the *Old Ship* hotel on 13 January 1825 they presented him with a piece of plate as a token of their esteem. This comprised a very handsome cup with a representation of the pier incised round it, handles in the form of special cables, which Captain Brown had invented, and a figure of Britannia on the lid. It is an immense pity that the whereabouts of this cup, if it still exists, are now known, as it ought to form part of the collection of plate in the Royal Pavilion.

In 1823 planning permission, as it would now be called, was granted for the construction of St. Peter's church because the diversion of the Lewes and Ditchling roads was required for its siting—a very foresighted piece of town-planning as the site of the church is most impressive. When the foundation stone was laid on 8 May 1824 the Town Commissioners accepted an invitation from the Church Commissioners of the Act of 1818 to take part in the procession to the site.

In 1823 the question of Russell House in the Steine came up. A proposal by Amon Henry Wilds for its altera-tion had been rejected in the preceding year. According to the court rolls, Russell House had originally been built on four tenements, but the Commissioners claimed that the land to the north of it was part of the Steine and in public use. The building had come into the hands of a solicitor named John Colbatch who practised at 19 North Street and later at 35 Old Steine, and who was also Clerk to the magistrates. He was proposing to demolish and rebuild the house. The Commissioners did not like the idea of this very much as they fancied opening up a view of the sea from the Steine, but as they were unable to prevent it they entered into negotiations with John Colbatch with the idea of buying Russell House from him. Relations with him in the past had been strained as on one occasion he had ordered the Commissioners' Beadle to be arrested. However, he proved quite reasonable on this occasion and expressed himself willing to sell Russell House for £3,105, though it had cost him £5,000. The Commissioners decided to purchase it in order to widen the road on the south, then called East Cliff, and to move the Battery to a site immediately adjoining Russell House on the east, provided that the proprietors of houses in the Steine would contribute £2,000 towards the cost. The proprietors must have proved unwilling because the purchase never took place. Colbatch continued with his new building—the *Albion* hotel—but was not granted permission for a bow window on the east elevation.

An almost similar situation to that of Russell House occurred in 1824 over the site of the *Castle* hotel. When the hotel closed down the site was bought by the King who converted the former assembly rooms into the Royal Chapel and demolished the other buildings. He gave a small strip of land to the Commissioners for the purpose of widening the road from Castle Square to the Steine. But a leasehold interest in the south-east corner of the site was acquired by William Boxall who was High Constable that year. He was given permission to build vaults beneath the road. It was soon found that, though no part of Boxall's new building encroached on the road or pavement, the cellars extended 13 feet beyond the foundations of the old inn. The Commissioners at first felt that they had no power to prevent further action. But it was soon realised that the building would obstruct the south-east view from the Royal Pavilion and would be objectionable to the King. The Vestry urged the Commissioners to revoke the permission. After sending a deputation to London to wait on Sir William Knighton they resolved that it was their duty to protect the Palace 'from every species of Nuisance and inconvenience'. They ordered the part of the new building which projected beyong the old inn to be pulled down and gave notice of their intention to rescind the permission for the construction of vaults. They informed William Boxall that they were willing to buy his interest, and he agreed to sell this at a figure to be fixed by arbitration. The Commissioners, however, felt that the acquisition of the leasehold interest was insufficient protection and entered into negotiations with the freeholder, R. G. Hall, who owned the *York* hotel in Old Steine. But as they were not able to buy the freehold for less than £10,000, which was probably £3,000 more than its real value, they did not proceeded any further with the purchase of any interest in the land. They did, however, take counsel's opinion whether they should institute any action about the projections of the cellars 13 feet beyond the foundations of the old building. The opinion was evidently negative as they decided not to take action. The result was the construction of the attractive small Regency terrace facing Castle Square and the Steine which subsequently became Needham's Stores. These were only demolished when the electricity showrooms were erected in 1930.

In the same year (1824) the Commissioners decided to widen the road from Middle Street to Mahomed's Baths, which was then called East Cliff, but did not sanction an enclosure there by Mahomed for his own use. Soon afterwards an interesting entry occurred relating to the *Cricketers* inn in Black Lion Street. This was about to be rebuilt, and the proprietor named Vallance offered to sell the Commissioners the frontage to the depth of three feet and to set back the new building behind this. At first the Commissioners were inclined to refuse the offer as serving no purpose. But in the end they agreed to pay £25 for a set-back of two feet on the understanding that the new building might have bow windows projecting 14 inches on the first and second storeys. The interest in this reference to the *Cricketers* is that, from the appearance of the hotel, one would have been inclined to date it at least 20 or perhaps even 30 years earlier than 1824. As a licensed house it is of course much older and was previously called the *Last and Fish Cart*. In quite recent times an inscription has been painted on it to the effect that it was founded in 1514.

The last planning entry of interest in the minutes under the Act of 1810 was a refusal in September 1824 of permission to Mr. Haines to erect a camera obscura under the cliff to the east of the chain pier.

Groynes

With the expansion of Brighton eastwards the necessity of building further groynes to protect Marine Parade became apparent. In 1819 the Commissioners recognised this and about a year later approached Thomas Read Kemp, who had offered £300 towards the cost of such sea defences. He repeated that he was prepared to contribute this sum as soon as the work was actually carried out. A groyne was therefore erected at Black Rock 100 feet west of the eastern boundary of the parish. The lowest tender received was from Samuel Bushill for £2,735. Edward Thunder, who was a Commissioner, was paid £50 for superintendence of the works. By some people the groyne was called 'Teddy Thunder's folly.'[1] At the same time the sea wall which extended to Royal Crescent was heightened and extended 100 feet eastwards. A year later a further tender of £487 was accepted from Thomas Furner and John Pocock for the Black Rock groyne. In November 1822, Kemp and the other private subscribers were asked to give their donations. The balance of the cost was paid out of the coal-tax, and as this proved insufficient, five debentures of £200 each were issued on the strength of the future coal-tax. Further debentures were issued to the value of £800 in August 1823 and £500 in September 1824.

This did not, however, complete the protection necessary for the east end of the town. The construction of Kemp Town began in 1823, and the Commissioners asked Thomas Read Kemp to submit his plans for the protection of the cliff. They subsequently agreed to pay him £800 towards the cost of this work.

The single groyne at Black Rock did not prove effective, and three more had to be erected. The cost of these amounting to £2,000 was paid by Kemp, but the Commissioners contributed another £800 towards it. Kemp also offered to be responsible for the future maintenance of these groynes if granted the exclusive use of them for the inhabitants of Kemp Town. But the Commissioners replied that their own Act of Parliament did not permit the grant of such exclusive use.

1. Edward Thunder invented a pedal for shifting the keys of a piano.

Bathing

One of the early concerns of the new Commissioners was to provide facilities for bathing. They appointed a committee to examine the best situations for erecting 'proper Houses for the accommodation of Ladies Bathing at the extremities of the Town' with a sloping approach to the sea. The already existing bathing-station east of Russell House was improved. When the committee reported in June 1810 an approach was made to the proprietors of two rooms beneath the West Cliff near the Battery concerning the terms on which they would let them to the Commissioners for a bathing-house. Handbills were issued prohibiting bathing after 9 a.m. without a machine between the *Norfolk* hotel and Royal Cresent on penalty of five pounds. In July contracts were approved for the erection of two bathing-houses. One was for ladies on the West Cliff and one for gentlemen on the East Cliff. The contractors were John Field, carpenter, for £88 18s.; Smith and Sons brick-layers and plasterers, for £62 15s.; and Smith and Sons, plumbers and glaziers, for £63 13s. But only one of the bathing-houses seems to have been built at this date. This was let to Messrs. La Mash and Howard in March 1811 for £51 a year. Soon after the lease came into operation a water closet was inserted in the building at the Commissioners' expense. In March 1812 the same tenants' lease was extended for three years at the rent of £30 a year. Bathing without a machine was permitted beyond the prescribed limits and a board was erected on the West Cliff in 1815 to indicate these places. Directions were given for vessels to avoid unloading coal where it would annoy bathers.

Hackney Carriages

In June 1810 the Commissioners gave notice that people who wished to obtain licences for hackney carriages, sedan-chairs, wheel-chairs, and bathing-machines should make application accordingly to the Clerk. Applicants were subsequently directed to attend a Commissioners' meeting to obtain their licences. Regulations for the use of such vehicles were drawn up, including the prohibition of the use of pavements by the bearers of sedan-chairs. In 1815 people having horses, ponies, or asses to hire applied to the Commissioners for a place to display them. This was refused as being liable to public inconvenience and detrimental to adjoining property. The Beadle was instructed to take action against anyone who exposed such animals for hire.

In June 1821 complaints were made about flys standing for hire in the streets and the nuisances to which these gave rise, namely collections of idle persons talking to the drivers and using indecent language. The Commissioners decided not to licence any hackney carriages, flys or sedan-chairs for 12 months. The expression used in the minutes on this occasion was very strong. The Clerk was empowered to put an end to such a 'glaring and abominable nuisance'. The ban did not last long, as by October a committee had surveyed the town and recommended the establishment of recognised stands for vehicles. In the following March a special meeting was held which rescinded the resolution of 6 June 1821 and promulgated a set of bye-laws for the use of hired vehicles. These limited the grant of licences to resident householders of good character and the number of vehicles to 24 hackney carriages drawn by horses or mules, 24 chaises drawn by asses, 24 hackney carriages drawn by hand, 24 sedan-chairs, and 80 bathing-machines. All vehicles were to operate from recognised stands, of which there were eight for horse-drawn carriages, six for chaises drawn by donkeys and two for hand-drawn chairs. The fares were also laid down.

It was reported three months later that the magistrates were refusing to convict people for using small vehicles for hire without a licence. The beadle was nevertheless instructed to proceed with the enforcement of the bye-laws, and a case was submitted to counsel whether a small carriage with one, or at the most two, seats, which was called a fly, was a hackney carriage within the meaning of the local Act of 1810. J. Gurney of Lewes advised the Commissioners that it was, and the magistrates were informed accordingly.

Some magistrates still refused to convict the proprietors of such vehicles on the grounds that they had no power to do so in the case of open carriages. They also failed to convict for the offence of throwing rubbish over the cliff. The Commissioners became so indignant at this lack of co-operation on the part of the magistrates that they issued printed handbills of a public meeting at which they proposed to take into consideration the conduct of the magistrates in failing to convict. At this meeting on 26 August, the Commissioners instructed their Beadle not to make any further applications to John Henry Bates and John Martin Cripps, nor to attend the magistrates at all. They informed the proprietor of the *Old Ship* hotel that they would no longer accept financial responsibility for the hire of a room in his hotel for Petty Sessions. They further sent a deputation to wait on the Lord Lieutenant for Sussex, Lord Egremont, to ask him to recommend additional names for the bench. The six Beadles were instructed to seize all carriages that had no licences and to secure them in an improvised pound in Ship Street, prior to their sale.

When the magistrates next met on 29 August they enquired through the High Constable, George Wigney, what was the position concerning the room for their meeting and whether they were under the obligation to move immediately. The High Constable pledged himself that there would be no inconvenience if they remained for that meeting. But they subsequently made arrangements to transfer the Petty Sessions to the *New Inn,* later the *Clarence* hotel, in North Street and met there for the first time on 7 November.

Meanwhile, on 30 August Sir David Scott ordered the Commissioners' Beadle, John Mills, to proceed to the Level to quell an affray near the *Richmond Arms* inn. The message reached Mills when he was in attendance on the Commissioners at the *Old Ship* hotel. He asked for their instructions. Acting mainly at the instigation of William Radley Mott, the Commissioners ordered the Beadle not to obey the message which he had received. As a result, at the next meeting of the magistrates on 5 September, J. M. Cripps, Sir David Scott, J. H. Bates, Thomas Read Kemp, who was himself a Commissioner, and A. Donavan issued a summons against the Beadle and, despite the defence on his behalf offered by the Clerk to the Commissioners, fined him £2. They also warned all the other Town Beadles that, though they were employed by the Commissioners, they had been sworn in by the magistrates and were bound to implement the latter's instructions. If they refused to do so they would be indicted at Quarter Sessions.

The Commissioners must evidently have instructed Mills not to pay the fine, for a distraint on his furniture was issued, which only raised £1 14s. They expressed their intention of appealing to Quarter Sessions for damages on behalf of the Beadle and of applying to the High Court for a writ of mandamus to compel the magistrates to convict offenders under the local Act, but they did not in fact do so. The magistrates, however, did take further action. They considered that they had been libelled by the handbills issued by the Commissioners prior to their meeting on 20 August and therefore applied to the High Court for a writ of criminal information against W. R. Mott and another Commissioner named Hargreaves who were the chief spokesmen of the 25 Commissioners who had voted in favour of the resolutions passed at that meeting. This writ was provisionally granted by the Lord Chief Justice Abbott and Mr. Justice Bayley in November. But when on 6 February 1823 application was made for it to be made absolute, after certain preliminary wrangling by counsel for the Commissioners, the application was, by consent, withdrawn. The Commissioners made an apology and said that they had no intention of bringing the magistrates into contempt.

Feelings ran very high in the town over this dispute, and when the Court's decision was announced the bells

of the parish church were rung, The reconciliation of the
two parties seems largely to have been the work of the
Dean of Hereford, who was also Vicar of Brighton, the
Rev. R. J. Carr. On 20 February a reconciliatory dinner
was held at the *Old Ship* hotel, at which he took the chair.
Most of the Commissioners were present, plus their joint
Clerks, Thomas Attree and Frederick Cooper; also the
magistrates, Sir David Scott, J. M. Cripps, J. H. Bates, and
Sir Edward Kerrieson, but not A. Donavan. Their Clerk,
John Colbatch, who was one of the leading progatonists
in the dispute, was not mentioned as being present either.
The poor Beadle whose house had been sold up, was
probably too humble a personage to be entitled to attend.
Not a word is said as to whether the Commissioners compensated him for the loss of his property in following their
instructions. He seems to have been the only loser in the
end as the *Brighton Gazette* records that the 'Dinner,
dessert, etc. were very sumptuously served up and nothing
but hilarity and good humour prevailed during the whole
evening'.

Following this dispute new bye-laws for the use of
hackney carriages and fares to be paid for them were
drawn up by the Commissioners in May 1823. Henry
Solomon was paid £20 to act as Superintendent of
Hackney Coaches for six months and thereafter at a salary
of £1 a week. A year later the Beadles were directed to
impound all donkeys or other animals that were found
standing or tied up in the streets. In June 1824 a Mr.
Williams objected to donkeys standing south of the *York*
hotel. The Beadle was instructed to prevent their plying
for hire at this spot.

Police

Though the Act of 1810 empowered the Commissioners
to appoint constables, no reference to the necessity for
such was made until January 1812, when it was resolved
that it was expedient to establish a nightly watch, and that
eight watchmen should be appointed: 'as many Inhabitants
as are willing to assist in superintending the Watch be

requested to divide their number in such manner as they shall think proper and taken on themselves the superintendence of the Watch, meeting each Night at the Town Hall at 10 o'clock'.

This was followed by an expressed desire for the establishment of resident magistrates in the town since the nearest Petty Sessions were at Lewes. A committee of Commissioners was appointed to consider the possibility of obtaining a police Act which would establish local magistrates. The committee reported in favour of the idea and the Commissioners requested the High Constable and the churchwardens to summon a public meeting. The result was the establishment of Petty Sessions in Brighton. Arrangements were made for the magistrates to sit first at the Town Hall, but later at the *Old Ship* hotel. The sessions were subsequently transferred for a short time in 1822-3 to the *New* inn, afterwards the *Clarence* hotel, in North Street, but then moved back to the Town Hall and eventually to the *Old Ship* again until 1830.

Nothing further seems to have been heard of the night-watch until July 1814, when a committee of four was appointed to provide firearms for the use of volunteers and the special constable was authorised to provide them with refreshments at not more than 9d. a head.

In October 1814 an advertisement appeared in the *Brighton Herald* to the effect that it was proposed to apply to Parliament for an Act establishing a paid Justice of the Peace in Brighton. This was signed Brooker and Colbatch, solicitors. John Colbatch was Clerk to the existing magistrates.

The chief argument in favour of the establishment of Petty Sessions had been to save the expense of the parish officers having to attend at Lewes. Coming so soon after the Act of 1810, the proposal to introduce a salaried magistrate gave violent offence to both the Vestry and to the Commissioners as a quite unjustified expense. Both bodies opposed the application so strongly that it was dropped.

By 1814 a serious situation seems to have developed for want of police. On 25 April a meeting of the Vestry was held 'to devise means for preventing nightly depredations to which the said Town Hall has been recently subject'. Twenty-four constables were to be appointed for night duty 'under whose directions shall be placed Gent. Inhabitants of the Town as shall volunteer their Services to Patrole the Streets'.

In November 1815 two magistrates, Sergeant Runnington and J. H. Bates, gave notice to the Commissioners that the Commissioners should use the powers given to them by the Act of 1810 to appoint as many watchmen as might be necessary. The Commissioners thought that 28 special constables would be required and that the patrol should consist of one special constable and 12 inhabitants. They should attend from 10 p.m. for eight months of the year and from 11 p.m. for the four darkest winter months and should be fined 1s. if 10 minutes late, 2s. if a quarter of an hour late, and the whole cost of providing a replacement, which was 2s. 6d., if they failed to turn up altogether. They would be provided with pistols, cutlasses with belts, whistles, and great coats. The cost of the cutlasses, which were made by Hyam Lewis, was £3. Refreshments for the patrol to the maximum value of 10s. would be provided by the special constable at the workhouse. These arrangements were put to a Vestry meeting and endorsed. Twenty-eight watchmen were enrolled on December 1815.

When the spring came the Commissioners were recommended to continue the employment of a nightly patrol of 12 men and to pay them 2s. a head per night, plus 6d. for refreshments. In December following a committee was appointed to approach all the inhabitants of the town to get them to act as volunteers for two special constables a night or, if they were not willing so to act, to pay 5s. a year in lieu. As the existence of a night patrol would reduce the fire risk the Fire Insurance Office was asked to contribute to the cost of the patrol. Training would be needed in the use of the fire-engine, for which the

Commissioners would pay 1s. a person per month. Thirty-seven special constables were appointed in March 1817. It was provided that, if they left their duty before being dismissed, they were liable to a fine of 7s. 6d. The amount of their refreshment seems to have been increased to 5s.

This patrol cannot have been satisfactory because in November disturbances occurred in the town, and a special meeting of the Commissioners was held to take precautions. Eighteen of the Commissioners themselves were appointed to preserve the peace of the town during the week and 'by conciliatory measures to allay the present irritated state of public Feeling'. On the four following days the town was reported to be in a 'perfect tranquil state'.

By February 1818 it was thought that, owing to the shortage of volunteers, the patrol would have to be abandoned. Two watchmen were, however, appointed, and 200 letters of appeal for further volunteers issued. A suggestion of employing three or five paid constables was made but seems to have been carried no further as in June 1818 34 people were enrolled as officers for keeping the peace. Early in 1819 the existing watchmen were dismissed and seven respectable housekeepers were appointed to superintend the new watch, one taking office each night for a fee of 5s. a night. Four watchmen were added in April, two in June, five in September, plus a special constable. These measures were, however, only a makeshift arrangement. So on 30 April 1819 the Vestry urged the Commissioners to levy a rate of 1s. in the pound to enable them to appoint 20 regular watchmen at a wage of £20 a year and six night constables at 15s. a week to patrol the town. They were to be provided with watch-boxes, greatcoats, staffs, rattles and lanthorns, and were to be instructed to call the hours of the night. The constables were to be superior officers, as two were to be on duty every night, one supervising the men on their beat and the other at the Town Hall. A committee was appointed to consider the matter but seems to have made no report.

It was not until January 1821 that serious professional measures were taken. The town was divided into eight districts for police purposes. Watch-boxes were erected in Steine Lane, Camelford Street, Portland Street, John Street, Cavendish Street, at the *Richmond Arms* and in two unspecified 'passages' for the western districts. The original resolution was to employ eight watchmen and two superintendents, but 12 seem to have been appointed and the number increased to 16 in October 1823. The watchmen were paid 15s. a week from Michaelmas to Lady Day and 12s. from Lady Day to Michaelmas. Later they applied for a rise, which was refused. Their hours of duty were from 11 p.m. to 4 a.m. But in May 1824 these hours were changed to run from 9.30 p.m. to 7 a.m. in summer, and from 9 p.m. to 7 a.m. in winter. The superintendents or officers of the night watch, as they were called, were paid £35 a year. In addition from time to time it was resolved to appoint four or five citizens to keep the peace and apprehend disorderly persons.

In February 1821 the magistrates enquired whether the Commissioners intended to build a Town Hall or could provide them with a room in which to hold their Petty Sessions. The Commissioners obtained from Mr. Shuckard of the *Old Ship* hotel the use of the Telemachus rooms in that hotel for two guineas a week. At the same time he undertook to provide a room for the Commissioners' own meeting for 21 guineas a year and for the Vestry meetings for £100 a year, plus £10 for servants and waiters. From March 1822 onwards the Commissioners' meetings were held regularly at the *Old Ship*.

In 1822 Samuel Simes, one of the officers of the night watch, whom the records show to have been a very sensible person, asked the Commissioners for directions on three points: whether the night constable might give shelter to travellers of decent appearance who were in want of a night's lodging; whether all vagrants were to be brought before the Bench; and whether some vagrants who had spent the night in prison might be permitted to go free on condition that they left the town. The answers which he received were not nearly so sensible: travellers were not to be lodged in the common prison; all vagrants were to be apprehended; while the reply to the third question was incomprehensible.

One volume of the night constables' report book, from April 1822 to December 1823, has survived and was recently presented to the Sussex Archaeological Society by Messrs. Howlett and Clarke. This presents a fascinating picture of night life in Brighton at this period.

When the report commenced the town was divided into eight districts with a watch-box to each, but from 4 October 1823 onwards the number of watchmen was increased from eight to sixteen. The costume worn by the watchmen was a cut-away black tail-coat, white trousers and a black top hat with a white band. They were armed with iron-tipped batons, lanterns and rattles which they 'sprang' to give notice to their colleagues of the fact that they needed help.

The two superintendents or officers of the night watch were named James Feldwicke and Samuel Simes. They took duty at the Town Hall on alternate nights. It was part of their functions to make up the night constable's reports. Attached to the Town Hall in Bartholomews was a lock-up which generally figures in the reports as 'the B. Hole', but occasionally is given in full as 'the Black Hole', and sometimes simply as 'the B.H.'. This contained several cells for men and women. In October 1823, after the Commissioners had taken over from the Directors and Guardians of the Poor the workhouse adjoining the Town Hall, further accommodation for female prisoners was made in this building as a temporary measure until a new gaol was built elsewhere.

The majority of entries in the constables' reports relate to disturbances created by 'drunks' or unruly characters who, on apprehension, were confined to the black hole for the night and were brought before the magistrate next day. One such, named James Penfold, was apprehended for following the watchman, Malthouse, and repeatedly calling the hour after him. When instructed to desist, he insisted that he had the right to do this for his own amusement. At the Town Hall he pretended to be drunk. Another, John Williams, was brought in on 5 October 1822 'for playing on the flute and behaving in a manner likely to make a disturbance'. These were very mild cases. Others were less so. A man named Charles Thomas, who was arrested on 12 February 1823, was described by Samuel Simes as 'one of those low characters who are continually insulting people in the streets. I never had a fellow before me who appeared to deserve to be punished more'. This man had first insulted and then assaulted a passerby. A band of similar characters escaped arrest on 11 October 1822. The watchman, Johnson, described then as 'ten or twelve of the greatest ruffians he ever saw' and reported that they 'with horrid imprecations threatened to throw him over the cliff which he believes they would [have] effected had not Mr. Walton of the *Norfolk* hotel interfered together with some other persons and protected him'.

The ordinary drunks were both men and women. But with the rather partial ideas of justice that were current at the period, those who were of higher social status than the average escaped being confined in the black hole. Two disturbances were caused during the period by officers of the 7th Hussars from the barracks. At half past two in the morning on 11 August 1823 Captain Molineux and a friend were found by the watchman, Cousens, making a great disturbance in Grand Parade. When remonstrated with they 'both began with all the abusive language to the watchman possible, calling not only him and the rest of the watchmen every ill name but further told him that the whole of the pollice magistrates and all was a set of base scoundrells and wished they had the opportunity of throwing them in the sea, desiring Cousens to carry a message from him to the magistrate of very extravagant abuse'. These officers were not arrested.

The same Captain Molineux and several others figured in another disturbance on the night of the 22/23 October

1823, when, on leaving the *York* hotel in the Steine between 2 a.m. and 3 a.m. 'and finding an empty fly belonging to a man named Vaughan, they shoved it over and broke the glass frame and assaulted the man with it with sticks and knocked in the crown of his hat kicking him at the same [time]'. They got away, but Vaughan followed them and, meeting with a watchman, gave them in charge. The captain retorted by giving Vaughan in charge, and both parties agreed to go to the Town Hall to settle the matter. But 'on the way thither Capt. Molineux swore he would knock the watchman down if he suffered the fly man [Vaughan] to speack. When they got about opposite Church Street Capt. Molineux and his party ran away and effected their escape the watchman being unfortunately unprovided with a rattle'.

One offender described as a 'commercial gentleman' named Norton, who was evidently considered to be in a category between a real gentleman and an ordinary disturber of the peace, was dealt with in a summary and improvised but most effective manner. He was brought to the Town Hall in a very tipsy condition by a Mr. Ireland who 'could not get him to bed in consequence'. He became very violent. James Feldwicke made two of the watchmen hold him and summoned 'Docktor Baldy [the surgeon at the workhouse] who gave him an emetick which after some time took effect'. Mr. Ireland called the following day and took him home 'perfectly reconciled', after having promised to inform the magistrates of the circumstances.

After disturbers of the peace, the most numerous class of offenders consisted of vagrants. The law affecting these unfortunates dated from the reign of Queen Elizabeth. After spending the night in the black hole, they were brought before the magistrates and then sent back to the parish of the origin for the latter to support them, so that they should not become a charge upon the poor-rate of any other district. Even children were apt to be found wandering in the streets. For instance, on 24 November 1822 the watchman, Willard, brought to the Town Hall a poor little sweep-boy who had come to the town from London to seek employment and was found half naked and alone. On 24 January 1823 two citizens discovered a child of nine in a wheelbarrow in the yard of the *White Horse* inn in Great East Street and brought her to the Town Hall. She had been turned into the street by her father and step-mother, who had been quarrelling that night. She was 'almost perished with cold'. Samuel Simes made her sit by the fire in the Town Hall all night. In the morning one of the watchmen took her to his home before bringing her in front of the magistrates.

In view of the well-known inhumanity of officials at the period, which Dickens and others have made plain, it is almost a surprise to read with what obvious kindness this night constable's report is written on most occasions. Frequently the head constable on duty allowed someone whom he was unwilling to treat as a vagrant to sit by the fire all night and then let him go in the morning without being committed, as the poor wretch technically should have been. One such case was an old man who had run away from Buxted workhouse. On 29 January 1823 he was found at 'the door of Mr. Tanner in St. James Street and Mr. Tanner brought him down both cake jelly and soup and some of the gentlemen who when just leaving the meeting at the hall wished me to take care of him for the night and send him away in the morning. So I kept him in the Hall by the fire until the men came in between five and six o'clock and as the weather was very severe and he was so very helpless and almost childish I thought it would be better to send him to the Black Hole for the disposal of the Magistrates unless the High Constable shall think fit to dispose of him any other way'.

All the same, the bumbledom of other areas raises its ugly head at times. For instance, on 4 August 1823 'a young woman about 21 years of aged named Sarah [? Jessop] was found by Willard near the Old Steine in a most deplorable state. She says she has been twice sent to Lewes Goal as a vagrant and passed to her parish where she cannot abide as she, when there, is nearly *starved to death* the officers allowing her no more than *eighteen pence* a week to exist on; and that, if she went out to work the *overseer* took her money which she received amounting sometimes to eight pence a day, *from her* and that in consequence of such usage she resolved to come again to Brighton and again run the risk of a jail'.

Another case was that of Martha Kenny who, on 23 April 1822, 'being destitute of lodging applied for a night's lodging in the B. Hole. She says she was a widow to a naval officer belonging to the Regulus 44 gun ship that after his death she cohabited with her present husband whom her parish Arundell compelled [her] to marry, as she was in the family way. He however left her at Deptford and she was returned to her parish but the Overseer refused to receive her unless she passed home and told her to come to Brighton to give herself up'. On 7 October 1822 two boys gave themselves up who had run away from the Brighton workhouse 'in consequence of the Governor beating them'.

On several occasions accusations and counter-accusations between men and women were made of theft on the one side and of sexual molestation on the other. The fullest of these occurred on 6 November 1822. Two soldiers of the First Life Guards met on the Level two domestic servants employed in a house in Richmond Place. According to the latter the soldiers then 'commenced a brutal assault upon them dragging them upon the grass and offering them money to gratify their lust'. The girls called 'murder' and a watchman thereupon came on the scene. The soldiers countered by saying that they had walked on the Level with the girls and that one of the latter had then stolen a sovereign and a pair of gloves from one soldier. After the watchman appeared the soldiers offered to stand the girls a drink and make it up, but the latter refused to accompany them. The maids were able to give reference to 'most respectable persons', and the gloves were subsequently found on the grass. The head constable clearly believed the girls' story and sent the men to the black hole for the night. But the next day he made the following note in the report book: 'The soldiers in the above affair were both of them dismissed and the women were directed if not satisfied with the decision of the bench to seek elsewhere for redress. And . . . Bates Esq *promised* to *see* the *officers* on *behalf* of the *men*. I thought this a most extraordinary proceeding for a *magistrate,* when men were brought before him for palpable misconduct, to promise on the bench to get that conduct passed by, by going on their behalf to the officers of a Regt. The bench almost blamed me for confining them. This was excessively *absurd* as I was clearly justified by the local Act., under which I am appointed to take into custody "all disorderly persons" '. From this one gather that in 1822, as in 1976, the decisions of the magistrates did not always give satisfaction to the police.

The greatest deficiency of the night constables' report is that it very seldom states what decision was made by the Bench the next day when offenders were brought into court. An exception occurs on 21 August 1822. That night a man was given in charge by a soldier of the Third Regiment of Light Dragoons, who was drinking with him at the *Duke of Wellington* public house in Pool Valley, for having offered him a sovereign and two shillings to go with him on to the beach with the purpose of committing an unnatural crime'. The offender's only excuse was intoxication. A note was made in the margin next day that the poor wretch was sent to gaol for two years.

A similar note was made on 15 August 1823. That night a man had been taken into custody in North Street for making a noise and using 'insulting epithets towards the watchman'. Next day the magistrates discharged him, and the watchman was told that 'he should *wink* at such things'.

On 30 November 1822 the watchman, Harman, 'by order as he states of Sir David Scott', who was chairman of the Bench, arrested a young man named Feldwick who was found tipsy in the Lanes. A note follows in Sir

David Scott's handwriting: 'Feldwick may be liberated if [there is] nothing more against him than drunkenness, provided his Father will be bound for his appearance— I gave no order to Harman whatever and knew nothing respecting the business on which he was employed. D. Scott'.

Several cases of suicide are mentioned. On 31 July 1822, for instance, a poor woman threw herself into the sea. Three days later another woman was seen first to be sitting by an open well and later, walking on the cliff, talking in a most incoherent manner, but she was prevented from doing herself any harm.

Several fires occurred. The town possessed two fire-engines which were kept at the Town Hall. The fireman in charge of them was Thomas Mason, who lived at 15 Claremont Place. On no occasion covered by this report was the damage resulting from a fire very serious, and the engines seem always to have been able to extinguish the fires. On 21 October 1822, for instance, a fire in a shed in a foundry yard in Spring Gardens was extinguished with the assistance of some soldiers from the barracks. On 10 January 1823 a fire in an unfurnished house on the east side of Regency Square was similarly quenched with the help of people from the neighbouring houses.

Two incidents defy classification except that they both belong to the age before borough surveyors and medical officers of health. On the night of 3 January 1823 a man was found by one of the watchmen 'under his house which had fallen with him in West Street about 3 o.clock this morning. He assisted immediately in extricating him. The Man escaped with[? out] material injury'. The second entry occurred on 31 August 1823. 'The Watchmen report that one of Mr. Tilstone's waggons loaded with night soil bursted in the night and has caused a very great nuisance down North Street and the north part of the town'.

In addition to the constables who were the servants of the Town Commissioners, a number of private concerns employed night watchmen on their own premises. The

Chain Pier Company did so; also the Bazaar in Grand
Parade. Two were on duty in St. Nicholas's churchyard
but do not seem to have been very efficient as, on
12 November 1823, they suffered a woman to run out
of the churchyard into Air Street crying 'murder'. Only
12 days later it was recorded that the same men 'are
drinking and making a great disturbance the whole of
the night', with the result that 'the church-yard has been
several times represented as a scene of nightly riot and
disorder'. Sentries stood guard at the Palace, as the Royal
Pavilion was then called. Revenue officers also occasionally
figured in incidents connected with the foreshore. On
8 September 1823 one of these seems to have run amok
and to have obtained admission by the back door to a
house in Nottingham Street, where he alarmed the family
by 'standing with his sword drawn and threatening saying
he wanted a girl'. A member of the family ran for the
watch, and the officer was disarmed but was subsequently
seen 'lying on the ground in George Street'. Feldwicke
commended: 'I shall report the base conduct of the
officer this morning to Mr. Harvey his Superior Officer
for his consideration'.

One cannot help wondering how successful the constables were in policing the town at this period. So
apparently did they themselves, judging by an entry on
12 July 1823. Samuel Simes then wrote: 'The Watch
are not strong enough to quell various disorders. Nor can
we venture to take one man from his round to assist
another as he is immediately missed from his own round.
The watchmen may not be able to take many robbers,
but it is impossible to tell how many distrubances they
do *suppress,* or robberies *prevent*'. Part of the trouble
may have been the darkness of the streets, as gas lighting
was not introduced until 1824, and that was actually
an early instance of its use. On 27 November 1823 it was
recorded that the north part of the town was left in total
darkness during the night as most of the lamps went out
before 11 o'clock and not one was to be seen by 2 or
3 a.m.

Still all the same, the watchmen seem to have been fairly efficient as the Comte de La Garde, when he visited Brighton in 1827, noted that these 'living clocks and barometers', as he called them in allusion to their habit of calling aloud the hours and weather of the night, seldom allowed their quarry to escape owing to their being able to give notice to one another with their rattles that they were giving chase. It would be interesting to compare this night constable's report of 1822-3 with its modern equivalent of today and to see whether the town has grown more or less law-abiding and whether the police have become more efficient and more humane. But at any rate it is unlikely that the present police record is written in such a picturesque and altogether attractive style as this old book of 150 years ago.

Miscellaneous Matters

There were a number of miscellaneous items of interest in the minute books between 1810 and 1825 which cannot be classified. In August 1810 the Commissioners were approached by Ralph Dodd concerning the possibility of erecting water-works on Richmond Hill to supply water on a voluntary basis to houses without wells. On 19 September they resolved that 'it is not only unnecessary to erect water Works for the purpose of supplying this Town with Water on account of the full supply of excellent Water obtained in all parts of the Town by the Common Wells, but that such Water Works, if erected, would in the opinion of this Meeting be greatly injurious to the Town and that therefore any application to Parliament for an Act for that purpose be opposed'.

Coal brought to Brighton was subject to a duty which was one of the principal sources of income of the Town Commissioners. Most of it came by sea, but instances evidently arose when it was brought by land to try to avoid this duty. In January 1811 it was therefore resolved that coal brought by land should not be unloaded until the carter had obtained from the Coal Meter a ticket specifying the amount of coal involved and therefore indirectly that the requisite duty on it had been paid. Failing such action a fine of 5s. per cart or waggon would be payable.

A very unusual entry occurred on 11 April 1811. The High Constable, the Headborough, the Beadle and seven other people gave evidence concerning a riot in North Street on the preceding evening in which an inhabitant had been assaulted, beaten and wounded by private soldiers and one officer (Lieutenant Bubb) of the South Gloucestershire Regiment which had been quartered in Brighton for more than 10 years. A number of other incidents had also occurred which were 'highly derogatory to the Character and Duty of Soldiers, dangerous to the Peace and security of this Populous Town and disgraceful to the army'. The Commissioners considered that the long period during which this Regiment had been stationed in Brighton was 'highly detrimental to His Majesty's Service'. They therefore presented a memorial to the commanding officer, Lord Charles Beresford, requesting him to have his regiment transferred elsewhere, and Lieutenant Bubb and his co-rioters court-martialled. No entry is made concerning any reply to the memorial.

Another form of bad behaviour, this time of domestic character, occurred in July 1814, when John Hargraves was censured and suspended from action on any committee of the Commissioners on account of having misconducted himself, abused other Commissioners and referred to the Markets Committee of the Commissioners in a court of justice as 'the Fire Brand Committee'. John Hargraves proceeded to have a pamphlet printed setting out his case. The Clerk was instructed to proceed against him and the printer, named Forbes, for libel. What was the result of this action was not stated. But he continued his hostility against the Commissioners, as a few weeks later the Attorney General, on the instigation of William Izard, abetted by John Hargraves, filed a Bill in Chancery against the Clerk, the Treasurer, the Collector and certain Commissioners for an offence which was not stated. The Commissioners resolved to defend the action jointly, except John Hargraves, who said he would conduct his own case. The Vice-Chancellor allowed a demurrer against this action. The Clerk and William Radley Mott were thanked for their zeal in defending this action. But the Commissioners recorded that William Izard and 'his abettor, John Hargraves', having involved the Commissioners in a great deal of unnecessary litigation and expense in a totally unprovoked manner, were 'utterly unworthy of the trust reposed in them as Commissioners and that they now deliberately pass upon them the most unqualified censure which it is in the power of language to express and enter it on their minutes as a perpetual memorial that these Individuals have forfeited their confidence and respect'. Both men, however, continued to sit and act as Commissioners.

In June 1815 an isolated entry occurred when a committee reported concerning the best plan for mooring chains. The estimate for the moorings and tackle necessary to heave up three ships at three different times at the same place or three ships at different places at the same time was £900 and to heave up one ship only would be £580. It was decided to carry out the latter. A premium of £30 for the best plan was paid to Henry Burchell.

In September 1815 a prosecution was undertaken against someone called Davis and others for assaulting the town Beadle, William Catling.

At about the same time the question was raised of acquiring the vicarage in Nile Street for conversion into a Town Hall where meetings of inhabitants could be held. The Vicar, the Rev. Robert James Carr, was authorised to set out his terms for the sale or exchange of the house. The Vicar informed the Commissioners he was prepared to exchange the vicarage for Sir Robert Bateson Harvey's house in West Street. This proposal was referred to a committee who reported that the volume of Sir Robert Harvey's house was greater than that of the vicarage. No action was taken. Ten years later, when the Rev. H. M. Wagner became Vicar of Brighton, he asked the Commissioners if they would like to purchase the vicarage in order to enlarge the market. But it was not until 1835 that the new vicarage was actually built near Montpelier Road.

At the same time as the exchange of the vicarage was discussed a decision was taken to allow a caravan belonging to a Mr. Weller at the bottom of the Steine to remain there until the following spring provided that it was lowered in height so that it obstructed the view as little as possible.

In 1816 a private Bill was presented to Parliament for the improvement of Shoreham harbour. The Commissioners considered this to be prejudicial to the interests of Brighton and petitioned the House of Commons against it. The petition was lodged the day before the third reading of the Bill. At the committee stage the Commissioners claimed that they had 'struck their opponents with dismay'. The Harbour Commissioners then conceded what the Brighton Commissioners asked, and the duty imposed on the goods landed at Shoreham for the use of the Brighton Town Commissioners was reduced to a fourth of the rate otherwise imposed by the Bill, which was in fact the existing rate. The report stated that 'a more complete victory your Committee could not have obtained'. A mystifying comment follows. The committee had satisfied themselves that the Shoreham Harbour Commissioners had no right to levy harbour dues under their two previous Acts, but they nevertheless felt that it would not be right to ask the Harbour Commissioners to repay 'what they have so long and so wrongfully taken from your Body'. The expenses of the petition against this Bill amounted to £210 12s. 7d.

At a meeting of the Commissioners on 5 May 1819 James Gregory used improper language and obstructed the proceedings to such an extent that he was, by resolution of the meeting, suspended from sitting as a Commissioner for six months. His signature does not appear again in the minutes until January 1820. In that month the lords of the manor instituted a prosecution against Henry Patching and William Izard, who was a Town

Commissioner, for taking sand from the beach. The Town Commissioners considered that this was a right practised by the inhabitants from time immemorial and decided to support the defendants in the action. Two years later they went further and instructed their Street-keeper, Thomas Harman, to take a load of sand from the beach in the presence of two witnesses. When the lords of the manor began a suit against the Commissioners its defence was entrusted to the Chain Pier Committee.

In July 1821 the Commissioners decided to confer with the magistrates as to the best method of celebrating the coronation of George IV, but the result of their delibera-tions was not stated in the minutes. Later the same month the Commissioners considered the possibility of erecting a platform on the beach to enable the King to pass in his carriage from the cliff to a barge on his departure for Ireland. Twenty pounds had been subscribed for the purpose. But the idea was abandoned because the King did not in fact leave from Brighton. The practicality of the scheme was in any case dubious.

A New Act of Parliament

The first mention in the Commissioners' minutes of a third Act of Parliament was made in February 1818, when the Clerk was instructed to prepare a petition to the House of Commons for leave to bring in a Bill to amend the Act of 1810. A committee was appointed to suggest what amendments were required. This committee consulted with a committee of the Vestry. Nine months later a petition was presented to Parliament in which the only details specified were that the new Bill would fix the tolls of the market and would seek to abolish the office of Surveyor of the Highways to the parish, which was a position independent of the Commissioners. The committee never reported fully, and in December 1819 they were asked to do so. The result did not prove satisfactory as in January 1820 a new committee was appointed to peruse the minutes of the meetings of the old committee. A week later the new committee reported that some of the amendments proposed were so injurious to the town and so objectionable that they could not recommend the Commissioners to proceed with the Bill. The Clerk was therefore instructed not to make any further application to Parliament until instructed to do so by a special meeting of the Commissioners and of the Vestry.

However, it was clear that some further action would have to be taken. By 1821 the population of Brighton had risen to 24,429 and the number of inhabited houses to 3,947. In the next decade these figures were to be doubled again. Therefore, in July 1823 the Commissioners instructed their clerk to give notice to the Michaelmas session of the magistrates that they intended to apply to Parliament for a new Act. However, they had learned little from past experience and did not submit a draft of the Bill to the Vestry before this was printed in March 1824. As a result the Vestry promptly refused to pay any share of the cost and resolved that this should be borne by the Commissioners alone. The Commissioners therefore instructed their Clerk to take no further steps with the Bill. The Vestry, however, appointed a committee of 31 people to examine the proposed Bill and report thereon. This committee included the Earl of Egremont, Thomas Read Kemp, the solicitor, George Faithful, the Rev. Thomas Scutt, and the Rev. Edward Everard.

The committee found the Bill unacceptable in its existing form. They truly stated that 'power cannot be safely entrusted to any body of Men (however upright their individual characters may be) without some efficient restraints to restrain the exercise of it within proper limits'. They recommended the elimination from the Bill of those parts which would 'invest the Commissioners with judicial powers and give them unnecessarily the Character of a local Magistracy'. Their suggestions were that the qualification for acting as a Commissioner should be extended to include possession of leaseholds; that Commissioners, instead of being elected for life, should be subject to periodic re-election, and that the appointment

of the Directors and Guardians of the Poor should revert
from the Commissioners to the Vestry. The Vestry consequently decided to oppose the Bill in its existing form if it
were proceeded with.

The Vestry committee presented their suggestions to
the committee of the Commissioners which had drafted
the Bill, and the two bodies formed a consultative committee to consider further action. In October it was
reported that the only point still at issue was the principle
that a proportion of the Commissioners should retire in
rotation. The Vestry proposed that the new Commissioners should retire after five years, but the existing ones
after two years. The Commissioners considered this to be
an unacceptable discrimination.

Notice of a new Bill was given in December, but
agreement between the Vestry and the Commissioners
was not reached until January 1825. The compromise
was that the existing Commissioners and the new ones
to be named in the Bill should all serve for three years,
unless they ceased to be qualified to act, and then a
seventh of them should retire annually. But the disagreement continued to smoulder even after the Bill had been
introduced into Parliament, and the Commissioners considered prosecuting one vestryman for having given vent to
'a tissue of falsehoods and a scandalous Libel'. The
Commissioners recorded that if the Bill, as agreed, were
not passed that session, they were not committed to
support any other Bill containing the same terms. At the
Committee stage the Commissioners threatened to withdraw the Bill and refuse financial responsibility for it if
any attempt was made in it to name the lords of the manor
as *ex officio* Commissioners. But with the assistance
of Thomas Read Kemp, who was himself one of the lords
of the manor, as well as Member of Parliament for
Arundel, the clause relating to the lords of the manor
was deleted.

In the House of Lords the Bill was so mutilated on
the motion of Lord Shaftesbury that the Vestry decided
to oppose its passage in that form. But on the return

of the Bill to the House of Commons the objectionable amendments were deleted, thanks to the exertions of C. J. Curteis of Windmill Hill Place and Walter Burrell of West Grinstead Park, the Members of Parliament for Sussex, together with the latter's brother, Sir Charles Burrell of Knepp Castle, who was one of the Members for New Shoreham, and also Thomas Read Kemp who sat for Arundel. As a testamony of the town's gratitude these Members and Lord Egremont, who had looked after the town's interests in the House of Lords, were entertained to a special dinner, the cost of which was defrayed by public subscription.

The Act was duly passed that session (1825). Its cost was recorded in the minutes of the Commissioners as £1,200. But a further sum of £4,192 0s. 4d. became due at a later date and was shared between the Commissioners and the Directors and Guardians of the Poor. Ill-feeling between the Commissioners and the Vestry still rumbled as the Commissioners complained that, owing to the extreme haste imposed by the Vestry, no provision was included in the Act, as had been provided by the Act of 1810, to furnish funds for the protection of the cliff.

3.—1825-1854

The Act of 1825 was a much more elaborate document than its predecessors and ran into 266 clauses, but it did not greatly extend the powers of the Commissioners. The preamble recited that, owing to the growth of the town, the market needed enlarging and it was necessary to establish separate markets for cattle and for hay, straw and corn. It was stated that all highways were henceforward to vest in the Commissioners, and the office of surveyor of the highways was to be abolished within the boundaries of Brighton. The Commissioners had agreed to buy the old workhouse in order to expand the market and also to purchase other property in Brighton for road widening. Great difficulty had been experienced in collecting the poor-rate. Therefore it was proposed to appoint a paid collector of this. Moreover, the payment of the general rates was also much evaded in the case of small houses let on short tenancies with frequent changes of tenants.

The number of the Commissioners was increased by 16, and the new Commissioners, both existing and additional, were named in the Act. *Ex officio* membership was abolished, but the Vicar of Brighton, the Rev. R. J. Carr, then also Dean of Hereford, was amongst those nominated. The existing members included Thomas Attree, Isaac Bass, John Colbatch, Charles Elliott, William Furner, George Faithfull, Thomas Read Kemp, Nathaniel Kemp, Hyam Lewis, Carter Thunder, George Wigney, and William Wigney the elder. Among the new members were Thomas Cooper, Lewis Slight, and Isaac Newton Wigney. All the Commissioners were to serve for three years. Thereafter 16, chosen by lot, were to retire annually until all the original members had ceased to hold office. From then onwards the 16 to retire annually would be the 16 senior members.

The qualification for action as a Commissioner was slightly increased. This was henceforward to be the occupation of a house worth £50 a year and ownership of other property of the same value, or of £30 and £70 respectively. The qualification for voters remained as the occupation of premises assessed to the poor-rate to the value of £20 a year. But to this was added a proviso that those whose assessments amounted to £50 would have an additional vote and above that figure a further vote for each additional assessment of £25 up to a total of six votes for £150 a year.

The total amount of the general rate leviable was not increased above 4s. in the pound. But in addition the Commissioners were empowered to arrange for the streets to be watered and a special water-rate of up to 1s. 6d. in the pound to be imposed on the owners of property in the streets which were actually watered.

Because of the difficulty of rate-collection when small houses were let on short leases, the new Act therefore provided that, in the case of houses worth less than £20 a year, if they were let for a shorter period than one year the Commissioner could compound with the landlord for the rates and, if he refused to agree to this, they could levy the rates on him compulsorily. In the previous Acts the rights of the Surveyor of the Highways had been reserved.

Henceforward the office of Surveyor of the Highways was abolished as far as Brighton streets were concerned, and all highways vested in the Commissioners. The provisions for lighting and scavenging the streets and collecting night-soil from privies were somewhat similar to those in the Act of 1810. As in 1810, the power was given to appoint watchmen; also beadles and town-criers. In addition the provision of a fire-engine and engine-house was authorised. The Commissioners could set aside a special place for the parking of boats, and those boats placed within 20 feet of the highway or in the gaps or sloping approaches to the beach could be removed.

The town-planning powers of the Commissioners were extended. Anyone building a new house or altering or demolishing an existing one must give notice beforehand to the Surveyor. In one respect this provision exceeds those of modern town-planning. At the present time demolition is not development within the meaning of the Planning Acts and does not need planning permission. All new streets were to be 30 feet wide, and any new house that was less than 15 feet from the centre of a new road was automatically declared to be a nuisance. Powers were given to lay drains in the streets and to charge the owners of adjoining properties therefor.

The Act includes a schedule of properties that could be acquired for road-widening or for the expansion of the Town Hall and the market. This could be by agreement, or, failing agreement on price, on appeal to a jury of 24 people summoned by the High Sheriff.

Under the preceding Act a total of £8,420 had been borrowed on the security of the general rates and £5,920 on that of the coal-duty. The Commissioners were now authorised to borrow an additional amount of up to one-third of the rates which had been received in the preceding year. But a sinking fund was to be established to pay off the debts on a basis of two per cent. or more a year on the total of £14,340 hitherto borrowed, and whenever this fund amounted to £500, that amount of debts were to be liquidated on the understanding that the oldest debts were to be paid off first.

The Directors and Guardians of the Poor had purchased a piece of land on Church Hill, as the lower part of Dyke was then called, on which they had built a new workhouse. They had borrowed £5,000 for the purpose, of which £666 13s. 4d. had been paid off. The Commissioners therefore agreed to buy the old workhouse in Bartholomews from them for £4,333 6s. 8d. They were empowered to build a new Town Hall on the site of the old workhouse, to extend the market, and to provide also a market for hay, straw and corn, a cattle-market, a weighing-house and a town pound. The tolls fixed in the Act were 5s. for every horse or cow, 3s. 6d. for a pig, 2s. 6d. for an ass or mule, 6d. for a sheep, 3d. for a lamb, 6s. for every load

of hay comprising 36 bundles, and 2s. for every quarter
of wheat. The tolls of the market could also be let by the
Commissioners.

The Act of 1810 had empowered the Commissioners
to licence hackney carriages, sedan-chairs and bathing
machines and to make bye-laws for their use. The new
Act added pleasure boats to this list, for which the licence
fee was to be 10s a year. The Commissioners were also
authorised to build bathing-houses and to impose a fine
of 20s. on anyone who bathed between 8 a.m. and 9 p.m.
without using a bathing-machine. Regulations could also
be made concerning porters in the town.

The coal-duty was not increased beyond 3s. a chaldron,
but the tax was extended to include 1s. 6d. a chaldron
on coke, 1s. a caldron on cinders and ashes, and 1d. a
chaldron on charcoal. The duty could also be let for
one year at a time.

A number of new provisions were made concerning the
poor and the workhouse. In the first place the 30 Directors
and Guardians of the Poor were no longer to be chosen
by the Commissioners but to be elected at a Vestry
meeting on Easter Monday, when the churchwardens and
Overseer of the Poor were also elected. The High
Constable, the Vicar of Brighton, the churchwardens,
the Overseer of the Poor and the surgeon of the workhouse were still to serve *ex officio* as Directors and
Guardians. The accounts of the Directors and Guardians
were to be passed by the Vestry. As in the case of the
Commissioners, the members of the Board were precluded
from being involved in contracts with the Directors and
Guardians. But strangely enough they were specifically
allowed to supply articles for consumption in the workhouse and to employ individuals amongst the poor
themselves. This provision was later to lead to great
abuses. The salary to be paid to the Assistant Overseer
of the Poor was increased from £200 a year to a maximum
of £300. The appointment of two deputy Assistant Overseers at £150 a year was authorised. Paid collectors of the
poor-rate were to be appointed and to be remunerated

on a commission basis of 6d. in the pound. The Directors
and Guardians were empowered to receive bonds from
people who had moved away from the town for the
maintenance of bastard children in the workhouse. Authority was given to borrow up to £10,000 on the security of
the rates for the improvement of the workhouse.

A provision was specifically made in the Act that
nothing precluded the trustees of the Brighton to Lewes
turnpike road from erecting gates beyond the west end of
the Brighton barracks.

The cost of the new Act was £4,192 0s. 4d. As in 1810,
half of this was paid by the Commissioners out of the
general rates and the other half by the Directors and
Guardians of the Poor out of the poor-rate.

The Election of Commissioners

The new Commissioners met for the first time on 29 June
1825 at the Town Hall. After the initial period of three
years there was a regular annual election of 16 Commissioners, but from time to time extra elections were
held to replace those Commissioners who had died or had
left the district, as for instance in March 1826 when 37
vacancies were reported, and which were duly filled in
April. Thirty-three Commissioners were elected in
February 1827, 12 in the following December, 24 in
March 1829, 24 in June 1831, 33 in February 1832,
and so on. The first election of 16 to replace those
retiring by lot took place in August 1827. Those retiring
included such well-known names as Thomas Read Kemp,
Charles Elliott and George Wigney, but they were
re-elected. Each Commissioner signed the oath on his first
appearance. The chairman was elected at each meeting
and henceforth he alone signed the minutes. On 26 June
1827 it was resolved not to admit the press to the Commissioners' meetings.

The Rates and Finances

The rate under the old Act had been 4s. in the pound. This
was continued under the new Act until 1832. To this was

added a new rate of 1s. 6d., or occasionally 1s. in the pound, for the purpose of watering the streets. This was confined only to the proprietors of the houses in the streets to be watered. But in 1833, without explanation the rate dropped to 7d. and the watering rate to threepence. However a second rate of 9d. was levied in the autumn. In October 1834 the rate was 9d. and the water rate sixpence. But in February 1835 it rose to 1s. 8d. and the water rate dropped to 3d. In October 1836 it was 1s. and the water rate of 3d. was not voted until four months later. The general rate continued at that figure until 1839, but in that year an additional rate of 9d. was voted to form a sinking fund to pay off debts. February 1840 brought a rate of 1s. 3d. and a water rate of 3d., but a further rate of 6d. was voted in April. In 1841 the rate became 1s. and the water rate threepence. The following year a rate of 2s. was recommended to pay off the arrears of debts that were due, but only 1s. was passed. From 1843 onwards it became customary to levy the general rate twice a year and the water rate once only. In most years it comprised 1s. each time and the water-rate generally 2d., but occasionally 3d. or even 1d. But 1844 was an exception and it then amounted to only 6d. each time. Many losses occurred through the non-collection of rates, and in 1844 it was resolved that these would be reduced if the rate was levied early in the year, say in January, but this never seems to have been carried out.

After the acquisition of the Royal Pavilion in 1850 a special Pavilion rate of 3d. was imposed annually. The last rate raised under the Act of 1825 was levied in March 1855. This amounted to a general rate of 6d., a watering rate of 2d. and a Pavilion rate of threepence.

As the years proceeded the Commissioners' finances, which in the early days had been very modest and were rather irregularly handled, became more substantial. Debentures to the value of £18,240 had been issued before the passing of the new Act, and £6,000 was borrowed on notes of hand soon after it came into force. In November 1825 a Vestry meeting recommended the execution of certain improvements such as the widening of Pool Lane, now Pool Valley, and of the approach to the Royal Pavilion, now Pavilion Buildings, which would cost the Commissioners £3,000. The Commissioners were not willing to increase the rates substantially and thought that all that was necessary could be carried out for £1,500 if the basis of the poor-rate was increased from one-ninth to one-sixth of the value of property. This step was taken, but it was, however, reported that unpaid rates to the value of £7,742 5s. 4d. were outstanding in October 1826.

A year later a full dress row developed between the Vestry and the Commissioners over the improvements which the Vestry had suggested and the method of financing them. The Vestry alleged that the improvements had not been carried out and that therefore the basis of rating should be reduced to its former figure. This produced from the Commissioners an outburst of furious complacency which is so often the reaction of elected persons to outside criticism. They recorded that 'they cannot but regret that the Vestry should have so far forgotten that dignity and respectability which they ought at all times to possess' as to have preferred charges which would, if true, have rendered the Commissioners 'utterly unworthy the confidence and respect of the inhabitants . . . As it is a matter of notoriety to every inhabitant that the business of the Commissioners is at present conducted with regularity, promptitude and economy' the Commissioners felt that it would compromise their powers and the sanctions given to them by Parliament if they permitted 'any dictation to be effectual in drawing them aside from that course which they in their Judgment and discretion might conceive would be conducive to the interests and prosperity of the Town'. The Commissioners were not, however, able to prevent the Vestry from reducing the rateable value back from one-sixth to one-ninth.

The Commissioners nevertheless proceeded with the completion of the disputed improvements but financed them by borrowing. In July 1828 £10,000 was borrowed on debenture at five per cent. from a Mr. Cunningham, but it was not until 1830, when the erection of the Town Hall and other costly improvements were begun, that the Commissioners had to embark on loans in a big way. In April a resolution was passed authorising the borrowing of £42,000 at four per cent., but no lenders were forthcoming. An increase of interest to five per cent. was authorised, but the clerk and treasurer seem to have found lenders who were prepared to accept four and a quarter per cent., provided that £2,100 in capital was repaid every year. This was agreed. At the same time the rates of interest on the existing debentures of £6,920 was reduced from five to four per cent. In October the loan of a further £20,000 was authorised. Of this, only £8,000 was obtained at four and a quarter per cent., £6,000 at four and three-eighths, and £6,000 at four and a half per cent. The Commissioners' total liability at that time amounted to £83,920. In April 1831 it was decided to borrow the further amount of £20,000. One hundred and eleven thousand two hundred pounds was in fact raised between 1825 and 1833, though in the same period debentures to the value of £32,820 were paid off. The Commissioners continued to feel that their income was inadequate to their necessary expenditure and in 1832 asked for a Vestry meeting to discuss the matter. This took place on 4 July 1832, when the Vestry was so far from being mollified that they recorded that, in their opinion, the Commissioners had 'wantonly and improvidently expended the funds of the Town entrusted to their care'. They appointed a committee to investigate the Commissioners' accounts and to report what steps should be taken to extricate the town from its difficulties without raising the rates. The Commissioners, however, refused to place their vouchers and records in the hands of the Vestry, although professing to be prepared to enable the Vestry to 'correctly investigate the accounts of the Commissioners'. Nothing therefore seems to have come of the matter.

In January 1834 a further amount of £30,000 was borrowed. A year later it was recorded that the amount borrowed on debenture or notes of hand was £127,920 and the current deficit on contract debts £1,600. The estimated expenditure for 1835 was £17,880, including £10,000 for the sea wall along Marine Parade. Nineteen thousand pounds of the debts would have to be repaid in 1836. So it would be necessary to borrow the further amount of £30,000 during that year, which was in effect done in January. But a resolution was passed in October to raise a further £15,000. Over a year later the Clerk was forced to report that he had only been able to raise £1,500 out of this last sum. He had therefore waited on Lord Egremont to tell him of the Commissioners' plight. As a result Lord Egremont lent them £11,000 on debenture at four and a half per cent to relieve them of their difficulties. Towards the end of 1838 concern was caused by the necessity of repaying a loan of £8,544 to the trustees of the late Sir G. F. Hampson, but this was surmounted by levying an additional rate to form a sinking fund.

In 1840 £9,000 was borrowed in May and £3,000 in September. At the beginning of 1842 a finance committee, which had been specially appointed for the purpose, reported that the arrears of debts amounted to £22,659, including a note of hand for £5,000. This was renewed and the remainder of the sum could be met from the rates if these were doubled, but the Commissioners declined to do this.

Ten thousand pounds was borrowed in November 1843. The following year the clerk recommended that the interest on all outstanding mortgage bonds should be reduced to four per cent. and those mortgage holders who would not agree to this should be paid off. The borrowing of a further amount of £20,000 for the purpose was authorised. A year later the clerk reported that he had secured the reduction of interest to four per cent. in the case of £140,300, which had decreased the interest payable by £644 a year. Holders of bonds to the value of

£35,000 had refused the reduction and had been paid off.

Sixty thousand pounds was borrowed from the Bank of England for the purchase of the Royal Pavilion in May 1850, and a further ·amount of £24,000 nearly a year later. The rateable value of the town was mentioned for the first time in 1852 and amounted to £304,573. The population at the time was 65,573. By May 1854 the public debt of the Commissioners stood at £134,220. A further amoung of £5,000 was borrowed in July 1854, which was the last sum raised by the Commissioners before incorporation of the town took place.

The Officers

The principal officers of the old Commissioners did not long survive the passing of the Act of 1825. The Clerk at that time was Frederick Cooper. Soon after the Act came into force the Commissioners, acting under a spur from a Vestry meeting to the effect that expenditure should be reduced, examined the nature of the Clerk's emoluments. They found that, as most of his time and that of several clerks was spent on Commissioners' business he was probably, if anything, underpaid. His actual salary only amounted to £100 a year, to which were added fees paid under Acts of Parliament amounting to £90 a year. But the bulk of his income came under law proceedings from acting as the Commissioners' solicitor. The Commissioners therefore decided to reorganise his emoluments and pay him a comprehensive salary of £300 a year from 25 December 1825. Four Commissioners (Lewis Slight, Nathaniel Bradford, John Pratt and Kenyon Masters Bradford) signed a protest at the foot of the minutes to the effect that this salary was much larger than was required. At a Vestry meeting on 1 December some members went even further and suggested that a competent person could be found to do the job for £50 a year. At this Frederick Cooper angrily resigned. The Commissioners asked him to withdraw his resignation, against which a further protest was recorded, this time signed by Lewis Slight, N. M. Bradford and Thomas Cooper. Two members of the Vestry sent a counter-petition in favour of Frederick Cooper continuing on the existing footing. Cooper agreed to withdraw his resignation on the basis of the Commissioners' original offer. But the advocates of retrenchment did not leave the matter at that. By a resolution on 9 August 1826, with Nathaniel Bradford in the chair, the Clerk's salary was reduced to £100 a year. As a result Frederick Cooper resigned with effect from Michaelmas.

Another committee then examined the Clerk's duties and re-defined them in a narrower fashion, on a full-time basis but excluding work as the Commissioners' solicitor. Henceforth the work as solicitor was discharged by Charles Cobby of 16 New Road. The Clerk's salary was therefore fixed at £50 a year, exclusive of all fees. A new appointment was made by ballot. The selection fell on Thomas Augustus Swaysland. But a few weeks later, again with Nathaniel Bradford in the chair, a resolution was passed allowing him to exchange the post for that of collector of rates at £120 a year. Thereupon Lewis Slight resigned his seat as a Commissioner and accepted the position of Clerk at the salary of £100 a year.

Lewis Slight was a man of considerable importance in the history of Brighton during the 28 years of his tenure of office. He became so influential that his enemies sometimes called him 'the emperor of Brighton'. But he started life in quite a humble way. He was born in Leicestershire in 1792 and moved to Brighton at the age of twenty-six. Here he opened a shoe shop in Poplar Place, which was the east end of Meeting House Lane that runs into North Street. This shop was moved to 31 North Street in 1821. At 32 North Street, adjoining, his first wife ran a business as a stay- and corset-maker, but this was removed to 23 Ship Street in 1831. Lewis Slight himself probably ceased to trade on his appointment as Clerk to the Commissioners. He was among the group of people who had actively campaigned for the local Act of 1825 and became a Commissioner under it. His resignation from this body and assumption of the duties of Clerk were somewhat symbolic of the high-handed behaviour which was to characterise him throughout his tenure of office and make him very unpopular with many people.

In October 1836 the duties of the officers of the Commissioners were reorganised. The Clerk, in addition to his salary of £100 a year, had for some years been receiving fees amounting to £168 a year. Henceforward he was paid £400 a year including fees and out of this was required to pay any clerk or clerks employed in his office. The first of these clerks was Frederick Drayson, but in June 1837 Slight was given permission to employ his son, also Lewis, as his clerk. Lewis Slight senior was a man of autocratic temperament who conducted municipal affairs in a very high-handed way, as many Town Clerks before and since have done. He was a radical in politics, but after his death it was said that the Conservatives agreed to allow him to rule the town's business provided he kept out of politics. He remained in office until January 1854, when he was involved in a big row.

After the Clerk the next officer in order of importance was the Treasurer, John Mills, who had been in office when the Act of 1825 was passed. He resigned in March 1826 and was succeeded by a member of the prominent Brighton family of Wigney. This was George Wigney, one of the two brothers responsible for the management of the brewery, Wigney and Sons. Ten years later his place was taken by his brother Isaac Newton Wigney who, with Clement Wigney, managed the bank of Wigney and Co., or the Brighton Bank, at the corner of Great East Street and Castle Square (60 Great East Street).[1] The failure of this bank in 1842 was one of the most spectacular events in Brighton's history and affected many people as its creditors only received payment of 1s. in the pound. Isaac Newton Wigney was declared bankrupt and his liabilities outstanding to the Commissioners amounted to £4,448 3s. 5d. One John Hamlin Borrer nobly agreed to advance this sum, upon which he resigned his seat as a Commissioner and was appointed Treasurer. The

1. I. N. Wigney was one of Brighton's first Members of Parliament, from 1833 to 1837 and again from 1841 to 1842.

Commissioners later had to apply to George Wigney, standing surety for his brother Isaac, for the balance of the debt due to them, but eventually all Isaac Newton Wigney's private creditors were paid in full.

The new Treasurer, John Hamlin Borrer, was also a banker, partner in the firm of Hall, West and Borrer (the Union Bank) of 7 North Street. He remained in office until April 1854, when he was replaced by his partner and friend Nicholas Eardley Hall. Following the disturbance which led to the resignation of Lewis Slight, and as the result of the aggressive actions taken by certain Commissioners, a new Treasurer was appointed. The transaction was recorded in the minutes in far from gentle terms. It was resolved that Mr. John Hamlin Borrer, having 'become mentally incompetent to the transaction of business, be and is displaced from the office of Treasurer'.

After the Clerk and Treasurer the other officers were less important. Amon Wilds, the joint architect of so many interesting buildings in Brighton, was appointed Surveyor in September 1825 and held the post until July 1828. Certain criticisms of his actions in certifying accounts were subsequently made against him. He had not been prevented from acting as a Commissioner during the time that he held office as Surveyor, though this was forbidden by the Act of 1825, and had even taken the chair at some meetings. Robert Chalkley had acted as his clerk of the works at a wage of 30s. a week. Wild's successors were at first Richard Rainger and later John Wright, who were each paid £200 a year. John Wright resigned in August 1836, having obtained a better post. David Laing took his place for only a year.

The next Surveyor was Henry Stiles Colbran. He was the grandson of the Rev. H. S. Colbran who had been Vicar of Brighton from 1705 to 1750. H. S. Colbran resigned in October 1846. The Commissioners were not dissatisfied with him and enquired why he wished to leave. They found that this was due to a difference between him and the Clerk as to how the Act of 1825 should be interpreted and also because his salary was insufficient. He professed himself willing to continue in office if he was given an increase in salary of £50 a year. This was not granted.[1] His successor was John Stead who was given £200 a year, which probably represented the extra £50 that Colbran had asked for. The poor man was soon in trouble: in June he was accused of executing work in Church Street which had not been authorised by the Commissioners. He countered by asking for an increase in salary and more assistance in the office. Both were refused, and he therefore resigned, 'having had to encounter many rebuts that ill become me as a man of business to encounter'. This incident led to a claim for money due to him which persisted over many years, sometimes in his name, sometimes in the name of his wife, and eventually of his widow.

The next tenant of the office was Richard Allen Stickney who was appointed in September 1847. His duties were to include the supervision of scavenging and watering of the roads. But the Commissioners seem at last to have appreciated that cheese-paring did not pay. He was given a salary of £250 a year and allowed a clerk or assistant and two foremen, who were each paid 30s. a week, Joseph Thomas Oddy being the· first assistant. R. A. Stickney resigned in April 1852 and Allen Anscomb was appointed in his place at the same salary.

The collection of rates had been put to commission under the 1810 Act, but soon after the passing of the Act of 1825, when the big row occurred over the position of the Clerk, T. A. Swaysland, who was first appointed to Frederick Cooper's position, exchanged the post of Clerk for that of collector in November 1826 at £120 a year. At the same time Robert Spice, who had been acting as collector of the watering rate since September 1825, was discharged because he was unable to pay the balance of £90 6s. 3½d. due from him to the Commissioners and the latter had to apply to his sureties for it. Swaysland's salary was raised to £150 in 1835 and he

1. H. S. Colbran died on 21 June 1856 and is buried in the Extra Mural Cemetery.

remained Collector of rates until February 1841, when he resigned after a long illness, leaving the town's finances in rather a muddle. He was succeeded by his assistant, Richard Rawley junior, at a salary of between £100 and £120, which was eventually fixed at £110, and back-dated. The office of assistant collector was suppressed and instead the Clerk was directed to give the Collector any assistance required. But in April Rawley resigned. In his place two collectors, John Chalk and William Tuppen, were appointed and paid by commission on a sliding scale: 1s. in the pound on the first £10,000 and thereafter 3d. in the pound for each extra £2,500 collected up to £20,000, plus £20 a year for collecting the watering rate. In January 1847 the Collectors asked for their remuneration to be changed to a fixed rate of three per cent., but this was refused.

This arrangement lasted until 1850 when John Chalk was still in office but was, in his own words, 'afflicted with very reduced power of personal Locomotion'. He was summarily dismissed and two new Collectors, William Westmore and John Pountain, were appointed at a fixed salary of £150 a year each. Poor John Chalk not unnaturally protested at his dismissal and asked for further employment, but the Commissioners reluctantly held that, in view of the state of his health, there was no office which they could offer him. They therefore offered him the sum of £50 compensation. Edward Bodle succeeded John Pountain as Collector in September 1851 at the same salary. In August 1854 the Collectors were refused an increase in salary.

An officer who was subsequently to play an important part in Brighton life was Henry Solomon. He was originally a watchmaker but had been in the service of the Commissioners since 1821. A year later he was appointed inspector of post horse duty and in 1823 superintendent of hackney carriages, bathing-machines and pleasure boats at the salary of £20 or £25 a year. In September 1826 his duties were extended to cover the watering of the roads, but 10 years later this job was passed to the Surveyor. In November 1826 he was given the additional office of superintendent of nuisances with a salary of £75 for both posts, and in March 1827 the office of inspector of gas lights at an extra fee of £10 a year. In 1832 he was made joint Chief Officer of Police as well with a composite salary of £120 a year. On the resignation of William Pilbeam through ill health in 1836 he was given sole responsibility as Chief Constable. Like other Chief Constables, he had his local enemies who at times accused him of being in league with the 'thimble and rig' men. He seems to have lived extravagantly in private life as, when two of his infant children died, they had to be buried at the expense of the local Jewish community.

His services terminated with one of the most spectacular events in Brighton's history. On 13 March 1844 shortly after 8 p.m. Solomon was on duty at the police station in the Town Hall when Constable John Barnden brought in a man named John Lawrence who had been apprehended for stealing. Lawrence and another man, after loitering outside Collins's shop in St. James's Street, had made off with a roll of drugget carpet. A shop assistant had pursued them. The other man escaped, but Lawrence was overtaken in Chapel Street and, after being taken back to the shop, was given in charge of the police.

Solomon proceeded to examine the prisoner. Three other people were present in the room at the time: Samuel Slight, an accountant, who was the son of the Clerk to the Commissioners; Edward Butler, the Collector of the poor-rate; and William Alger, a draper; in addition to John Barnden who was standing outside the door. When the examination was finished Lawrence was told to sit down, but subsequently started up in great agitation, removed his cravat and asked for a knife with which to cut his throat. Shortly afterwards the shopkeeper, Collins, arrived, but failed to identify the prisoner. Lawrence was again told to sit by the fire while the chief constable proceeded with other affairs. The other people present in the room were not attending to Lawrence, and Edward Butler was actually reading the newspaper. When the Chief Constable crossed the room Lawrence seized the poker from the grate and hit him with it on the right side of the head above the ear so violently that it caused a gash two and a half inches by one inch wide. So great was the force of the blow that it bent the poker considerably, as was proved in evidence at Lawrence's trial. Solomon recovered consciousness but died early the next day. He was buried in the Jewish cemetery at Hollingdean which had been given to the local Jewish community by Thomas Read Kemp in 1825. He left a widow and nine children.

Lawrence was a native of Tunbridge wells, aged 23, who had been apprenticed to his father as a plasterer. His father died, and his mother re-married a farmer at Speldhurst. After working for a while for his step-father he left home and drifted into a dissolute life. He was convicted of passing base coin and twice of a felony. Eventually he spent six months in Brighton with a gang of thieves and prostitutes, among whom he was known as 'Mag'. In particular he associated with and was maintained by a prositute known as 'Hastings Bet'. But he quarrelled with her as the result of having pawned some of her clothing. He kicked and beat her so savagely that she asked for police protection. He had been drinking hard for several days before the crime was committed, though all the witnesses at the trial agreed that he was not in liquor at the time of the assault.

Henry Solomon died at 10 a.m. on 14 March. Shortly after 11 a.m. on the same day Lawrence was brought before the magistrates. He was committed for trial at the Assizes which were due to be held at Lewes on the 19th of the same month. The inquest on Henry Solomon's death was held on the following day, the 15th, and resulted in a verdict of wilful murder against John Lawrence.

His trial was held on the second day of the Assizes (20 March) before the Lord Chief Justice, Lord Denman. Three jurors who were Jews were replaced by the judge. As there were three eye-witnesses of the murder and no witnesses for the defence the trial only lasted three hours. Counsel for the defence could only allege that the crime was committed in a momentary fit of insanity. But the Lord Chief Justice had little difficulty in showing that the circumstances did not come within the scope of the recently-formulated McNaughton rules. The jury did not retire and only took 12 minutes to arrive at a verdict of guilty. Lawrence was removed from Lewes to Horsham gaol the next day and was there publicly hanged at 12 noon on 5 April in the presence of a crowd of between 1,000 and 3,000 people. The whole proceedings since the date of the murder had taken little more than three weeks.

A public meeting was held in Brighton on 23 March to launch a subscription for the widow and children of Henry Solomon. The meeting expressed the hope that the Brighton Commissioners, whose employee Solomon had been, would make a generous gift. As a result, at their next meeting on 27 March the Commissioners subscribed £500. They expressed their 'abhorrence and detestation of the cold-blooded deed which had deprived the Town of an old, faithful and valuable Servant, the country of a most zealous and vigilant Officer and a Mother and nine children of the only support on which they depended for subsistence'.

At the instigation of the Lord Lieutenant of Sussex, the Duke of Richmond, the Government subscribed £30 out of the Royal Bounty. The Queen contributed £50. The Jewish congregation themselves subscribed £52 10s. A circus contributed the proceeds of one night's performance. The total sum received was £1,030 14s., and was invested to bring in £2 a week for Solomon's widow.

When the post of Chief Constable to replace Henry Solomon was advertised in the press 40 applicants came forward. Five were short-listed and ballotted upon. A further vote was then taken on the candidates placed first and second in the ballot. The man eventually chosen was Thomas Hayter Chase, aged 30, Chief Superintendent of the Police in the Isle of Wight. An interesting note was attached to the name of one of the other five runners-up: John Savage, who was Chief Superintendent of the Police of the London and Brighton Railway. It was said that he had 'great knowledge of the improper characters in the habit of coming to Brighton' and of 'the improper characters residing in Brighton'. The new Chief Constable's salary was £150 a year. In August he was appointed also inspector of nuisances, apparently without extra salary. But he received one rise of £50 a year in October 1846. The office of inspector of hackney carriages, pleasure boats and bathing-machines, which Henry Solomon had also held, was in July 1845 given to Isaiah Barnden, who was one of the Inspectors of Police, at a salary of £75 a year. When he was promoted to Superintendent in August 1847 he was succeeded by Inspector Terry.

Thomas Hayter Chase had a chequered career as Chief Constable. In June 1850 he applied for a further rise in salary, but was turned down. However, in the following October the principle of an increase in salary seems to have been agreed on the basis that all fees arising from his services should be paid to the Commissioners and that he should not accept gratuities. But no increase had in effect been voted by August 1851.

In that year he ran into trouble for the first time. A respectable resident named John Poune was in possession of a constable's staff which had been given to him by Thomas Palmer in 1829. The Chief Constable met Thomas Poune in the street when Poune was carrying the staff. Under the impression that Poune had purloined it from one of the town's officers, the Chief Constable ordered him to hand it over. When the latter refused, he wrenched it from Poune's grasp. Poune complained to the Commissioners and was able to prove his case. The Commissioners recorded that 'the conduct of Mr. Chase in wresting the Staff from Mr. Poune was unjustifiable seeing that the Staff is clearly the property of Mr. Poune'. Chase was directed to return the staff and to make an apology.

Only a few months later another incident occurred of which full details are not given but relating to the removal of a dead body from the King's Road baths.

Mr. Brill made a complaint to the Commissioners, as the result of which they recorded that 'Mr. Chase manifested a great want of discretion and judgement and they regret that the feelings of a respectable Inhabitant should have been wounded by an Officer of the Commissioners'.

In February 1853 a constable named John Lang, who had not been promoted to first class but had apparently been engaged in detective work, was ordered to go on duty in uniform in the normal manner. He objected so strongly that in consequence he resigned from the police force, though he later expressed his willigness to rejoin the service as a detective officer in plain clothes. The Commissioners naturally recorded that 'it would be subversive of all discipline and good conduct to permit any Constable to be appointed to perform Special duties of his own selection only'. But during the discussion of the matter one of their number, Thomas Cooper, accused the Chief Constable of acting out of pique. Cooper was reported in the local press as saying that 'there were few people who would submit to his [Chase's] orders, a man who had been out in Spain shooting people!' If Lang was not reinstated he [Thomas Cooper] 'certainly should not spare any pains to get the other customer [Chase] into the same position'. Chase complained to the Commissioners that such language overstepped the bounds of fair criticism and asked for protection against its repetition. The letter was entered at the foot of the minutes, but no action seems to have been taken thereon.

Only three months later Chase was dismissed from his post. The events leading to this action began as far back as November 1851, when a woman named Eliza Maria Amphlett was brought into the police station from London on a charge of obtaining goods from Hanningtons on false pretences. She had formerly lodged with Mrs. Chase's mother in the Isle of Wight, when Chase had been Chief Constable in the island. On her arrest she claimed acquaintance with Mrs. Chase who, out of kindness, lent her a nightdress for the night. She was sentenced to a year's imprisonment in Lewes gaol and when this sentence expired, was transferred to the debtors' side of the prison as the result of a detainer for debt. Mrs. Chase frequently visited her there during this period.

Had this been all, no harm might have been done. But Mrs. Chase also persuaded her husband to allow their address, 37 Great East Street, to be used by Miss Amphlett for her correspondence. Letters and parcels were sent to her there under the name of Mrs. Benyon, which was said to be her mother's maiden name, and also in that of Miss Howard. A constable named Reeves testified to the fact that, when he took prisoners over to Lewes gaol, he frequently carried letters and parcels for Miss Amphlett. Letters were a daily occurrence, and parcels were taken about once a week. Chase afterwards stated that he had only given his consent for the delivery of letters and personal necessaries. He was also influenced by the fact that Miss Amphlett was well connected and that her family was endeavouring to obtain for her property amounting to about £10,000 to which she was said to be entitled.

Whatever Chase may have thought or intended, it is clear that Miss Amphlett conducted a regular business of buying and selling goods, mostly female apparel, from prison. But in due course she became too venturesome and wrote to a hosier named Cherton of Oxford Street to order some samples of ladies' clothing, and to a jeweller named Laurie of Pall Mall asking him to send her a few rings 'not to exceed £15 or £20 in price'. These traders became suspicious and approached the London Association for the Protection of Trade.

The secretary of that body, Thomas Blakeman, had evidently had dealings with Miss Amphlett before and at once suspected that the hand-writing of the letter sent in the name of Mrs. Benyon resembled Miss Amphlett's writing. He thereupon took steps to ascertain who was the occupant of the house, 37 Great East Street, from which Mrs. Benyon's letter letter had ostensibly been written. Communications with the Chief Constable followed in which the latter was singularly evasive. One letter said:

'The party mentioned are not staying with me; but I have every reason to believe that the money is safe and will be paid in good time'. He was most reluctant to reveal that the real address of the writer of the letter had been Lewes gaol. When pushed into a corner he did in due course call on the association in London and revealed the full circumstances. The association then laid the whole story before the Brighton magistrates. The latter did not feel that the facts warranted any action by them. The Chief Constable, in a further interview with the association, expressed his regret for the indiscretion of his conduct. In view of this the association also came to the conclusion that, though his conduct had been highly reprehensible, they did not propose to press for any further investigations.

This debtors' prison incident has a wonderful 'Little Dorrit' atmosphere about it. Naturally it became known to the Commissioners. At the same time attention was drawn to another failing on Chase's part. Each policeman was supplied with two uniforms which were used for two years. At the end of that time they were sold to an old clothes dealer and the proceeds credited to the super-annuation fund. It was found that Chase had not always paid these amounts into the fund at once, but had used some of the money for the necessary police disbursements. In fact he claimed that, as he was not supplied with petty cash, he had no other source on which to draw for such, except his own money. But the explanation did not carry full conviction. The Commissioners held that 'in consequence of the improper conduct of Mr. Chase in connection with Miss Amphlett' he was 'unworthy of the confidence of the Commissioners and that he be hereby discharged'.

For six months the senior Superintendent, named White, whose appointment dated from 1842, acted as Chief Constable 'with great efficiency and energy'. In December he was appointed Chief Constable and was voted the same salary as his predecessor had received, namely £200 a year, in view of his 'long and faithful services, his numerous family and the peculiar advance in the cost of maintenance at the present time'. He remained Chief Constable at the time of the incorporation of the town.

In April 1830 the new office of Engineer was instituted at 20s. a week. Robert Newton was appointed to the office with three foremen under him who were only paid a retainer of one guinea a year. But this office seems not to have lasted.

George Cherriman was appointed Town Crier in September 1825, and Eastman Barnard and William Giles in March 1827, all at £10 a year plus fees of 3s. a cry. The existing Beadles (William Catling, John Knight, William Sheppard, and Henry Martin) were all discharged at the same time, but Catling, Knight and Sheppard were reinstated two days later at 18s. a week. George Cherriman died in January 1838 and was replaced by Samuel Cheeseman. William Giles died in 1846 and was succeeded by his son, John.

The Market and the Town Hall

In 1825 the Commissioners decided to continue the arrangement whereby the market was kept in their own hands. The yard of the adjoining former poor-house, which the Commissioners had purchased from the Directors and Guardians of the Poor in 1822, was laid out for additional market space. George King was appointed collector of market tolls at a salary of £2 12s. 6d. a week, out of which he had to pay a cleaner. Nearly a year later he reported that he had been unable to collect some of the market tolls because the magistrate, Mr. Iremonger, had refused to convict those who evaded payment. A delegation of the Commissioners waited on Mr. Iremonger and Sir David Scott. As a result, misunderstandings were cleared up and the magistrates agreed to convict where appropriate.

The existing market, even including the adjoining poor-house, was inadequate for the needs of a town expanding as fast as Brighton was then doing. Therefore one of the first tasks of the new Commissioners, as indeed one of the main reasons for the passing of the new Act of 1825, was to build a new market and Town Hall. A formal resolution to build such was passed on 6 March 1827. In addition to the council chamber and offices, the Town Hall was to include a few cells of a prison and a suite of rooms for public meetings and assemblies. But the assemly rooms were subsequently omitted as a result of a resolution passed by a Vestry meeting. The site of the existing Town Hall and market was chosen for the new building.

A public competition for the design of the building was arranged and the drawings were submitted anonymously. Three of these were selected by a committee, and out of them the winning design was chosen by ballot at a full meeting of the Commissioners. The first choice was Thomas Cooper, himself a Commissioner, who was awarded a premium of £50. He designed the *Bedford* hotel at almost exactly the same time in 1829, and the original Eye Hospital in Queen's Road in 1846. The runner-up in the competition was an architect named Clisby who was the first Surveyor to the Brunswick Square Commissioners. He was awarded £30. The third successful competitor was Henry Kendal, who subsequently designed the Kemp Town Slopes. He was awarded £20. Kenyon Masters Bradford, who was often in disagreement with the proceedings of the Commissioners, protested against the decision made, though the grounds of the protest are not stated.

The plan of the building, as designed, was to be that of a Greek cross, but the south wing was never built. According to Erredge this was because the Commissioners were not able to purchase the necessary land to the south which did not belong to them. Advertisements for tenders for both the Town Hall and the new market were made in August 1828. William Doubleday offered to build the Town Hall for £12,491 1s. 7d., and the market for £2,948 14s. 4d. His securities were Major Russell and Joseph Fenton. These tenders, as the lowest offered, were accepted. But Erredge records that the total cost of the Town Hall was over £60,000. The Commissioners borrowed more than £80,000 at this time on the security of the rates for various improvements including the Town Hall. The materials of the old Town Hall were sold by auction. In the interim period the Commissioners rented a room for their own meetings in the *Sea Horse* hotel. Their solicitor, Charles Cobby, provided a first-floor room in his office in Steine Lane for the use of their Clerk.

The foundation stone of the new Town Hall was laid by Thomas Read Kemp in April 1830, the Earl of Egremont having declined the Commissioners' invitation through ill health. In 1831 a delay in the building seems to have been caused by inefficiency on the part of the surveyor, Richard Ranger, who subsequently resigned. Further discord arose because plate glass was used in glazing the windows without the authority of the Commissioners. Public subscriptions were raised to place portraits of the King and Queen, by Simpson, in the building. In 1845 a portrait of the first Marquess of Bristol was also placed in the Great Room.

At first the Town Hall does not seem to have been heated, except presumably by coal fires in the individual offices. In November 1836 it was specifically decided, after consulting the magistrates, to heat the police cells in the building 'as they were not of sufficient warmth to justify placing of Prisoners therein during the Winter Season'.[1] At the same time reference was made to a plan prepared by the former Surveyor, John Wright, for heating the whole building, which would secure the results desired by the magistrates in a more beneficial manner. But there is no record of whether or not this heating system was installed.

The question at once arose of using parts of the Town Hall for public purposes. In 1833 S. W. Bennett suggested that a portion of the building should be let as an inn or coffee house, but nothing came of this. Three years later a meeting of the Vestry recorded that 'it would be highly

1. Erredge described these cells in 1862 as being 'underground dungeons similar to which criminals convicted of the darkest crimes would not by any British Government be permitted to be consigned'.

expedient and promote the amusement and pleasure of the Visitors and Inhabitants of this Town if an organ were placed in the Large Room at the Town Hall'. A committee of inhabitants, under the chairmanship of George Wigney, raised the necessary money and offered an organ to the Commissioners. The offer was rather grudgingly accepted on the condition that the organ became the property of the Commissioners and was installed to their directions. No thanks were recorded to the donors. What became of it is not certain, as in 1848 the Lord Chamberlain, on behalf of the Queen, presented the Commissioners with the organ from the Royal Chapel at the Royal Pavilion, and this was installed on a temporary stage at the eastern end of the ballroom at a cost of £25. This organ was subsequently moved back to the Royal Pavilion and inserted in the place of the original organ in the Music Room which had been moved to Osborne House.

The large room in the Town Hall was at once made available for private and public events, much as the rooms of the Royal Pavilion are now. Private individuals could hire it to give a concert. Madame Tussaud rented it in 1833 for the exhibition of her waxworks at a charge of a guinea a day. The free use accorded by the Commissioners included a dinner in 1833 to entertain the first two Members of Parliament for Brighton, George Faithful and Isaac Newton Wigney, a Fancy Fair for the Sussex County Hospital in 1833, and the more dubious cause of a public meeting to protest against compulsory church rates in Brighton in 1836. The line between what qualified for free use and what needed payment was at first not very clearly marked. So in 1837 the Commissioners drew up general principles on the subject. The room was henceforward to be available free for the use of the Vestry and town meetings, for all other meetings connected with the commercial or trading interests of the town, to public, charitable, literary or scientific institutions which made no charge for admission to their meetings. This provides a somewhat marked contrast to the stiff rates charged to local societies for rooms in the Royal Pavilion today. For other public or private use the great room was to be available for lectures for a fee of one guinea, for morning concerts for seven guineas, for balls for 14 guineas or £21 for the whole suite of rooms.

The Commissioners subsequently had doubts about charging for the rooms at all. In December 1839 they recorded that it was 'conducive to the interests of the inhabitants at large that the rooms of the Town Hall should be at all times be open to the public free of other charge than the attendant expense of lighting, fitting up, etc.', and agreed that the rooms should be available free of charge for meetings connected with the trading, commercial or political interests of the town; for charitable, literary or scientific institutions; and for balls, concerts, or lectures 'conducted of given by inhabitants': a wide and generous reference. But in 1847 gratuitous use was discontinued and a graduated scale of charges introduced, based on a percentage, though it was not stated what charge would be made for charitable events.

In May 1840 the Commissioners received a request from William Furner, the newly-appointed judge of the Brighton Court of Requests for the recovery of small debts, asking whether the Commissioners would provide a room for the sessions of the court in the Town Hall. As a result they agreed to spend £450 in fitting up a room on the ground floor beneath the Commissioners' rooms which could be used for the new court, the Sheriff's court and the Magistrates' court. The old court room, previously used for Petty Sessions, was then fitted up for use by the Commissioners. Occasion was taken to instal gas lighting in the main rooms at the same time.

Seven years later, at the request of the Lords of Treasury, the use of the court-room was also accorded to the County Court. This led to the Magistrates asking the Commissioners for an additional room once a fortnight when the County Court was in session. The Commissioners took the opportunity to remove from the Town Hall the offices of the Assistant Overseer of the

Poor as the assemblage of paupers there was highly offen-
sive. The Directors replied with great indignation that
this would involve the complete removal of all parochial
offices from the Town Hall and the erection of new offices
elsewhere. As the transaction of parochial business was
in their view second only to the requirements of the Commissioners themselves the latter had exceeded their powers
in giving such notice. As a result the Commissioners
climbed down and agreed to confer with the Magistrates
about the use of the Commissioners' own room when
necessary.

When paupers were not concerned the Commissioners
were more generous. In 1846 they agreed to grant the
temporary use of two ante-rooms on the first floor and
the south room on the second floor to the newly-founded
Brighton Athenaeum and Young Men's Literary Union
for use as a reading-room and as classrooms.

There was a fairly persistent demand for the erection
of a clock on the Town Hall. For instance in March 1842
188 inhabitants, and in May 1845 160 inhabitants signed a
petition to that effect. But on both occasions the Commissioners replied that the state of the finances at the time did
not justify the required outlay. Six years later the idea
met with more success. A committee recommended that
it would be a great public convenience to have a public
clock in a prominent situation and recommended 'a
Tower over the north entrance of the Town Hall' for the
purpose. The Surveyor was instructed to prepare plans
and estimates, but no action seems ever to have been
taken.

In January 1855 the Commissioners agreed to allow
the Quarter Sessions of the new borough to be held
in the Town Hall, and the south room was fitted up
for the use of the grand jury.

After the new market was built tolls continued to
be let annually. In 1837 Henry Grymer and William
Brooker were appointed collectors of the tolls at a salary
of 30s. a week each. Brooker was also appointed weigher
at a salary of 18s. a week. In 1839 William Shopland the

elder and Isabella Shopland took over the collection, though Brooker remained weigher and, after 1844, collected the first tolls for 3s. a week. At the same time Jonas Levy rented the market tolls for £1,700 for one year. In the following year the collector was William Shopland the younger. Jonas Levy continued to rent the tolls for £1,730 in 1840, and £1,840 in 1841, for £1,750 in 1842, and for £1,1610 in 1843. The next year the tolls were kept in hand by the Commissioners. Robert Rutherford was appointed collector of them. The commission subsequently fixed was four per cent. on the first £1,500 and slightly less thereafter. By this method the tolls fetched £2,086 14s. 4d., less expenses of £126 9s. 5d. The arrangement was therefore continued. But during the next eight years the receipts gradually dwindled to £1,627 14s. 1d. in 1853. The collector's commission fell in proportion to £75, which even the Commissioners agreed was insufficient remuneration. The basis of his commission was therefore changed to a uniform rate of six per cent., which was calculated to produce a total commission of about £100 a year. The decline in the amount of the market tolls was attributed to the failure of the potato crop and to the large quantity of fruit and vegetables which were brought to the town by rail and delivered direct to shops instead of being taken by country people in carts direct to the market. In other words the rural England of the pre-industrial age was beginning to disappear.

Lighting

An agreement to light the town with gas had only been made a few months before the 1825 Act came into force. The contract with Gatton, Lashmar and Vallance involving 463 lamps was signed in the following August. In the interim period, oil lamps still had to be used, and Thomas Harman continued to be paid a guinea a week to look after them. The company was evidently dilatory in instal-ling the lights, and in June 1826 it was decided to prosecute .the contractors if they did not fulfil their contract. In December the company reported that they were unable to light with gas some of the streets in the outskirts of the town and were allowed to substitute oil lamps for gas in those streets, but no further money was to be paid to them until they had complied fully with the terms of their contract. When matters were working smoothly in 1827 Henry Solomon was appointed inspector of gas lights, in addition to his other duties, at the extra salary of £10 a year.

In the autumn of 1827 Thomas Read Kemp enquired whether the Commissioners would be prepared to extend the gas lighting to Kemp Town. The Commissioners agreed to provide 36 lamps in Kemp Town and six lamps along Marine Parade between Royal Crescent and Kemp Town in return for a special rate to be fixed by them and and payable on all the 105 houses in Kemp Town until these became assessable to the poor-rate.

The contract with the Brighton and Hove Gas Company to light the town ran out in 1839, and the Commissioners gave notice in May, under the terms of the contract, they would acquire the lamps and apparatus that had hitherto been the property of the company. The price subsequently agreed was £1,457 18s. 1d. At the same time a Bill was being promoted in Parliament for the incorporation of the General Gas Light and Coke Company. The Commissioners thought that certain amendments to this Bill were desirable and instructed their Clerk to attend the Committee stages in both Houses to this end. The Commissioners proceeded to consult other towns concerning the conditions under which these were lighted. Following this they negotiated with the two companies (the Brighton Incorporated Gas Light and Coke Company and the Brighton and Hove General Gas Company) and entered into contracts with them to light the east and west districts of the town in winter from one hour after sunset to one and a half hours before sunrise, and in summer from one and a half hours after sunset until two hours before sunrise, at the price of £2 7s. 6d. per light of two and a half cubic feet per year, and of £4 3s. 9d. per light of five cubic feet. At the option of the Commissioners the use of half the lights could be discontinued for a period of 10 weeks at the height of summer for a discount of 4s. 6d. per light.

In April 1846 a committee of the Commissioners reported that these contracts, which were for 14 years, could be broken at the end of seven years. After enquiries at other towns they had come to the conclusion that gas could be supplied more cheaply and that, if they built their own gas works and supplied individual consumers at the same rate as the companies were then charging, the Commissioners would make sufficient profit to enable them to light the streets without cost to themselves. This led to negotiations with both companies and they both eventually agreed to light the streets from sunrise to sunset, an average of 12 hours a day instead of nine, for £4 a year per lamp and to reduce their rate for supplying private consumers from 9s. to 7s. per thousand cubic feet until June 1847 and thereafter to six shillings. Both contracts were signed on this basis.

An interesting entry occurred in the minutes of 20 December 1848. Thomas Willson, architect, of 22 Grand Parade wrote to the Clerk to draw the attention of the Commissioners to the valuable discovery of electric light. 'As soon as I am favored with the apparatus and fittings for maintaining this extraordinary light I shall hope to render it available for the gratification of the Inhabitants of the Town of Brighton'. The letter was entered in the minutes, but nothing further seems to have been heard of him.

In 1853 it became possible to break the gas contracts and the Commissioners informed both companies that they proposed to do so on 25 December.

New contracts were negotiated for another 14 years. The price per lamp remained at £4 a year and the hours for which they were lit were unaltered. But the rate for private consumers was reduced from 6s. to 5s. per thousand cubic feet. In 1854 £3,001 5s. 2d. was spent on lighting the town.

Scavenging and Drainage

Keeping the streets in reasonable condition involved two, later three, processes: watering the roads, scavenging and later collecting the ashes. Only certain selected roads in the centre of the town were watered, and on the inhabitants of them was levied a special rate which varied from 1s. to 1s. 6d. in the pound per year. At first John North was paid £27 10s. a year, apparently to water all the chosen streets, but in April 1826 the contracts were split into two areas. North was paid £1 18s. a day for the eastern district, and James Phippen £2 12s. 6d. a day for the western. In May 1828 three districts are mentioned: William Sharpe being paid £1 19s. a day for the eastern, John North £2 6s. for the western, and Charles Bishop £1 12s. for the northern. In 1837 the Water Company was paid £3 a day and in 1839 John Hill £7 a day. His contract was discontinued after a year as he did not have sufficient equipment. By 1840 the amount paid to the contractors, Sharp and Shallcross, had risen to £9 7s. 6d. a day for four months. In 1842 John Still, Henry Stringer and Charles Still submitted the lowest tender of £8 14s. a day.

The contracts for scavenging the town ran out in the summer of 1826. The Commissioners then decided to separate the collection of ashes from the actual scavenging. They entered into a contract with the Directors and Guardians of the Poor for the scavenging to be done by the paupers of the parish for £400 a year. Arrangements were made for the deposit of night soil 'in the bottom west of the Bear Inn on the Lewes Road' between midnight and 4 a.m.

Scavenging by the poor did not prove satisfactory to either party and, as the Directors and Guardians demanded an extra £100 a year for the renewal of the contract in 1827, the Commissioners accepted a contract from Robert Jackson to do the work for £399 a year, though this, too, only lasted for one year.

When the collection of ashes was separated, this collection was entrusted to Carter Thunder who had been superintending the work since 1822. He had at first been paid on a commission basis, but henceforward seems to have been allowed to make what money he could out of it by re-selling the ashes. In February 1831 it was decided to put up to auction the right to collect ashes for three years, together with the right to collect the coal-duty for one year. Jonathan Streeter and Charles Ever paid £4,600 for the latter in 1831, and A. J. Lamprell £4,700 in 1832. But it proved impossible to sell the right of collecting ashes as Carter Thunder had not only refused to give up his rights but, strictly against the Commissioners' instructions, had seen to it that the brick-makers of the district had previously been supplied with seven hundred pounds' worth of ashes, with the result that no bids were received for the right of collection. Thunder was dismissed from his office.

The Directors and Guardians of the Poor must have continued to employ the parish paupers to scavenge the streets for a few more years, as in September 1835 they gave notice of their intention to end the contract. They were asked to continue, but declined to do so beyond 24 July 1836. In the following January they did agree to employ the poor in cleaning snow from the streets. Private tenders for the scavenging were then incited, and the contract for one year was given to John Hill for £639.

In March 1838 the Commissioners recorded that it would be highly desirable for a general system of drainage to be adopted for the whole town. But nothing seems to have been done about it. In fact, in March 1840 the Directors of the Chain Pier wrote to complain about the drains from the houses in Marine Parade between Old Steine and Rock Gardens discharging onto the beach above high water mark, instead of into the sea below low water mark, as had been agreed two years previously. The Commissioners agreed to remedy this defect.

After eight years of direct collection of ashes by the Surveyor this was again put out to tender in 1840. John North agreed to collect and deliver them to the Commissioners' depots for 1s. 11½d. per cartload. In the following year his tender was only 1s. 5¾d. a cartload. Four months later he also agreed to scavenge the town for three years for £335 a year.

In April 1842 Charles Hill and James Longhurst submitted the lowest tender for collecting ashes, namely 1s. 4d. per load. Their sureties were not however accepted. So the contract was re-advertised. This time John Hill made a tender to collect the ashes for three years for 1s. 1d. a load, which was accepted. But his performance was unsatisfactory, and six months later the Commissioners declared that John Hill had himself rendered the contract void. On being challenged he claimed that the contract price was so low that he made a loss on it. The Commissioners replied that the wages he paid were such that his employees were driven to ask for tips. They condemned this objectionable practice and called on Hill's sureties to perform the contract.

At almost the same time (March 1843) the question of scavenging the streets gave trouble again. A committee reported that no-one could be expected to clean the streets of so large a town as Brighton properly for £335 a year, which was what John North was being paid. They therefore gave him his discharge. The Directors and Guardians of the Poor were not this time interested in employing the poor of the parish on the job. The Commissioners therefore had no option but to employ direct labour. This they appear to have done.

In July 1849 occurs the curious entry of the Directors and Guardians of the Poor writing at the instigation of the medical officers of the parish to complain that the back streets, courts and alleys of the town were insufficiently scavenged and watered. The Commissioners undertook to remedy this defect.

There was no further mention of scavenging in the minutes until 1854. The collection of ashes was then costing £112 a week, or £6,000 a year. So it was decided to return to the practice of putting up to auction the right of scavenging the town and of collecting the ashes. Bids were accepted from John North and C. F. C. Barnes to scavenge for one year the first, second, third, fifth and sixth districts for £380, £443, £477, £420 and £430 respectively, and from Samuel Matthews to do the same for the fourth district for £525. The following year, after incorporation had divided the town into six wards tenders were accepted from Shallcross and Packham for four wards for the total of £1,245 and from John and Henry Still for the remaining two wards for £681. This represented a saving of £749 on the preceding year. At the same time the Commissioners considered the possibility of installing their own equipment for watering the roads. But the estimate for doing this amounted to £6,469 1s. 6d., plus £773 10s. in annual maintenance. They therefore agreed to accept from the newly-formed Brighton, Hove and Preston Constant Service Water Works Company an offer to water the roads on the same terms as the old company had provided, namely £780 a year, plus £11 12s. 9d. per acre for any new streets added to the list of those that were to be watered. But this decision seems not to have been implemented because two months later it was resolved to accept the tenders of John North and C. F. C. Barnes to water the streets at the cost of 5s. 11d. per day and 3s. per half day. A dispute with the old Water Company ensued in which the company claimed £391 15s. 7d. from the Commissioners. The County Court judge, William Furner, awarded them only £190 18s. 7d., plus half the cost of his award, amounting to £20 13s.

In 1847 the subject of main drainage came before the Commissioners for the first time when Parliament was considering the Health of Towns Bill on the subject. The surveyor, Richard Allen Stickney, was instructed to investigate the position in the original old town and to prepare a drainage scheme for it. He found that the

Commissioners had no power to compel the insertion
of private drains and that, when public sewers existed,
the owners of adjoining houses had not always taken
advantage of them to connect their houses with them.
But as Parliament was about to legislate on the subject
he recommended that, as in the case of Lancaster and
Liverpool, no steps towards compulsion should be taken
until a full survey of the existing drainage in the whole
town had been completed. In January 1848 he was
authorised to carry out such a survey. This cost
£1,566 15s. In April 1849 the General Board of Health,
acting under the newly-passed Act, appointed an inspector
named Edward Cresy to report on Brighton's drainage.
When he did so in November the Commissioners recommended that the Public Health Act, 1848, should be
adopted for Brighton but that its procedures should
be amalgamated with those of the local Act and administered by a single body of 50 persons with the qualification of real or personal estate to the value of £1,000 or rateable to the poor-rate to the amount of at least £30 a year.

No further step was taken until November 1850, when
the surveyor was instructed to prepare an estimate for a
drainage system in the central district. This came to
£36,000 for 28 miles of piping. At the same time the
Electric Telegraph Company was given permission to
lay pipes for their wires below the roads from the railway
station to their proposed office in Old Steine.

In May 1852 the main sewer was continued along
Marine Parade to connect with Kemp Town, and from
Chichester Terrace to the eastern boundary of the parish
in 1854. In November of that year the surveyor presented
an estimate for a complete system of drainage for the
town amounting to £37,760 18s. But in view of the
approaching transfer of powers to the Town Council the
Commissioners decided not to authorise its execution.

Road Improvements

Beside the construction of a new market and Town Hall
there were other improvements which the Commissioners

of 1825 wished to carry out. Kemp Town was being built and a new groyne was required to the south of it which would cost £1,400. Thomas Read Kemp advanced £600 in July 1825 and the Commissioners agreed to pay the balance. Their next task was to widen Pool Lane (now Pool Valley) and to improve the approach to the Palace (now Pavilion Buildings). In June 1826 it was decided to build a sea wall from Middle Street to Mahomed's Baths (where the *Queen's* hotel now stands) with arches in this to house the boats that had formerly lain on the beach, but the owners of each house along what was then called East Cliff would be responsible for making the arch opposite his house. Six months later it was proposed to form a road from Marine Parade to the west side of Old Steine along the north of the *York* hotel, though this was not actually done until 1831. The improvements in Pool Lane and East Cliff led to the construction of what came to be called Grand Junction Road to the south of the *Albion* hotel to avoid the use of the narrow road to the north of the baths (now King's Road). When the decision was made in March 1827 to build this road, George Vallance protested against this in the minutes as being beyond the powers of the Commissioners. Some of the fishermen also opposed the plan because it involved removing some of their capstans from the beach, but their protests were disregarded and the road was opened in 1829.

In September 1830 the Commissioners contracted with William Lambert to erect a wall in front of Marine Parade from New Steine to Royal Crescent and in December to form a cattle market at the north end of the workhouse garden in Church Hill (now Dyke Road).

In July 1832 all public works were suspended on account of 'the present state of the funds', but two months later the Directors and Guardians of the Poor requested the Commissioners to employ the paupers of the town in necessary improvements. The Commissioners agreed to do so for the purpose of finishing the sea wall from New Steine to Royal Crescent at the rate of 10s. per square foot. This work lasted until June 1833, when the paupers obtained other work.

The next work of any public importance was in Old Steine. This open space still retained a somewhat rural atmosphere since a certain Mr. Myrtle had been allowed to graze his sheep on it from September 1826 until April 1827 for a fee of £20.

Early in 1834 a request was made by some inhabitants for a road to be made across the enclosure from east to west. The Commissioners agreed to make not only this road but also a principal approach to the town from the north of the Steine. These plans were approved by the Vestry on 27 March 1834, but they did not find favour with other inhabitants, and Messrs. Colbatch and Upperton gave notice of their intention of applying for an injunction against the roads. John Colbatch, who owned the *Albion* hotel, and Henry James in fact filed a Bill in Chancery against the trustees of the Steine. What happened to this Bill is not recorded because in fact the road across the Steine was made that year.

In the next year it was agreed to employ a man to keep order in the Steine. In 1838 at the request of the Commissioners, Colonel Barton, the Commanding Officer of the newly-arrived regiment of the 12th Lancers, agreed that the regimental band should play on the site on Tuesdays and Thursdays.

Seven years later John Cordy Burrows of 46 Old Steine obtained permission from the Commissioners to erect a fountain in the Steine south of the new road. This was designed by Amon Henry Wilds and sculptured by one Pepper. It cost £989 16s. 7d., plus £114 7s. 6d. for its erection. Of this, £961 11s. was raised by public subscription, and the balance was presumably paid by Cordy Burrows himself. It was inaugurated on 24 May 1846, the Queen's birthday and thus called the Victoria fountain. A special piece of music named the Fountain Quadrilles was composed for the occasion by the local musician, Charles Coote, a copy of which is still in the

Public Library. At the same time both parts of the Steine, which had previously been only a grass enclosure, were planted with trees.

No sooner had the sea wall from New Steine to Royal Crescent been started than the Commissioners realised that this would have to be extended to Kemp Town. The decision to do this was taken in January 1835. The proprietors of Kemp Town, acting through William Hallett, agreed to provide the material and labour required to back up this wall, which would then connect with the esplanades that the proprietors were themselves building below Kemp Town at that time. Two thousand seven hundred pounds in private subscriptions were raised among them. Work proceeded satisfactorily until 1838, when the contractor, William Lambert, was held up for want of materials. The private subscriptions had run out. The Kemp Town proprietors offered a further sum of £800 to complete their obligations, which was recognised to be about half what remained to be spent. The Commissioners accepted this in view of the large sum which the proprietors had already spent, on condition that a site was also provided from which the necessary materials could be taken.

A strange entry occurs in the minutes of 21 September 1836. The Vicar of Brighton, the Rev. H. M. Wagner, had recently built himself a new vicarage near Montpelier Road to the design of George Cheeseman. The old vicarage in Nile Street, which had been built by the Rev. Thomas Hudson[1] in 1790 on the site of the Prior's lodgings of St. Bartholomew's chantry or grange, had been acquired by a Quaker named Isaac Bass, who was a Commissioner. He offered to convey the old vicarage to the Commissioners and to effect an exchange of land with them in order that Market Street could be widened and a new approach made from Ship Street to the Town Hall, at the same time converting Nile Street into a pedestrian way. The Commissioners made the curious reply that they saw

---

1. Thomas Hudson was Vicar of Brighton from 1789 to 1804.

'no reason to interfere in the proposed plan of Mr. Bass
for the formation of a street from Ship Street to the Town
Hall further than they may be called upon by the powers
vested in them by the act'. Many subsequent communications took place between the Commissioners and Isaac
Bass concerning the removal of the wall in front of the
old vicarage in order to widen the road, but no agreement
was ever reached, though the house itself was demolished
in 1837. The Commissioners continued to negotiate with
Isaac Bass on a somewhat similar basis, as in 1842 they
agreed to pay him £800 to take down three houses in
Black Lion Street in order to make a road 30 feet wide
across their site to connect Black Lion Street with Ship
Street. This was the west half of Prince Albert Street.[1]

The year 1841 brought the opening of the railway
from London. The Commissioners therefore approved
a plan prepared by Thomas Cooper for the creation of
what is now Queen's Road and the widening of the west
end of the north side of North Street by the demolition
of courts known as Petty France and Durham that lay
between North Street and Air Street. This seems to have
been a very insanitary part of the town for as late as 1846
a slaughterhouse in Air Street gave rise to the most lurid
description of a public nuisance arising from its condition. The cost of acquiring the necessary land for the
road widening was £2,500. As the result of the steps
taken by Thomas Cooper in connection with this widening
a debenture of £1,000 was issued to him. The Directors
of the London and Brighton Railway gave £2,000 towards
the cost of the road, and three years later agreed to be
responsible for the expense of a bridge over Trafalgar
Street to complete the connection of Queen's Road with
the station. The Commissioners undertook to finish the
road from Gloucester Lane (now Gloucester Road) as far
as the bridge.

1. Isaac Bass also gave land to the town for the creation of what
was then called East Street Avenue, or the direct access southwards
from East Street to the Front.

No improvement scheme of any great importance seems to have been carried out after this until January 1852, when the surveyor produced an estimate for widening King's Road between West Street and Mahomed's Baths. The total cost of this, arranged in three sections, was £7,843. The Commissioners decided to embark upon the west and centre sections stretching from West Street to Ship Street at a cost of £5,076.

Planning

The planning powers given to the Town Commissioners were somewhat widened by the Act of 1825. After that date perhaps the majority of entries in the minutes relate to planning matters. As formerly, the prevention of nuisances in the streets was a constant occurrence. Equally often it was a question of stopping bow windows from projecting further into the street than was permitted, or securing that houses were built with party walls. For instance, in September 1827 the Clerk was instructed to institute proceedings against any person who began to erect houses or altered the exterior of existing houses without giving notice of their intentions. The majority of these entries are routine items of little interest. But a few are worth recording.

For instance, in September 1827 Mrs. Fitzherbert requested that the 'boulder pitching' in Steine Lane, adjoining her house, should be taken up and the surface 'Mac'Adamised'. The Commissioners refused the request on the grounds that they had very recently improved the lane at Mrs. Fitzherbert's request. However, she returned to the charge by offering to pay for the work suggested, and on this basis the Commissioners agreed to have the work carried out.

A year later Lord Northland was permitted to erect a temporary passage between the drawing-room windows of nos. 48 and 49 Marine Parade during his Lordship's occupation of both houses.

In 1830 Thomas Attree, the Clerk to the Vestry, built his house in Queen's Park, originally called Brighton Park.

This was intended to be the first of a series rather in the style of Calverley Park, Tunbridge Wells. At his own expense he laid out roads right round the Park. The Commissioners agreed to lower the surface of Egremont Place in order to connect with the new roads that Thomas Attree was then making, which are now called West Drive and Park Hill. They contributed the sum of £50 to Attree so that he could have the work done.

In March 1831 William IV was granted permission to 'build the intended Entrance Gateway to His Majesty's Palace in a line as per plan now produced'. This was the North Gate, designed by Joseph Good, Nash's successor, and was completed the next year. The new pavement in front of the gateway was paid for by the King.

Police

The Act of 1810 had empowered the Commissioners to appoint constables or watchmen, and the Commissioners had in fact done so since 1821. The Act of 1825 continued this power. But one curious entry occures in the minutes of 15 August 1826. It was recorded that it was 'highly necessary to appoint three Officers as a Police' but that the Commissioners 'have no power to pay the present Police and that the salaries paid to them be discontinued at Easter next'. A month later a committee recommended the appointment of a silent patrol instead of watchmen crying the hours of the night, and that the numbers of Beadles be reduced from four to two, plus two Criers who would also act as Beadles.

This seems, however, to have been only legalising the existing situation. Samuel Simes, who was already acting as night constable, was re-engaged at a salary of 25s. a week, likewise James Feldwick as his assistant. Fourteen permanent watchmen were engaged at 14s. a week or 2s. a night for the 14 districts into which the town had already been divided, plus six supernumeraries, of whom two were employed each night to collect tickets from the watchmen to ensure that these were at their posts. But they were still instructed to call the hours of the night. All the watchmen were provided with greatcoats, bludgeons and rattles. The Beadles were paid 18s. a week.

In July 1827 the Vestry asked the Commissioners to 'appoint Police Officers at Salaries as heretofore to be paid out of consolidated rates . . . under the sole control of the Magistrates'. Four men were named as 'Officers of the Commissioners to keep the Peace of the Town'. But six months later it was recorded that this resolution was illegal as the people concerned were 'subject to other authority' and therefore incapable of carrying out the Commissioners' orders. Neither had they accepted the appointment. Nevertheless, it was thought advisable to appoint four persons 'as special watchmen to keep and preserve the Peace of the Town'. This seems to have been an attempt to follow the lead then being set by the Government in establishing a proper police force who were more efficient than ordinary night watchmen. But it proved a very controversial measure. Correspondence with the Home Secretary, Sir Robert Peel, followed in which the Commissioners pointed out that they had been prepared to appoint four police officers but had not done so because they considered that they already had efficient arrangements for keeping the peace. But they ended the letter by saying that 'a paid Police is not only unnecessary but the System is degrading to the character and feelings of the Town'.

Nevertheless the four policemen who had been named in the original resolution were in fact appointed on 6 August 1828, out of 42 people who volunteered for the post. At the same time the wages of the existing night watchmen were increased from 2s. to 2s. 6d. a night. When the new policemen took up their duties in April 1829 the principal officers of the Commissioners were also sworn in as special constables. In September 1829 at the request of the proprietors of Kemp Town, three watchmen and one beadle were appointed for that area, to be paid by the proprietors themselves.

When the controversy had been settled the whole police system was reorganised on the basis of the system recently established in London. William Pilbeam, who was one of the newly-appointed special watchmen, was given the position of Chief Officer of the Police at a salary of £120 a year. The other three men, whose duties had hitherto consisted principally of apprehending felons, were appointed superintendents of districts at £90 a year. Samuel Simes remained night constable at 25s. a week and presided nightly at the Town Hall. The body of the force comprised 14 constables who paraded by night, and seven by day. In addition one man operated in Kemp Town, who was paid by the Kemp Town proprietors. Each constable was provided with a baton and rattle, but they were instructed not to call the hours of the night as hitherto. This practice, which had been instituted as a precaution against fire and for the protection of lives, was thought to have become a drawback and almost a forewarning to housebreakers. The watch-boxes in the streets were removed. But when these regulations were adopted Thomas Mills entered a protest in the minutes to the effect that the new method of watching the town would not be so effective as the previous system, particularly in the early discovery of accidents by fire, and would cost £500 a year more. The High Constable, J. G. Sarel, however, represented to the Commissioners that it would be advisable to supplement the paid force by a body of special constables, and in November 1830 it was decided to enrol such.

In February 1832 James Feldwick who had been Samuel Sime's principal assistant as night constable since 1821, fell ill and was thought unlikely to recover. Henry Solomon, who was already acting as superintendent of hackney carriages, bathing-machines and pleasure boats, superintendent of nuisances, and inspector of gas lights, as well as superintending the watering of the roads, for which he was given the composite salary of £85 a year, was appointed Chief Officer of Police to act jointly with William Pilbeam at the salary of £120 a year, but was to continue to perform all the duties of his other offices as well.

In 1836 a committee found the then police service highly defective, and the existing policemen were discharged. William Pilbeam had been ill for a long period previously, and therefore Henry Solomon was appointed sole Chief Officer at the same salary of £120 a year. He remained Chief Constable until he was murdered. James Thoburn and John Wise were engaged as Superintendents at £90 a year. A night constable at £70 a year, three inspectors at 21s. a week, and 24 watchmen at 18s. a completed the force. The men were divided into three sections, of which two worked by night and one by day in rotation. In Henry Solomon's first monthly report to the Commissioners the only crimes to occur were robberies of lead. Seven people were apprehended for these, three committed to trial and two convicted and sentenced to transportation for 14 years. A month later he mentioned that all the police had been told not to solicit Christmas boxes, but they had nevertheless done so. A committee of the Commissioners investigated the matter and found that the three inspectors (Holman, Cooke and Cackett) had organised a systematic house-to-house collection. The whole force that was then off duty had assembled at the *Pelham Arms,* Great Russell Street, on the morning of 30 December, where they breakfasted and had received their share of the collection amounting to £1 11s. each. As a result, the three inspectors were discharged. So also was a poor watchman named Richard Gates. His offence was that he had allowed a man to escape who had been given into his charge by one of the sentinels at the Palace. This man was charged with having 'made a proposition of a disgusting nature to the said sentinel'.

In November 1837 Henry Solomon asked for a rise in salary. In view of his length of service and efficiency he was granted £30 a year, but this 'should not be considered a precedent on the appointment of a new Officer'. However, his salary was again increased by £50 a year in 1840. Despite a general ruling in 1834 that no constable should be paid when off duty, wages were frequently granted to individual members of the force for short periods of illness—an unusual provision for the period. However, in 1836 John Moody, who was presumably a policeman, asked for superannuation in view of long service. The Commissioners replied that they had no powers to grant such. In 1841 the sum of £25 was voted to John Cordy Burrows for the medical inspection of the police, which he had carried out gratuitously during the past two years.

In 1840 a Bill for the establishment of county and district constables came before Parliament. Both the Commissioners and the Vestry petitioned for exemption from it for Brighton as a town of 50,000 inhabitants, as they had been from a previous Bill of the year before, under a clause which disallowed its application to towns of 10,000 inhabitants and upwards.

In June 1841 a curious incident occurred, though it was not reported in the minutes until April 1842. During the Lewes elections, about 18 voters from that borough were secluded in the *Globe* inn in Edward Street on the instructions of Messrs. Harford and Elphinstone, apparently acting on behalf of the whig party to prevent them being bribed to vote for the tory candidates. The publicans, father and son named Streeter, were friends of Superintendent Jesse Maynard of the Brighton police who was not only himself present for several nights during the election, in the bar at the *Globe*, but also stationed police constable John Knight there to see that the electors were not taken away. John Knight gave evidence before the House of Commons concerning the election, and as a result of the incident Superintendent Maynard was dismissed from the Brighton police and George White appointed in his place.

In August 1842 another odd incident was recorded. Seargeant Simpson of the Barracks lost five sovereigns at the thimble table during the races, but as betting was contrary to military regulations, when the matter came to the ears of the officers of the Barracks Sergeant Simpson invented the story that he had been robbed. With the connivance of several comrades, he claimed to identify the thief and gave him in charge to Superintendent Elme. He then alleged that the superintendent recommended him to settle the matter by accepting two sovereigns. At the hearing the chairman of the Magistrates animadverted adversely on the police, but with the assistance of the adjutant at the barracks, Captain Deacon, the Commissioners were able to establish the truth and clear the superintendent.

The relations of the Magistrates and the Commissioners through the police remained consistently bad. In February 1845 a dispute took place between a certain Miss Penfold of 22 Preston Street and a shoemaker named John Day, concerning a pair of shoes made for her which she said did not fit. A second and third pair were made and not paid for, though Miss Penfold had said that the second pair would do for her maid. When the shoemaker came to demand payment for at least the third pair she summoned Constable George Packham. The constable refused to give any opinion as to whether or not the shoes fitted, and after a quarter of an hour Miss Penfold agreed to pay 6s. for the shoes, instead of 8s. which had been demanded. Packham then left without any request having made to turn the shoemaker out of the house. The lady, on the advice of John Colbatch, who was Clerk to the Magistrates, brought a summons against Packham for neglect of duty. He was fined £1 by the Magistrates. The Commissioners appealed to Quarter Sessions, but expressed the view that 'the existence of a good understanding and cordial co-operation with all the constituted authorities acting in this Town' was most desirable, and hoped that all possible measures would be adopted 'to prevent a disarrangement of such understanding'. The appeal was not allowed, but in the meantime George Packham was dismissed for other misconduct.

An addition of 10 men was made to the police in April 1845. At about this time a statement occurred in the press to the effect that many burglaries in Sussex remained undetected because the burglars escaped into

Brighton, where the stolen goods were never recovered, and that this was due to jealousy between the East Sussex constabulary and the Brighton police. The Chief Constable of East Sussex, Captain H. F. Mackay, made a report repudiating this allegation, saying that his men had always carried out the fullest co-operation with the Brighton police. Nevertheless the Lewes Magistrates put on record their view that this report showed the Brighton police to have been 'extremely inefficient in the detection of Crime'.

The Brighton Commissioners were most indignant about this. A committee interviewed Captain Mackay, who said that he had had no intention in his report of making allegations against the Brighton police. From the exposed position of the town, opening onto the downs, it was impossible to prevent stolen property being brought into Brighton, but that the recent increase in the number of Brighton police would probably make this practice more difficult. The Commissioners therefore wrote to the clerk of the peace for East Sussex expressing the pain which they felt at receiving a communication from the Lewes Magistrates which they considered to be quite unjustified. The Lewes Magistrates were not in the least mollified and went on to recommend that the Brighton police be placed under Captain Mackay.

From this recommendation the Brighton Magistrates unanimously dissented. But the Commissioners were really roused. They expressed the view that 'there can be but one feeling pervading all classes of the inhabitants of Brighton' and decided to prepare a memorial to be signed by the inhabitants, praying the Lewes Magistrates 'not to interfere with the Police management of this Town, since any interference with the municipal regulations of this Town by persons nor resident or proceeding from any authority nor identified with it would be highly prejudicial to its [Brighton's] prosperity'. There the matter rested.

In November 1846 the Chief Constable, Thomas Hayter Chase, recommended an increase of 20 men in the police owing to the current growth of Brighton. The almost exactly comparable town of Bath had a total of 100 policemen, which was double the number employed in Brighton. He also recommended that the rates of pay be varied to rise from 16s. to 18s. and £1 on promotion, instead of a fixed rate of 18s., and that inspectors be paid 25s. instead of 21s., to encourage good men to accept responsibility. The police committee accepted the recommendation but the Commissioners, as usual, were reluctant to increase their expenditure. However, in June 1846, perhaps influenced by a number of recent evening robberies, they agreed to the addition of one superintendent and 10 constables. Simultaneously a claim was made by the existing men for an increase of wages on the grounds of 'the present high price of provisions'. Though the police committee felt that this increase 'applied to all persons in the employment of the Commissioners', the Commissioners as a whole were rather more discerning. In fact they went further than the Chief Constable had suggested and agreed to pay a minimum wage of 20s. a week, rising to a maximum of 24s. for good conduct and long service, and 30s. for inspectors. Moreover, they recommended the establishment of a superannuation fund, to which constables should contribute 6d. a week and inspectors one shilling. They also confirmed that sick pay, when applied for, were almost invariably granted. These provisions were most unusual at the time.

In December 1851 a complaint was made by the inhabitants of the north part of the town that their area was insufficiently policed. The police committee thought that the total number of constables should be increased. But no action was taken other than to refer the complaint to the Chief Constable.

In 1852 the police comprised 50 constables and 10 officers. Their cost for the year was £4,096 5s. When Superintendent White was promoted to be Chief Constable in December he was not replaced as a superintendent, but an increase in salary was given to his two colleagues, Superintendents Crowhurst and Barnden who had been in office since 1844 and 1847 respectively. Henceforward they were to receive £130, instead of £110, and the inspector of hackney carriages, James Terry, £91. In future in the absence of the Chief Constable and the superintendents one of the first-class constables was to be placed in charge at the Town Hall.

In March 1854 the question of amalgamation of the town and country police again came under consideration by the Government. The Commissioners resolved that they were strongly opposed to this measure as being 'an unjustifiable interference with local self government, its privileges and independence'.

A few months later the Chief Constable was authorised to release a quantity of lost or stolen property which had accumulated over a long period of time at the Town Hall to the people who had found it or otherwise as he thought fit.

At the incorporation of the town the Borough took over the organisation of the police and the Commissioners transferred to the new authority all the uniforms, money and other assets that had been under their control. But no appointment was given by the Borough to the former night constable, James Thoburn, who had been incapacitated from carrying out his duties for some years on account of 'age, infirmities and injuries received in the public service'. As he had been a policeman for 39 years the Commissioners granted him a pension of 20s. a week out of the superannuation fund.

The Coal Duty

The Act of 1825 empowered the Commissioners, as had the Acts of 1773 and 1810, to levy a duty of up to 3s. a chaldron or 2s. 6d. a ton on all coal brought into Brighton by sea or land. After the town rates, this duty was in fact the principal source of revenue to the Commissioners. The Coal Meter who actually weighed the coal at the time of the passing of the Act was John Lucas, but he died in June 1826. He was succeeded by Humphrey Downes, who was paid £25 a year, plus 4d. a chaldron for the amount of coal weighed. Humphrey Downes was still in office at the time of incorporation in 1854 and was the only one of the Commissioners' officers to serve for the whole 29 years of their existence. He is buried in the Extra Mural cemetery.

The office of collector of the coal duty had been given in 1822 to Carter Thunder who also superintended the collection of ashes, but he seems subsequently to have been replaced by someone named Hargreaves. In September 1826 Carter Thunder offered to collect the coal duty gratuitously. Hargreaves was therefore discharged, but this arrangement cannot have lasted long, and the right to collect the duty was subsequently put up to auction each year.

A new general Act which came into force on 6 January 1836 slightly altered the rate of the tax by reducing the sum due on coke to 1s. 2d. a chaldron. This Act caused the Commissioners at first to think that it would no longer be legal for them to let the right to collect the duty under the local Act of 1825. They therefore appointed Richard Patching as collector of coal duties at a commission of two and a half per cent., with three assistants at salaries of 20s., 10s. and 7s. a week respectively. The difficulty about letting must have been surmounted as a year later it was resolved to auction the right of collection for one year for not less than £5,000. The successful bidder was John Cheeseman, junior.

In 1837 Richard and John Patching paid £5,350 for the right to collect the duty and a similar sum again in 1838. John Patching incidentally often acted as chairman of the Commissioners. In 1839 the auction raised £5,250, in 1840 £5,320, and in 1841 £5,420. In 1842 it was decided to keep the collection in hand and the clerk was appointed collector. In April 1854 the general management committee recommended the appointment of a chief collector to the Commissioners who would be responsible for the collection not only of the coal duty but also of all other fees and rents due to the Commissioners. But this recommendation came too late in the

life of the Commissioners to be implemented and the
Clerk remained responsible for coal duty collection until
their demise. The net returns of the duty during these
years were:—

	£	s.	d.		£	s.	d.
1842	5,811	14	7¼	1848	7,231	0	0
1843	5,901	16	8¼	1849	6,774	0	0
1844	6,235	15	7¾	1850	7,701	0	0
1845	6,602	13	5½	1851	7,450	0	0
1846	6,909	17	7	1852	8,082	0	0
1847	6,537	0	0	1853	7,858	0	0

In June 1854 a new note was struck. Some residents
of an unstated area of the town, including one Commissioner, had been obliged to apply for police protection
'against the inroads of crowds of poor starving persons
. . . in search of Cinders'. As a result the audit and finance
committee gave their attention to the matter of the coal
tax. They found it quite out of date, extensively evaded
and unjust both to people and places.

When the tax had first been imposed most of the
coal delivered in Brighton came by sea; the duty was
therefore easy to collect. By 1854 virtually all the supplies
came by land: if this was by rail then again collection was
easy, but if brought by road, wholesale evasion of the
tax took place. There was, moreover, the anomaly that
residents in Hove were exempt from it. If the duty was
retained the committee recommended that toll-bars and
weighbridges should be erected at the boundaries of the
town to prevent further evasion of the duty.

More important still were the social consequences of
the tax. The local Act had empowered the churchwardens
and Overseers of the Poor to grant the poor a 'drawback'
or remission of tax on up to two chaldrons a year. But no
such exemption was given, at least in recent years. The
committee therefore recommended the abolition of the
tax and its replacement by an increase in the general rate.
But if it was retained they suggested that 'drawbacks.
amounting to about £1,300 a year should be granted

to 'the industrious and poorer classes who are so numerous in the Town'—possibly 4,000 families occupying houses at £10 a year or less. If these steps were taken it might well reduce the revenue derived from the tax to about £2,000 a year. The committee had, however, little confidence that their advice would be taken since this tax had been one of the Committioner's principal sources of revenue since 1773. The committee's forecast proved perfectly correct: the tax was not abolished and in November, Thomas John Bolton and Elisha Ambler paid £8,250 for the right to collect the duty for another year. This was the last occasion before incorporation of the town on which the coal duty was let, but the tax was not abolished until 1887.

Miscellaneous Matters

Some entries in the minutes are of too miscellaneous a character to be considered under headings. For instance in July 1826 complaints were made by inhabitants of houses on the cliff about 'persons indecently exposing themselves while bathing'. This was said to prevent the inhabitants letting their houses and to annoy visitors walking along the cliff. The Commissioners therefore decided to provide 32 bathing-machines at four different places along the front and that two Beadles were to attend between 7 a.m. and 9 p.m. at the extremities of the beach to caution people against bathing other than from machines. One rather enlightened touch for the period was provided by the fact that two machines were to be supplied for those who could not pay the normal charge. These were to be painted a special colour and marked 'Bathing Machines for the use of the Poor'.

A curious entry occurs on 20 October 1826. The meeting having been irregularly called was dissolved without transacting any business, but two reports were entered in the minutes on the same page. One of these stated that John Colbatch, the owner of the *Albion* hotel and Clerk to the Magistrates, with whom the Commissioners had had difficult relations in the past, had enclosed with a wall a piece of land to the east of his hotel, including the Commissioners' rope vault, which he had sold to the Commissioners in 1824 for £150. But there is no mention of whether any enforcement action was taken against him.

In November 1826 the inhabitants of the Royal Colonnade complained 'of the State of Riot and alarm in which they are constantly kept by the great assemblage of Boys and other disorderly persons in the Colonnade every evening'—a very modern note. The Beadles were directed to attend and abate the nuisance.

In April 1827 the first steps were taken towards forming a fire service. The two existing engines were adapted so that they could be drawn by either horses or men. A third engine and a fire escape, which were previously the property of the Sussex County Fire Office, were procured from the Guardian Fire Office. A paid engineer was appointed at a salary of 20s. a week, plus fees of 5s. for each fire attended and 2s. 6d. per alarm. The other staff were assembled for the occasion when the fires occurred, though the three foremen were paid a retainer of one guinea a year. Each fireman received 6d. an hour when attending a fire, plus a bonus of 20s. to be divided between the crew of the first engine to throw water on the fire. They were provided with white leather hats, and the foreman also with canvas frocks. After a fire the engineer was instructed to assess his bill and proportion it between the various insurance companies for insured property and the churchwardens for uninsured property.

In 1835 the judges refused to hold the Assizes at Horsham as the Magistrates there declined either to repair the courthouse or to build another. Therefore Quarter Sessions were temporarily held at Lewes. But, as it was thought most inconvenient that the assizes should be at 'so very distant a place as Lewes', a petition was sent to the Privy Council by the Brighton Member, Captain Pechell, urging the claims of Brighton. A Vestry meeting supported this and the Commissioners offered the Town Hall free of charge for the Spring Assizes. Nothing came of this.

In December 1839 'in view of the late lamented accident' it was decided to provide a lifeboat for the benefit of those landing on the beach. A shed was duly erected for its reception a year later.

In November 1844 it was decided to lay out the Level or cricket ground with trees which the Earl of Chichester had offered to the town for the purpose.

By June 1850 the tunnel at Black Rock that had been built to take coal from ships to the gasworks had fallen in and was dangerous. The Commissioners ordered it to be blocked up at each end.

In May 1851 the Clerk reported that he had objected to certain proposed clauses in the Brunswick Square Amendment Bill which extended the authority of the Brunswick Square Commissioners to cover Adelaide Crescent. These mostly related to the right to take shingle from the beach or to deposit rubbish thereon.

A modern note occurs in the entry of the minutes for 4 June 1851. The hackney carriages in the town went on strike for several days, but it is not clear from the wording of the minutes whether this was because the Clerk on licensing day refused a licence to the proprietors of 38 cabs, or whether this refusal was a result of the strike. In either case the Commissioners ordered the 38 licences to be issued.

In March 1852 the Commissioners authorised A. H. Wilds to plant the road from the *Hanover Arms* inn to the racecourse with trees in accordance with a plan prepared by him. Charles Call and Thomas Wisden protested against this decision without success. As the result of this planting the road was subsequently named Elm Grove.

The Royal Pavilion

Queen Victoria visited Brighton for the last time in 1845. As early as August the clerk reported that from certain proceedings in Parliament it appeared to be the Government's intention to sell the Royal Pavilion, and the Commissioners appointed a committee to consider

what steps could be taken to avert the sale or disposal of
the palace. This committee interviewed the Chief
Commissioners of Woods and Forests, Lord Carlisle,
but did not report until June 1849. In the meanwhile
the Commissioners of Woods and Forests announced
their intention not only to sell the building but to
extinguish all rights of way over the grounds and to
open a road along the line of Great East Street northwards which had been closed at George IV's request when
he gave the town the site of New Road in order to take
the thoroughfare farther away from his windows. A Bill
was introduced into Parliament authorising the Commissioners of Woods and Forests to apply the proceeds
of sale in the repair of Buckingham Palace. This alarmed
the Brighton Commissioners, particularly the idea that the
lawns to the east and north of the Pavilion would be
built on. They instructed the committee to continue
negotiating for the prolongation of the existing restric-
tions and conditions of the land. The committee lost
no time in summoning a public meeting of the Vestry
which met on 27 June 1849. It resolved unanimously
that 'every means should be adopted by the Inhabitants
and the public Authorities in the Borough to prevent
such an injury—the demolition of the Pavilion—being
inflicted on the Town' in view of the fact that the
building was 'a Palace endeared to the affections and
loyal attachment of the Inhabitants from having been
from its earliest commencement erected under the
auspices of the great Patron of this Town, His Majesty
King George the fourth, when Prince Regent'. It was
thought that a means of opposing the sale might be
found in the contention that the original sale of parts of
the land to George IV had been subject to certain restric-
tions which would be nullified by re-sale. It was decided to
petition Parliament against the sale as 'an act of injustice
and injurious to the Town of Brighton'. Seven thousand
four hundred and six people signed the petition.

A deputation, accompanied by the two Members for
Brighton, Captain Pechell and Lord Alfred Hervey, waited

on Lord Carlisle. But at first the Government seemed unwilling to give up their Bill, which went to a second reading. This Bill would have empowered the Government, not only to demolish the Pavilion, but to sell the site for the building of houses. Thomas Cubitt was reported to have offered £100,000 for the property for this purpose. A petition of Brighton inhabitants against the sale was presented to the House of Commons by Captain Pechell, and the Bill was referred to a Select Committee, of which he and Lord Alfred Hervey were members. Before the Select Committee met, a further deputation had an interview with Lord Carlisle, at which the principle of sale to the town for £53,000 was agreed. The Bill was amended accordingly and received the Royal Assent on 1 August 1849.

Meanwhile at a further public meeting in Brighton on 27 July it was unanimously resolved that it was desirable for the Pavilion to be purchased by the inhabitants and a committee was appointed to treat with the Government for the purchase. The Vestry confirmed that the offer to sell for £53,000 should be accepted and appointed a committee of 14 people, of whom seven were Brighton Commissioners, in whose name a contract was made out. But at the same time the Brighton Commissioners resolved that they and not the Vestry were the only official body in existence which really had the power to effect a purchase and instructed their clerk, Lewis Slight, to execute this on their behalf. When the contract was received from the Commissioners of Woods and Forests, Lewis Slight, without consulting the Vestry, substituted his name for theirs on the document.

This characteristically high-handed action on his part gave his enemies, of whom there were many, and opponents of the purchase, the opportunity to come forward. At a meeting of the Vestry on 8 November, which lasted five hours, much opposition was expressed for the first time. No conclusion seems to have been reached, but when the opponents of the purchase demanded the requisition of another meeting on 1 December the parish officers declined to call one on the grounds that inhabitants had already made very plain their approval of the proposed purchase.

A meeting of the Vestry was however held on 20 December to approve the new draft Bill for the purchase of the Pavilion. At this Lewis Slight announced that he, on behalf of the Brighton Commissioners, had signed the contract for the purchase on the preceding day. So great was the animosity against Lewis Slight that, after a session of seven and a half hours an amendment was carried by a majority of 93 to 71 rejecting the purchase of the Pavilion. A poll of voters was demanded by George Faithful.[1] An unsuccessful attempt to prevent this was made on the grounds that Faithful had not paid his poor-rate at that date. The poll took place on 21 and 22 December. By the end of the first day's poll the opponents were leading by 555 votes to four hundred and eight. But the final result was 1,343 in favour of purchase and 1,307 against. A majority of 36 was a very small number for the conclusion of so momentous a matter.

The leader of the opposition to the purchase, John Colbatch, as well as being a Town Commissioner, was a solicitor, Clerk to the Magistrates, and proprietor of the *Albion* hotel. The leader of the party advocating the purchase was Dr. William King—a man of far greater distinction. He was born at Ipswich on 17 April 1786. After being Senior Wrangler at Cambridge he became a Fellow of Peterhouse, but moved to Brighton in 1823. He lived from 1828 to 1830 at 1 Regency Square (part of St. Albans House) and subsequently at 23 Montpelier Road. He was a strong advocate of the co-operative system and from 1828 to 1830 edited a journal, *The Co-operator*. In recognition of this support the Co-operative Society recently erected a tablet in his memory on his house in Regency Square. He also advised Lady Byron on improvements on her estate for the benefit of the poor. He was a

1. One of Brighton's first Members of Parliament, from 1833 to 1834.

Town Commissioner and the first president of the Medico-Chirurgical Society of Brighton and Sussex when this was founded in 1847. He died on 20 October 1865 and was buried in the cemetery of the old parish church at Hove.

The poll in December 1850 really ended all effective opposition though, when the new Bill was presented to Parliament, a further petition was submitted against it. But a petition in favour contained more than double the number of signatures. The Bill authorising the Commissioners to purchase the building therefore went through both Houses without opposition and received the Royal Assent on 17 May 1850 as the Brighton Improvement (Purchase of the Royal Pavilion and Grounds) Act. The total cost of the Act was £1,709 9s. 9d., of which £1,332 15s. 5d. amounted to the legal costs paid to the Commissioners' solicitors, Charles Cobby, and £89 19s. 8d. to Somers Clarke, the Clerk to the Vestry. William Furner, the first County Court Judge, and Haslar Hollist were appointed by the Vestry as auditors of the accounts. Though the idea of purchasing the Pavilion is said to have originated with Thomas Cooper, the main credit for its execution lies with the redoubtable Lewis Slight and his principal allies George Faithful and Dr. William King.

In June 1850 the public were admitted to the grounds of the Pavilion for the first time and seats were provided. The bye-laws subsequently drawn up prohibited the flying of kites, the throwing of balls, the shooting of arrows, the trundling of hoops, and the playing of any games. Some inhabitants subsequently requested that an entrance into the grounds should be made from New Road. The Commissioners rejected this request on the grounds that two lodges would be required and that it would probably involve the creation of a further entrance from Pavilion Parade with a thoroughfare between the two. The decision was confirmed by a Vestry meeting.

In September the expenditure of £4,500 was authorised to repair and fit up the 10 state rooms. In making a recommendation to this effect the Pavilion committee stated that they were 'guided by a desire to economise in every department [and] at the same time impressed with the great importance of doing everything in a manner worthy the Town'. They remained so divided in mind for about 100 years. The re-decoration was entrusted to Christopher Wren Kirk, who had done work on the building for William IV and Queen Victoria. It is interesting to note that, of the magnificent interior, only the ceilings were, in the then denuded condition of the building, 'in a perfect state and are data as to the style in which the fittings must be carried out'. They were cleaned and re-gilded. The walls were canvassed and papered 'in a style corresponding as far as practicable with the general character of the said ceilings'. 'Appropriate' chimney-pieces, chandeliers and looking-glasses were provided. Unfortunately, the municipal idea of appropriateness for chimney-pieces left much to be desired. Most of them are still there. The organ from the Town Hall was transferred to the music room. The sum of £873 4s. 3d. was spent on new furniture and moveable fittings. But in 1852 the Commissioners refused an offer from the Thames Plate Glass Company to sell them the two largest pieces of silvered glass in the world which had been exhibited at the Crystal Palace in 1851. These had cost over £1,000 to make, but were offered to the Commissioners for £525. The Commissioners proceeded to insure the Pavilion, but only for £15,000, though the purchase price had been £53,000.

As soon as the Commissioners drew up bye-laws for the use of the Pavilion a row developed with the Vestry about public access. The Commissioners suggested that free admission should be limited to the ratepayers of Brighton, with their families, on one Monday a month by ticket only. On all other weekdays the admission charge would be 6d. a head. The Vestry considered that free admission should be on at least two Mondays per month and that this should be for any member of the public, without tickets, but subject to the limitation of not more than 500 people being admitted at any one time. The Commissioners accepted the extension of two days a month, but insisted on the right being confined to rate-payers and by ticket only. As the Vestry still contended that the Pavilion Act specifically provided that the acquisition of the building was intended for the benefit of 'inhabitants and visitors' the Commissioners referred the bye-laws to counsel to settle. Counsel advised that it was not *ultra vires* to confine the free admission to rate-payers and even recommended that one Monday a month was sufficient as a free day. A special meeting of the Vestry was summoned for 4 September 1851 and seems eventually to have accepted the bye-laws as originally drafted by the Commissioners.

The social inauguration of the Pavilion in its new ownership came with a grand ball on 21 January 1851 which was attended by about 1,400 people. Thirty-five lady patronneses distributed the tickets costing 10s. 6d. each (one guinea on the day of the ball). The president of the 13 stewards was the Duke of Devonshire, who led the first quadrille with Lady Willoughby de Eresby. Dancing lasted until 4.30 a.m. next morning. A picture of the scene in the music room was painted by an artist named Penley which is chiefly of interest as showing what the room looked like without its original wall-hangings. A series of similar balls was held at the Pavilion during the year which realised a profit of £603 19s. 7d.

The first free assignment of the public rooms was made in February 1851 to Gavin E. Peacock and John Cordy Burrows for the purpose of holding a Fancy Fair for the benefit of the Brighton Dispensary Building Fund. This event raised £700.

From 1851 to 1853 the Brighton Artists, whose honorary secretary was F. H. Woolege, held an annual exhibition in the hall. A charge of 1s. was made for admission, which amounted to £201 10s. 10d. in the three years. This was used to purchase pictures to form the nucleus of a Brighton picture gallery. The artists whose pictures were purchased were G. B. Potts, R. H. Nibbs,

F. Earp, G. Earp senior, H. Earp, J. Leathem, and H. Downard. In addition in 1852 a special subscription was raised to buy Frederick Nash's picture of Brighton by moonlight for 60 guineas.

In 1853 the band of the 17th Lancers played in the Pavilion rooms every Tuesday afternoon from January to May. An admission fee was charged which raised £198 10s. 6d., against which the only expenses were £19 to convey the band from and back to their barracks.

In the same year the first notable cultural event occurred in the Pavilion, when gratuitious use of the whole building and of the Town Hall was granted to the British Association to hold its annual meeting.

The Royal Pavilion, having been a palace, was much larger in 1850 that it is now. The 'offices', as they were called, extended as far south as Castle Square. These comprised not only the domestic quarters but also the Lord Chamberlain's office. To the east was a courtyard, now Palace Place, beyond which was the Royal Chapel, the servants' hall and certain other rooms. At the south end of what is now Pavilion Buildings stood the South Lodge which had been designed by Joseph Good for William IV in 1831. This found favour with no-one and had even been compared to a prison. It joined the main building of the palace to two houses on the north-west and the dormitories for royal servants in Prince's Place, which also dated from 1831.

Agreement was reached at once between the Commissioners and the diocese of Chichester for the transfer to the diocese of the former Royal Chapel at the price of £3,000. This was then re-erected in Montpelier Place as St. Stephen's church. In November 1850 the Commissioners decided to pull down the South Lodge and place a new gateway further north in order both to open up a view of the west front of the Pavilion and to re-continue Great East Street up to this gateway on the line of which it had formerly run until its closure by the Prince Regent in 1806; to demolish the houses to the east of this road on what is now the east side of Pavilion Buildings; and to let the houses on the west side, together with the buildings facing Castle Square and what is now Palace Place. A Vestry meeting was called to confirm this action. But the Vestry only favoured the demolition of the South Lodge. The rest of the proposals were referred back to the Commissioners for reconsideration. On second thoughts in March 1851 the Commissioners recommended the retention of only the two houses to the north-west of the South Lodge, and the demolition of all the other office buildings. This recommendation was duly confirmed by the Vestry.

The only part of the offices which was excepted from this demolition was the clock tower which stood in a small internal courtyard towards the south and west ends of the office buildings. This had been erected in 1816 for the storage of water. In July 1851 Thomas Cubitt, who was then building Osborne House in the Isle of Wight for Queen Victoria, on the instructions of the Prince Consort, gave back to the Commissioners the dial-faces of the clock from this tower which had been removed from the building by the Commissioners of Woods and Forests along with the rest of its fittings. It is interesting to note that this was the first instance of fittings from the Pavilion being returned by a member of the Royal Family, and not as has hitherto been thought, the wall-hangings and chandeliers which were given back by Queen Victoria several years later, and also that it was the Prince Consort, with his particular interest in the arts, who was responsible for the gift. Though thanks were returned for this both to the Prince and to Cubitt, the Commissioners do not seem to have been very pleased about it, as two months later they resolved that it would be undesirable to heighten the clock towers unless it was decided to have a public clock, which they did not propose. In April 1852 the pump and dome over the well in the clock tower were removed and the rooms in the tower let to George King, the tenant of 9 Pavilion Buildings, for £10 a year.

The Commissioners do not seem to have taken any steps with regard to the stables, now the Dome, until

February 1853. They then resolved to let the building for £50 a quarter to the Board of Ordnance for the use of the artillery stationed at Brighton Barracks. Curiously enough there was no mention of the riding school, now the Corn Exchange, at the same time. But in September 1854 Captain Wright, the Barrack Master, asked for the use of the building. The Pavilion Committee recommended that free use be accorded. The Commissioners referred the matter back for consideration of the financial angle. But when the Duke of Richmond, as Lord Lieutenant of Sussex and Colonel of the Royal Sussex Light Infantry Militia, renewed the request two months later the Commissioners gave in and accorded free use daily during a portion of the middle of the day. However, when the officers of this militia, emboldened by this consent, enquired whether the Commissioners could provide them with a mess-room, sitting-room, kitchen and bedrooms in the Pavilion this was turned down flat.

When the Pavilion was sold to the Commissioners the sale did not include the ice-house at the extreme south-west corner of the estate at the end of Regency Row, North Street. In February 1854 it was used as a soup kitchen. When the Town Commissioners offered to rent it in order to continue this use the Commissioners of Woods and Forests countered with an offer to sell the building and the garden adjoining it for £500. At this the Brighton Commissioners tried, on very slender grounds, to maintain that the ice-house was amongst the property which they had agreed to buy in 1850. But as no reference to it was made in either the conveyance or in the Act of Parliament for the purchase they were unable to substantiate their claim, and the Commissioners of Woods and Forests disposed of the building to someone else. As a result the ice-house does not now exist.

The first Curator of the Royal Pavilion, as we should now call him, was Francis Edmund De Val, who sub-sequently played an important part in the history of the building. He had begun life as an assistant in Kramer's china shop in North Street. As such he was employed to deliver a parcel of china to the Royal Pavilion, where he incurred the ire of one of the French cooks by placing this on a kitchen table. A fight ensued which came to the ears of the Prince of Wales, who sent for De Val. The Prince seems to have taken a fancy to him and, according to J. G. Bishop's *Strolls in the Brighton Extra-Mural Cemetery* subsequently entrusted to him the odd commission of paying Phoebe Hessell's weekly pension.

When the Pavilion was dismantled in 1847 De Val, presumably then still employed at Kramer's shop, had a hand in packing up the fittings which were detached from the building and in despatching these to London. This proved to be a useful experience for him when subsequently, as Manager of the Royal Pavilion, he was able to procure the return of some of these fittings.

He began his official connection with the Pavilion in the humble capacity of porter. But in 1853 he was called the 'laborer in charge'. His wages were £1 10s. a week. Under him were a hall porter at 14s. a week and three house porters. Two of the latter were paid 12s. a week and the third 10s. This was William De Val, probably F. E. De Val's son. In 1854 F. E. De Val's status was raised. He was appointed Manager of the Pavilion with complete responsibility for the letting of the rooms, the maintenance of the building, and the collection of the whole revenue of the estate. He was provided with a residence in the building, and, jointly with his wife, was paid a salary of £2 2s. a week. He was given an assistant or clerk at the wage of £1 1s. a week, who also acted as ticket-collector.

F. E. De Vall, having helped to pack up the fittings of the Pavilion when they were dismantled, was fully aware of their nature and value. He was also convinced that though some of them had been inserted in the new wing of Buckingham Palace, others were not being used at all. He continued to make representations to this effect to the Town Commissioners, and subsequently to their successors, Brighton Corporation. Eventually in November 1863 the Lord Chamberlain gave permission for De Val

and the Borough Surveyor, P. C. Lockwood, to visit
Kensington Palace, where the unused fittings were stored.
De Val's forecast was fully substantiated. After the
Queen's pleasure in the matter had been taken, permission
was given for all these unused fittings to be returned to
Brighton. These included the wall-hangings, doorcases,
and five chandeliers from the music room and the
chandeliers and some of the wall-paintings from the
banqueting room.

In return for his services in this matter De Val was
given a bonus of 20 guineas by the corporation. But as
they made a profit of £420 from the celebrations of the
re-decoration of the building, the gift to F. E. De Val
was not over-generous, as H. D. Roberts remarks in his
History of the Royal Pavilion. Fortunately, a better
memorial of him exists. When one of the tall narrow wall-
paintings in the north-east corner of the banqueting-
room was replaced in position the face of the Chinaman
holding a standard was found to be damaged. This was
replaced by a likeness of De Val. He died on 9 May 1867
and was buried in the Extra-Mural cemetery.

Lewis Slight and Quarrels with the Officers

The enterprise shown by Lewis Slight in arranging the
purchase of the Royal Pavilion had very happy results
for all concerned. But not all the differences of opinion
between him and his many enemies were resolved as
satisfactorily.

The first sign of trouble occurs in the minutes of
21 July 1852, when a committee of nine Commissioners
was appointed 'to enquire into the mode of managing
the business at the Town Hall' and other matters. The
chairman of this committee was Thomas Cooper, who
designed the Town Hall and the *Bedford* hotel, of which
latter he was the proprietor for some time. In September,
Lewis Slight complained to the Commissioners of the
treatment that he had received at the hands of Thomas
Cooper and prayed them to protect him from a recurrence
of it. This was an unexpected development as Cooper

and Slight had been close allies on the Commission at the time when Slight first became clerk. Cooper was himself a man of little restraint who was characterised as a 'rough diamond'. He was the son of a builder who had been killed in a fall from a house in Brunswick Square during its construction. A quarrel between the two men must have subsequently taken place, due no doubt to their dominant personalities. As a result of the Clerk's complaint, the committee was dissolved, and a new one of nine other Commissioners, excluding Thomas Cooper, was appointed. This is one of Cooper's last appearances in the minutes as he died on 27 December 1854 and was buried in the Extra Mural cemetery in Brighton.

The new committee made their first report in August 1853. The Commissioners took the extraordinary step of referring this report to the dissolved committee of July 1852. The general management committee made their final report in November 1853 which, after a further reference back to them, was circulated to all the Commissioners. The document constituted a formidable attack on the Clerk, who in the meantime had provided additional grounds for complaint against himself. Incorporation of the town was at the time under discussion. For some reason or other Lewis Slight considered this proposal to be a personal reflection on himself and opposed it tooth and nail. He even went so far as to accompany a deputation of opponents of incorporation when they waited on the Lord President of the Council. As the Commissioners were not at that time opposing incorporation this was too much even for those who were not personally antipathetic to Slight. They at once informed Lord Granville that the Clerk had no authority to accompany such a delegation which opposed incorporation.

The general management committee maintained in their report that, according to the decisions of the Commissioners in 1826 and 1836 it was the Clerk's duty to reside in Brighton, not to engage in any other form of business; to attend the office every day from 10 a.m. to 4 p.m., and to keep a journal of daily transactions and accounts. Instead of this the Clerk lived at Burgess Hill, carried on business as a farmer there, frequently absented himself for a whole day at a time without leave, regularly left the office between 2 p.m. and 3 p.m. every day, and did not keep a journal. Moreover, the accounts were not satisfactory. In them the Clerk called debtors creditors and vice versa, passed for payment a bill of £27 13s. for printing pamphlets against incorporation, and refused to produce accounts relating to the Level.

Some of these complaints were very unwisely framed and were the result of animosity. Lewis Slight had little difficulty in showing in reply that the committee had not examined the minute books in which were recorded reports signed by some of the members of the management committee who had previously approved what they were now condemning. The Level was the property of trustees, over whom neither he nor the Commissioners had any jurisdiction. To the general charges he replied that he was not obliged to live in Brighton or to refrain from carrying on other business. It is true that he usually left the Town Hall between 2 and 3 p.m., but on the other hand he arrived at 8.30 a.m., and the office itself remained open until 5 p.m. The accounts were, until 1850, kept in the same form as when he had taken office, and in that year they were changed to double entry, as followed by other commercial concerns. The accounts were always audited by a committee and the item of £27 13s. had been specifically passed for payment. He had accompanied the anti-incorporation deputation to London because the Commissioners had themselves resolved that incorporation was not in the town's best interest. This last was a very weak argument, because, although the Commissioners had in fact passed such a resolution, they had at a later date passed another in favour of incorporation.

The committee's report, including the Clerk's reply, came up for discussion at a meeting of the Commissioners on 28 November 1853. Richard Edwards and Elias Taylor moved that the clerk's reply was not satisfactory. Edward Cornford and Dr. William King put forward an amendment to the effect that 'the Clerk has always in his official capacity been actuated by a desire to promote the best interests of the Town And that the Commissioners have perfect confidence in his integrity'. W. D. Savage and James Bull then proposed a second amendment suggesting that the whole matter be referred to an accountant for a report. On this Edwards and Taylor withdrew their original resolution. The first amendment was put as the substantive motion and carried by 50 votes to thirty-six.

Despite this fairly substantial victory the Clerk took the town by surprise and resigned in January 1854. His letter said that 'whatever my failings may have been I can most conscientiously declare that the promotion of the welfare of the Town has, invariably, been the object in view. From that object no personal considerations shall divert my attention, and, in the hope that my retirement will facilitate the attainment of it, I now beg to tender my resignation'. One cannot help feeling sorry for him that his long period of office should have ended so distastefully.

Despite the resignation of Lewis Slight the finance and audit committee continued to probe into his method of keeping accounts in which they found 'abuses and irregularities'. They said that he had not kept a daily journal of financial transactions, as he should have done. He had illegally and at his pleasure varied the fees charged for licences for sedan chairs, boats and bathing-machines, and so on. But the only specific charge that they seemed able to make against him was a demand that he should pay to the Commissioners the sum of £1 14s. received by him in the previous October as discount for buttons from the sale of police uniforms. So great was the malice shown by some Commissioners against Lewis Slight that they could not let matters rest at that. The general management committee returned to the charge in July 1854. They discovered that in 1842 a cheque for £102 2s. had been drawn in favour of Messrs. Still and Stringer for watering the roads on behalf of the Water Company for which no voucher or receipt was to be found. They demanded an explanation. Slight replied that at the time Still and

Stringer were insolvent and the cheque was cashed and distributed as a 'matter of arrangement between the parties interested'. The committee proceeded to examine both John Still and his partners, Henry Stringer and William Packham. All three denied receiving the money or giving any authority for it to be paid to anyone else. The committee then requested Lewis Slight to attend upon them, which he not unnaturally declined to do. But he subsequently wrote to explain how the majority of the sum had been paid to the late Henry Faithful, solicitor, acting for the Water Company and William Packham, and the remainder had been handed 'by the direction of Mr. Stringer' to creditors of the firm. This reply was considered by the Commissioners to be 'evasive and unsatisfactory', and they resolved to institute legal proceedings against Slight for the recovery of the money.

The committee, however, had enough sense to take counsel's opinion before doing so. Ten months later they reported that counsel had advised that a case against Lewis Slight was very unlikely to succeed that in any case, as the facts dated back to 1842, he would be able to plead the Statute of Limitations in defence. On 16 May 1855 the Commissioners therefore resolved to take no legal action, but recorded that the conduct of their late Clerk in this matter was 'highly reprehensible and deserving the censure of the Commissioners'. Again so great was the prevailing malice that a copy of the resolution was sent to Lewis Slight. But it was little more than a gesture of defiance before the long night as only two further meetings of the Commissioners were held after this entry was made.

Lewis Slight did not wholly disappear from sight after his resignation. Having resigned without notice, he received no pension, and therefore in 1857 was presented by his admirers with 260 guineas, a silver epergne and a service of plate. The epergne was inscribed to the effect that he had 'rendered eminent services to the town of Brighton during a period of nearly thirty years' and the presentation was made by the Mayor. He even became for a short time a member of the Town Council whose creation he had so strongly opposed. He later entered into partnership with George Robertson as auctioneers, appraisers and general commission agents at 126 North Street, but this business was not a success. His first wife pre-deceased him and he married again. His second son, Frederick, was Secretary to the London, Brighton and South Coast Railway for 17 years but died in 1866.

At the end of his life Lewis Slight moved back from Burgess Hill to Brighton and in 1864–5 he was living at 36 London Road. By 1868 he had moved to 63 Upper Brunswick Place, Hove, and there he died on 28 March 1869, aged seventy-seven. He was pre-deceased by his daughter and his three sons, but survived by his second wife. He was buried in the churchyard of Keymer parish church, near to where he had lived.

The agitation against existing practices did not end with Lewis Slight's resignation. A week later the Commissioners asked the original committee of July 1852 to consider and revise the duties of the Clerk, the mode of keeping accounts and other matters. The committee reported in March, but for some unexplained reason only eight of the signatories were those of the original members. Two names were missing, and in their place appeared the name of Elias Taylor, who was to prove a fanatical critic of the existing system.

But once Lewis Slight had disappeared the burden of attacking existing practices passed from the general management committee to the audit and finance committee. This was an even more hostile body and comprised only three members: Elias Taylor, Thomas West and Alex Williamson. They turned their attention to the Commissioners' solicitor, Charles Cobby. They reported that, over the last 27 years, his bills came to 'the enormous amount of above £500 a year' or £15,000 in all. In view of 'the magnitude of this evil' they thought that in future legal costs should be abated, either by taxation, by resorting more frequently to arbitration, or by paying fixed salaries. They went on to criticise the practice of buying cloth for police uniforms outside the town and having it made up, instead of purchasing the clothing ready-made. In view of the wastefulness of past practices they recommended the appointment of an audit committee of five Commissioners which would meet once a week to exercise more supervision over the Commissioners' accounts.

Charles Cobby replied that all his bills had been passed for payment by the audit committee which existed at the time. Moreover, the total of £15,000 that had been mentioned included all disbursements such as stamp duties, counsel's fees, expenses of witnesses at trials, and the like. Parliamentary agent's fees for Royal Pavilion Act alone had come to £1,200.

The audit committee's fury at this reply was quite unbridled. They expressed astonishment that Charles Cobby did not 'remain quiet and satisfied with his share of gain during so many years, but he appeals to your [Commissioners'] compassion or generosity as if he had neglected to take sufficient care of himself and had not had enough of the public money. He seems to offer himself as a voluntary and injured champion and defender of an ill paid and disinterested class of Gentleman, to avenge whose wrongs he takes up a gauntlet never intended for him'. They went on to say that in view of the approaching incorporation of the town, when the whole system of administration would be changed, it would be wisest to make no further comment, instead of 'recalling with much severity the lax, wasteful and vicious system of long bygone times in his [Cobby's] and other departments; which they hope is now, with his single exception, fully and generally repented of, and which may therefore be safely forgiven and forgotten'. It would be difficult for such self-righteousness to be exceeded.

Having demolished, as they thought, the Commissioners' solicitor to their satisfaction, the audit and finance committee then turned their attention upon the surveyor, Allen Anscombe. They had received several complaints

against his first assistant (unnamed) who seems to have
kept a public-house. They therefore laid down that henceforward no officer of the Commissioners should engage
in any other occupation, for, it such were permitted,
'the largest staff would not suffice for their [officers']
public duties'. The committee stated that the surveyor
had 'unhappily been too long left to execute his important
duties without any, or with a very imperfect control'.
They found past contractors' accounts excessive and that
the surveyor's explanation of this only showed 'a pertina-
ceous adherence and preference for a very faulty and
expensive mode of executing the works of the town.
'He seemed', they said, 'more to sympathize with the
Contractors than with his Employers, whose interest it
is his especial duty to watch and protect against every
one. For that he is paid, and for that is his expensive
establishment maintained'. They considered that he
offered 'nothing worthy of the name of defence' for
authorising the disbursement of large sums of money
without the sanction of the Commissioners.

They then laid down that in future the Surveyor should
not have authority to incur any expenditure without the
express sanction of the Commissioners and that all contractors' accounts should be submitted to the finance
and audit committee who would meet monthly to
examine them. A separate committee of five Commissioners was appointed to meet weekly for the purpose of
surpervising the Surveyor. His accounts would be
presented to them for eventual submission to the finance
and audit committee through the Clerk.

The new Surveyor's office committee did not however
give satisfaction to the stringent finance and audit
committee. In January 1855 the latter reported that they
had been 'placed in a very painful situation by the failure
of their expectations'. The Surveyor's bills still came to
them un-countersigned. When enquiry was made concerning the degree of supervision over the Surveyor that the
other committee had exercised, it was established that
little or nothing in that line had been carried out, and

several members declared that 'they could not neglect their own avocations to give the necessary time to the attention to this public duty'. The Commissioners, however, had too little time left to them to take any further steps concerning this matter before their jurisdiction ceased.

Following Lewis Slight's resignation, his son of the same name was appointed acting Clerk in April 1854 at the salary of £250 a year. Luke Ford and Isaiah Richardson were voted a salary of 25s. a week each as assistant clerks. A fortnight later poor Lewis Slight junior broke his thigh. His father offered to help the Commissioners during his absence. But they did not think it advisable to avail themselves of this offer. The audit and finance committee undertook to supervise the Clerk's office during the acting Clerk's absence. The latter returned to work on 23 June. He must have been a remarkable young man, because, without apparently ever quarrelling with his father, he retained the confidence of the Commissioners to the end. The last entry in their minutes, for 28 May 1855, recorded that the Commissioners 'have much pleasure in expressing their approval of the obliging and efficient manner in which Mr. Lewis Slight Junr. has discharged the duties of the Office of Clerk to this Body, and to express a hope that as the said Office is about to expire he may succeed in obtaining some other appointment commensurate with his abilities'. Their wish was granted, for he became Borough Accountant to the new Town Council and held the position until his death in 1862.

Incorporation

After 1809 no further mention of incorporation was made in the Commissioners' minutes for 35 years. In fact, the Act of 1825 seems to have given general satisfaction. In March 1830 a Bill was presented to Parliament which would have general provisions for lighting, cleaning and watching streets in towns. This would have involved the repeal of certain clauses in previous Acts of Parliament for special towns such as Brighton. The Brighton Commissioners therefore petitioned Parliament against this Bill.

In 1834 the Municipal Corporations Act was passed for the reform of existing municipalities which, in the words of the report of the Commission that recommended the Act, 'neither possess or deserve the confidence or respect' of His Majesty's subjects. In fact there prevailed 'a distrust of the self-elected Municipal Councils whose powers are subject to no popular control'. Brighton of course was not a borough, and the process of choosing its Commissioners had been made more democratic by the Act of 1825. But a certain measure of distrust between the Vestry and the Commissioners often existed. In this instance both bodies joined together in petitioning Parliament against the application of the new Act to the town on the grounds that Brighton already had resident magistrates and an efficient police force and did not desire to incur the expense of employing a Recorder or of building a gaol.

The first subsequent occasion on which incorporation was mentioned was 21 October 1844, when a committee of nine inhabitants was chosen to consider the matter. This committee reported in favour of incorporation, including the area of the Brunswick Square Commissioners and the rest of Hove. Brighton then had a population of 50,000, which was a fourth of the population of East Sussex. It contributed £3,000 a year towards the county rate. If a new gaol was shortly erected at Lewes, as was to be expected, Brighton would have to bear a third of the cost of its construction, since out of the average number of 142 prisoners which were to be found at any one time in Lewes gaol, about 55 came from Brighton and Hove. Construction of a local gaol containing 90 cells would therefore be little more expensive than such a liability. Incorporation would cost £1,000, but the annual expenditure of administration would probably be reduced by about £200 a year. The number of municipal representatives would be reduced from 124 Commissioners to 49 councillors, but the amalgamation of the three authorities (Brighton, Brunswick Square and Hove) would be a great advantage. This report was printed, but when the adjourned meeting of the Vestry considered it on 16 December 1844 it was rejected on the grounds that incorporation would 'not be beneficial to the Inhabitants'.

In 1847 the introduction into Parliament of the Health of Towns Bill stimulated further thought into the structure of local government. This Bill, which related to the provision of drainage and water supply, empowered the Queen in Council to appoint a Commission of Health and Public Works. This commission would appoint inspectors whose job it would be to visit towns to decide whether or not the Act, when passed, should apply to them. If, as a result of a report from an inspector, the Commission decided that the Act should be applied to any town the Commission would direct that a local committee of 27 should be constituted for that town of which two-thirds would be elected and one-third nominated by the Crown. This local commission would be given power to levy rates, to appoint a surveyor and a medical officer of health, to superintend the drainage, the water and gas supply of the town, and, if necessary, to take over all the existing powers of the Town Commissioners.

On 22 April 1847 the Vestry appointed a committee to consider this Bill. The committee consulted people in other towns and attended a meeting in London at which it was resolved that an efficient system of drainage was of the utmost importance, but that the Bill, as constituted, was objectionable and subversive of existing arrangements for local government. As a result, the Bill was amended in Parliament, and at a subsequent meeting on 1 June the Vestry resolved that, if the Bill became law, it was highly desirable that it should be brought into operation in Brighton.

The provisions eventually included in the Bill in 1848 laid down that it would not come into force in any area until the inhabitants of that area petitioned the General Board of Health to that effect. The number of inhabitants making such a petition should be not less than 50, but the committee of the Brighton Vestry thought that this should be increased to one-twentieth of the inhabitants rated to the poor-rate. On the receipt of such a petition the General Board of Health would despatch a superintending inspector to report on the needs of the district. A local board of health would then be elected. The Bill fixed the constituent number of such a board at 27, but the committee thought that this should be increased to 37 in towns of over 40,000 inhabitants and to 47 in towns of over 50,000 inhabitants. Qualification would be local residence, the possession of real or personal estate to the value of £1,000, and assessment to the rates of not less than £30. The committee thought that the qualification should be confined to real estate only. Each elector would have one vote for each £50 of the rateable value of his property up to the maximum of six votes. The local committee was instructed by the Vestry to support the Bill but to try and secure such amendments as they considered necessary.

This situation led straight back to consideration of incorporation of the town. The position had not greatly changed since 1844. No new gaol had been built at Lewes. The number of prisoners which the existing gaol contained was two hundred and twenty-six. The governor stated that this was 'about double the number that the prison is capable of accommodating'. Of these, 70 came from Brighton, An additional argument in favour of incorporation was that in elections for councillors ratepayers would only have one vote each, whereas, both the Brighton Act of 1825 and the new Bill allowed a plurality of votes up to a maximum of six for high rating assessments. When the committee's printed report in favour of incorporation had been considered they were instructed to carry it into effect. But at a subsequent meeting on 13 April 1848 incorporation was again rejected as being 'highly injurious to the interersts of the Town'. The motion in favour of incorporation was carried on a show of hands, but a poll was demanded, and this brought a vote of 1,148 for and 1,749 against such a step.

The protagonists of incorporation did not leave the matter there. Four days later, as the result of a requisition signed by 300 inhabitants and published in the local newspapers, a further meeting was held at which it was moved that a committee of 21 people should be appointed to investigate the matter further. This was carried on a show of hands, but lost on a poll by 1,419 votes to seven hundred and forty-six.

Meanwhile the Public Health Act, 1848, was passed. Though the minutes do not say so, a petition was made to apply the Act to Brighton, but not Hove. An inspector named Edward Cresy was sent down to make a report. This painted a very bad picture of health matters in Brighton, It recommended the substitution of drainage for cesspools, the improvement of the water supply, the provision of public baths,[1] the removal of slaughter-houses, the discontinuation of burials in churches and chapels, and the establishment of vagrant lodging houses. It transpired that, in a case like Brighton where a local Actt of Parliament existed, if the town petitioned for the Public Health Act to be brought into force, the local Act would first have to be repealed. The Vestry therefore wished to be reassured that this repeal would only affect matters of public health and not the powers of the Directors and Guardians of the Poor to maintain entire local control of the poor. The Vestry therefore petitioned the General Board of Health to extend by one month the time for the submission of statements on the inspector's report. This the board agreed to do, but a subsequent request for a further extension of a month was refused.

The board proceeded to make a provisional order for the introduction of the Public Health Act, 1848, into Brighton. When a Vestry meeting was held on 11 July

1. In September 1851 the Vestry had appointed a committee to consider the best means of establishing public baths and wash-houses, but evidently nothing came of this.

1850 to welcome this action the proposal was rejected by a large majority, both on a show of hands and at a poll. In this decision the Town Commissioners concurred. At the same time a memorial with 1,638 signatures against the order was presented to the General Board of Health. The order was therefore dropped.

In January 1852 the General Board of Health produced a fresh order. A committee of both the Vestry and the Town Commissioners was appointed to consider under what form the Act could satisfactorily be applied to Brighton. The committee reported against acceptance of the provisional order. The principal objection was that the new Local Board of Health would be automatically composed of the Town Commissioners who numberd 114, but no elections would take place until this number had been reduced by deaths or resignations to forty-two. After that a third of the board would retire annually and be subject to re-election. As the board was to receive greatly increased powers under the Act and order, this was highly objectionable. Secondly, if the town was subsequently incorporated, the local board of health would continue to co-exist with the new Town Council. The General Board of Health by this time was evidently incensed at Brighton's reluctance to fall into line and consequently acted with a lack of communication that the committee designated as 'not characterised by the usual courtesy observed by officers of public boards'.

When the board therefore made a second provisional order on 3 February 1852, without withdrawing the first one, and a Bill was introduced into the House of Commons to confirm this, the Vestry requested the local Members of Parliament, Sir George Brook Pechell and Lord Alfred Hervey, to oppose the Bill. As a result of action by these Members the chairman of the General Board of Health, the Earl of Shaftesbury, and three other members visited Brighton for a conference with the Town Commissioners and the committee of the Vestry. Following this conference two of the main objections to the order by the Vestry were surmounted, namely that the powers of owning and managing the Royal Pavilion should be transferred to the local board of health with the rest of the powers formerly vested in the Town Commissioners, and that the members of the local board should be elected from the inhabitants at large and not from the number of the Commissioners. Brighton was therefore struck out of the schedule of the Bill before Parliament, but agreement was not reached about the qualification of electors or the number of the local board. The General Board of Health subsequently agreed to the number of the Commissioners being increased from 30 to forty-two. Therefore when an amended provisional order was submitted in September 1852, the Vestry was able to approve this.

However, opposition was not finally silenced, and on 8 February 1853 a further resolution was passed to the effect that it would be 'highly inexpedient' to apply the Public Health Act to Brighton. The local Members of Parliament were asked to use their influence against adoption of the order which was before the House of Commons. This was confirmed at a poll on 21 February by 2,983 votes to 934, but a separate Bill for the establishment of the Brighton, Hove and Preston Water-works for the supply of water on the constant service principle found favour and was unanimously endorsed by the Vestry on 10 March 1853.

Meanwhile the question of incorporation of the town was being pursued as a current alternative to the adoption of the Public Health Act, 1848. In April 1852 a memorial in favour of a charter of incorporation, signed by 2,099 people having rateable assessments of £50,000, was lodged with the Privy Council. The opponents therefore summoned a Vestry meeting in June at which it was declared that incorporation would be 'highly injudicious to the interests of the Town and unjust to the Female Rate-payers in respect of their being disenfranchised'.

A counter-petition was deposited with the Privy Council signed by 1,054 people whose rateable assessments amounted to £64,000. In view of this opposition and of the fact that some of the petitioners' grievances could be alleviated by other means, the Privy Council declined to recommend the grant of a charter. In April the petitioners had an interview with the President of the Council, Lord Granville, at the instance of Lord Alfred Hervey, M.P., at which Lord Granville advised them to try again.

In April 1853 the Town Commissioners passed a resolution to the effect that the Act of 1825 should be amended and the Commissioners' powers extended. Following this a Vestry meeting was held on 2 May at which George Faithful moved the expediency of the Brighton Act of 1825 being amended to secure more effective local government and that the Vestry should consult with the Town Commissioners to that end. An amendment to defer the matter for two months on the grounds that the majority of the Vestry was debarred from voting by reason of the partial collection of the poor-rate was carried on a show of hands, but defeated at a poll, when the original motion was carried by 1,344 votes to one thousand and sixteen. A fortnight later it was proposed to appoint a committee of the Vestry for consultation with the Town Commissioners. But an amendment to the effect that it was not expedient to do so was carried by 118 votes to thirty-four. A poll was demanded, but a protest signed by Henry Verrall was also handed in to the effect that the amendment was out of order and should not have been put to the meeting by the chairman (the Rev. H. M. Wagner). The poll confirmed the show of hands by 2,020 votes to 1,655, with 'the majority of votes under protest 365'.

Up to this point, though opinions in the town had been severely divided, there had been general agreement between the majority view of both the Vestry and the Town Commissioners. Henceforward a clash of views between these two bodies developed. In June 1853 the Commissioners passed a resolution to the effect that incorporation would be 'highly injurious to the best interests of the Town'. The protagonists of incorporation asked the High Constable, H. P. Tamplin, to call a public

meeting, which he at first refused to do. However, a
Vestry meeting was held on 27 June which resolved
that the Commissioners' resolution 'did not represent
the opinion of the Inhabitants of Brighton' and that
therefore no amendment of the 1825 Act would be
satisfactory unless it was accompanied by a charter of
incorporation. The High Constable was severely reprimanded for refusing to call a public meeting. This
resolution induced the Commissioners to change their
minds and at a meeting on 14 July they recorded that,
should the Queen be disposed to grant a charter to the
town, they would be prepared to hand over their powers
to the new body corporate. However, this mood did
not last. In December the Commissioners again resolved
that incorporation would be highly injurious to the town's
best interests and appointed a delegation to bring this
view to the attention of Lord Granville. Meanwhile both
parties pursued their objectives vigorously outside the
council chamber. A petition in favour of incorporation
was submitted to the Privy Council, signed by 2,108
ratepayers, whose assessments amounted to £90,064, and
of whom 1,605 were parliamentary electors. A counter-
petition was signed by 1,241 ratepayers, with an assessment of £80,796, and of whom 735 were parliamentary
electors. The Privy Council must evidently have thought
that, despite the fact that the opposition nearly equalled the
amount of support for the proposal, the latter was well
grounded as the next reference to the matter in the
minutes of the Commissioners is to the arrival of the
charter in April 1854. The returning officer was Colonel
John Fawcett, who became the first Mayor of Brighton,
and the first town clerk Charles Sharwood, who had
previously been a Town Commissioner.

The incorporation of the town did not, however, extinguish the existence of the Brighton Commissioners, and for
a short period the two bodies continued to co-exist with
different functions and in control of different buildings.
The Commissioners, for instance, still owned and con-
trolled both the Town Hall and the Royal Pavilion.

In June a committee of the Commissioners was appointed to confer with the Town Council about the transfer of their powers to the new body. An attempt was made without success, to obtain an opinion from the Attorney General. Counsel, named E. D. Creasy, was therefore consulted and advised that most of the powers exercised by the Commissioners under their Act of 1825 could be transferred to the Town Council under the Municipal Corporations Act, 1835, but that there was some doubt whether this could be done in the case of the ownerhip and management of the Royal Pavilion under the Brighton Improvement (Purchase of the Royal Pavilion Act), 1850. He therefore suggested that both bodies should seek a special Act of Parliament for the transfer of powers. This recommendation was approved by a Vestry meeting on 16 October 1854.

The Brighton Commissioners Transfer Act, 1855, was duly passed and came into operation on 29 May 1855. The Commissioners held their last meeting on the preceding day. The minutes were signed by John Patching as chairman. Thus ended a form of local government in Brighton which had existed with some modifications since 1773. Incorporation also put an end to Vestry meetings in the form in which they had previously existed. But the Vestry seems to have continued to hold meetings of a kind to discuss special subjects, such as the extension of the cemetery, until 1856. Their Clerk, Somers Clarke, survived until 1892.

INDEX